CW01332856

THE NEW CENSORSHIP

Ayala Panievsky

THE NEW CENSORSHIP

HOW THE WAR ON THE MEDIA IS TAKING US DOWN

FOOTNOTE

First published in 2025 by
Footnote Press

Footnote Press
An imprint of Bonnier Books UK
5th Floor, HYLO, 105 Bunhill Row,
London, EC1Y 8LZ

Owned by Bonnier Books
Sveavägen 56, Stockholm, Sweden

First printing
1 3 5 7 9 10 8 6 4 2

Copyright © 2025 Ayala Panievsky

The right of Ayala Panievsky to be identified as the author of this work has been asserted in accordance with the Copyright, Designs and Patents Act 1998.

All rights reserved.
No part of this publication may be reproduced, stored in a retrieval system, or transmitted in any form or by any means without the written permission of the publisher, nor be otherwise circulated in any form of binding or cover other than that in which it is published and without a similar condition being imposed on the subsequent purchaser.

A CIP catalogue record for this book is available from the British Library.

ISBN (hardback): 978-1-80444-111-4
ISBN (audio): 978-1-80444-307-1
ISBN (ebook): 978-1-80444-112-1

Typeset by IDSUK (Data Connection) Ltd
Printed and bound in Great Britain
by Clays Ltd, Elcograf S.p.A.

The authorised representative in the EEA is Bonnier Books
UK (Ireland) Limited.
Registered office address: Floor 3, Block 3, Miesian Plaza,
Dublin 2, D02 Y754, Ireland
compliance@bonnierbooks.ie
www.bonnierbooks.co.uk

This book originates from hundreds of conversations with journalists who trusted me to tell their stories. It is dedicated to my grandma, Hava Weinkrantz, a tough and loving Holocaust survivor, who would have hated my politics – but shaped it deeply in ways we never had the time to discuss.

Contents

Foreword by Emily Maitlis	ix
Prologue	xv
Between the Li(n)es	1
The Populist War on Our Right to Know	23
The Playbook: Choose Your Weapon	47
The Nigel Farage Effect: Mainstreaming the Far Right	65
Strategic Bias: How Our News Universe Shifts to the Right	83
When the War on the Media Meets War	111
Deride and Conquer: The Populist Crackdown on Solidarity	125
Welcome to the Upside Down: The World of Anti-Media Media	153
The Fight to Know	177
Afterword	205
Endnotes	207
Bibliography	221
Acknowledgements	257

Foreword

By Emily Maitlis

THE AUTHOR OF THIS BOOK, Ayala Panievsky, is my first virtual friend. Come to think of it, she's my only virtual friend. We met, rather randomly, after I DMed her through Twitter. I had read some of her academic work online and thought she was brilliant. I wanted to hear more. I needed, in a very concrete sense, her guidance to steer me through something I was itching to say – but could not yet enunciate. A week earlier, in August of 2022 I had been approached to give the prestigious MacTaggart Lecture at the Edinburgh Television Festival. It was a few months after leaving the BBC, and the invitation had put me in a total panic. I had only 17 days to think, write and deliver what felt like the sum total of my journalistic life's work. The subject, the MacTaggart team said, 'could be anything media related'. I'd just entered the podcast world. Did I want to talk about podcasts? I didn't. I knew that. The only thing I wanted to talk about in fact, was the struggle journalists like me were having making sense of the new populist landscape. Politics had changed. Politicians had changed. But somehow, we, the media, had not. Our rules and norms and practices remained stuck in some dying past. And we were losing relevance with our audiences. We had stopped speaking their language.

I had been at the helm of *Newsnight* for the past five years. They had been incredible years and I could not be prouder of the work that the team and I put out there: we covered the first Trump Administration, the Brexit vote, the Theresa May and Boris Johnson governments, the fire at Grenfell, the bomb in Manchester Arena, the migrant crossings, the Paris Bataclan attacks, the Covid pandemic, the fall of Harvey Weinstein and the interview with Prince Andrew. It was a rich time to be in news. Journalists had the best job on the planet.

But increasingly, I was struck by a sense of foreboding. Our cosy neat world of facts and research, data and checks was losing ground to a world where feelings and assertion – and occasionally conspiracy and misinformation – could dominate. When MAGA politicians accused us of 'fake news', I knew it was meaningless. But I didn't have the tools to rebut it. When conspiracy theorists took us down a whataboutery rabbit hole instead of answering my question, I could feel what was happening, but I nevertheless tumbled headfirst. As lie after lie in the Brexit campaign got repeated as fact – to the point where they ended up as bus slogans and posters – we realised that the old world of polite correction had stopped working.

This wasn't a mistake. It was full-on antibiotic resistance. They were using disinformation as a propaganda weapon in a shit-flooded zone. I turned to Panievsky, because she'd seen it all before. And she'd taken away its potency by giving it a name.

Ayala worked as a print journalist in Israel under Netanyahu. A leader so canny about political message sharing, that he'd began a PhD on 'The power of the computer in the art of political communication'. This was in 1976. 1 9 7 6! Long before the birth of the World Wide Web. He got it. And, as she explains in *The New Censorship*, his blueprint three decades ago set the tone now followed by many autocrats and populist world leaders. Under Netanyahu, those who dared criticise Israeli government policy would be accused not merely of bias but of disloyalty. Occasionally even anti-Semitism. Their journalism somehow recast as treachery against the state. In America under Trump those journalists were framed as 'enemies of the people'. Even in the UK – under Johnson and Covid – we were warned 'now is not the time for asking questions' (of government policy) 'when the whole country needs to pull together.' In this framing, the journalist is the one betraying their country by daring to query those in power. I remember interviewing the prominent leave campaigner and then-leader of the House of Commons, Andrea Leadsom, for BBC's Newsnight, one year after the Brexit vote. When asked about the negotiations with the EU, she told me: 'It would be helpful if broadcasters were willing to be a bit patriotic'. Now, you could argue that my patriotism – at that moment – was shown in an attempt to do the job well, and interpret for our licence fee-paying public the state of government negotiations. But I think that's missing the point. It's certainly missing the strategy.

This is how populists effect the shutting down of scrutiny. Panievsky described a process she'd seen many of us use as 'strategic bias'. How broadcasters – fearful of those accusations – end up leaning towards their accusers, just to prove them wrong, and in so doing, lose their journalistic distance and judgement. They end up – ironically – enacting the very position they were trying to avoid.

It was Ayala who first made me understand how insidious this could be and how widespread it had already become. Her research provided me with the basis for my speech, and the backbone to be able to say it. On stage in Edinburgh that night, I talked about 'false equivalence'. How often on *Newsnight* we would present a 'balanced panel of guests' without letting our audience know that one viewpoint was so prevalent we'd find 50 speakers in five minutes, and the other would be so esoteric we'd had three researchers looking for three days. We would just present 'both sides' as if they were equally weighted within the country or the community.

I talked about what it was like, as a broadcaster, to face guests who didn't just contradict you, but tried to stamp down your right to ask the questions at all. And I talked about the trap television presenters sometimes got into – unsure whether to correct false information online, thereby attracting more attention to a possible conspiracy, or to let it go – thereby becoming part of the silent problem.

I remember finishing the speech that night with a palpable sense of relief. It was front page news in many of the UK and international papers by the time I'd finished talking. I was thinking: 'Thank god we've got this – before it's too late'.

But we hadn't. And it was.

Three years on, autocracies outnumber democracies for the first time in 20 years, according to the V-Dem Institute which analyses the state of Democracy in 202 countries. It is almost impossible to have a thriving free media within an autocracy.

And it is almost impossible to end up in autocracy if the media is free and thriving. That's why all this matters. It's not about whinging narcissistic individual journalists. It's about whether we – as citizens – want to retain the right to know what's really going on.

This lies at the centre of the book you're about to read. Ayala puts the public's right to know at the heart of her argument. And she shows that failure 'to know' can, literally, kill you. She talks us through the lessons learned from Netanyahu's Israel – where many citizens *do not know* what's taking place in Gaza. She shows us the weapons of the populist playbook: how lawsuits and SLAPPS are used to silence investigative reporting. And she looks, with a critical eye, at the part we all played – still play – in normalising figures that would once have shocked us. There are places in *The New Censorship* where our thoughts diverge; I'd be shocked if we saw eye to eye on everything (plurality of thought is, after all, at the heart of press freedom). But her arguments are profound, compelling, and fascinating.

And as ever, I read her words with awe, and a deep gratitude I can call her my inspiration – but also, my friend.

Prologue

Not the Book I Planned

THE 2023–2025 ISRAEL–GAZA WAR caught me writing a very different book. After years of research into the campaign of populist politicians, parties and movements to transform the media, I was working on a popular guide for *knowing* in populist times. From Europe to the Middle East, from the United States to Latin America, the war over the news has become a dominant feature of current politics, mainly, but not exclusively, on the right.[1] Journalists – especially those raising critical voices and practising investigative reporting – have become used to orchestrated ruptures of online rage and public hate intended to intimidate and silence them.[2] Populist leaders around the world invest considerable efforts and resources into eroding our belief that journalism could be fixed; that we could have a common source of knowledge about the world at all. The book I thought I was writing focused on what happens to our right to know when the media is under attack in the name of 'the people'. How do journalists navigate these conflicts, and at what costs? What can we, the people, do to save the media? And which media is it that we are willing to save? These questions will still be addressed in the following chapters, but behind them came crawling a new urgency.

Weeks after 7th October, 2023, the day Hamas attacked Southern Israel, killing and kidnapping thousands of women, children and men, I travelled from my home in London to my hometown, Tel Aviv, to find my community grieving, traumatised and despairing. The media landscape has altered quickly. The news was on 24/7, loud and clear, telling and retelling the national trauma. The sense of loss and pain was everywhere. The day of the attack was recounted compulsively, immersive, like a collective PTSD ritual. Have we truly survived that? The collapse of the state authorities. The mutilated bodies. The burned homes. Footage of Hamas terrorists capturing and torturing young, beautiful partygoers dancing in the desert. The redheaded Bibas babies, held in captivity for months, were staring at us from every frame, featuring in street graffiti and improvised murals. The growing number of soldiers returning from Gaza in coffins. There was enough pain to fill newscasts for days, weeks, months – perhaps forever. But the terrifying loss on the other side of the border remained invisible. As have large chunks of reality.

The haunting visuals from the Gaza Strip, which I witnessed in London on BBC and CNN, were entirely filtered out of the TV screen in my mom's living room and my friends' newsfeeds. The many thousands of Palestinian bodies buried under the rubble of what used to be their homes, the starving women and children queuing for food, the horrid mounting death toll, the newborns freezing to death in defunct hospitals. Those maimed by IDF snipers and Hamas militants, those bombarded defenceless in their tents, those who came to provide humanitarian aid and ended up buried in the sand, those scarred forever. On Israeli TV, you could see the distant explosions in Gaza but not their gruelling aftermath. You could witness empty, destroyed buildings but not the unfathomable human suffering surrounding them. And it was not just the suffering in Gaza that seemed to have disappeared as my flight was making its way from London to Tel Aviv. Debates of the future, of both Israelis and Palestinians, were scarce. Opposition voices were almost entirely ignored. One famous TV pundit was suspended for carefully suggesting, early on, that this war must end. By the time the opposition to the war started gaining traction, it was too late for too many of us, on both sides of the border.

Why were my friends and family, living one hour's drive from Gaza, not watching what the entire world was watching at this crucial, consequential, historic moment in time? Would these blind spots and silences have become so ubiquitous if there hadn't been two decades of populist assault on journalism? And how can we make sure that we establish an information environment where such silences and caving no longer take over our right to know – in Israel or anywhere else?

In times of crisis – and especially following an unprecedented collective trauma like 7th October – it is not unheard of for people (and reporters) to turn a blind eye to the casualties on the other side of the border. Researchers have already exposed how hyper-nationalism took over the US media after 9/11,[3] how little the BBC bothered showing UK audiences the human toll of the Iraq war,[4] and how Ukrainian media ignored Russian casualties.[5] During the Persian Gulf War, US audiences were shown a sanitised version of war – despite the estimated 100,000 Iraqi soldiers killed, and a similar number of civilian casualties. Even during the Vietnam War, which became a founding myth for modern war reporting, Vietnamese civilians drew very little media attention from US reporters.[6] In previous conflicts in the Middle East – and God knows we've had enough of those – Palestinian casualties got little traction in the Israeli press.[7] And yet, since my entire life growing up in Israel was shadowed by wars, intifadas, terror attacks and military conflicts, I knew this war was covered differently. And thanks to years of research into the guts of the Israeli media, I felt like I knew why. There was just one problem: I couldn't speak.

For months after 7th October, I fell silent. As someone who speaks and writes for a living, who was at the time studying and teaching media and populism at Cambridge University and City, University of London, giving public lectures and media interviews, and for years editing other people's sentences, I was struck by my inability to find the words. Every conversation was gut-wrenching. Everyone close to me was hurt. In Tel Aviv, my peace-activist friends were physically attacked by police officers and right-wing goons for speaking their minds. Pro-Palestinian voices were targeted in universities around the globe and beaten up in the streets of London. My Jewish friends in the United States and the UK met anti-Semitism and harassment on campuses. Islamophobia was on the rise. While many of us were losing our loved ones, we also seemed to have lost the words. It seemed futile to talk; no one was listening. But it was crucial to talk. People were dying. My country was breaking down, taking with it the future of my people and everyone else in the region. That realisation was chilling, but it finally broke through: by keeping silent, I was practising the very same strategy I have seen journalists entertaining for years. It was *The New Censorship*, in all its glory. This book is my very personal attempt to overcome it.

I went back to the manuscript, trying to find my shattered voice again. The research materials I had collected over the years, I hoped, could help us make sense of the blind spots in the Israeli media and consciousness, and the diminishing of our right to truth.

It matters. Not just for Israelis and Palestinians, but for all those facing unleashed illiberal authoritarians, who weaponise democracy against itself. Wars, like pandemics and natural disasters, are critical crises, and an indicative litmus test. When they erupt in a broken information environment, the ramifications can be fatal. The bloody conflict between Israelis and Palestinians has always drawn massive global attention,[8] but the 2023–2025 Israel-Hamas war has quickly become a bone of contention in political battles far beyond the Middle East. Not only have neighbouring countries like Egypt and Jordan become central protagonists in this excruciating round of violence, terror and fear, Joe Biden's (and then Trump's) America, Rishi Sunak's (and then Starmer's) Britain, Emanuel Macron's France, Olaf Scholz's Germany and even Cyril Ramaphosa's South Africa have all found themselves torn apart around their governments' policies in the region.

It is not easy to jump headfirst and open-eyed into this political minefield. For now, I will confess that after years in journalism, academia, activism and even bits of politics, writing this book was probably the hardest thing I've ever done. I am aware that for certain readers it might be too critical of the Israeli media, government and society. For others, it might be too focused on Israelis rather than Palestinians. To all those readers I say: I criticise Israel because I belong there, and belonging is both powerful and painful. Some of you might find even this last sentence difficult to read; after all, how can one love a place that is absorbed in war and blood, displacement and hunger, revenge and despair? This book is born out of this paradox of dreadful belonging. I love the place I grew up in, am attached to its people, and heartbroken every day by the path it took. I am shaped by its past and potential future, while broken by its devastating present.

Written as we mourn over 500 days of bloodshed, this is not a book about the war. It remains anchored in the long and quiet 'war' that preceded this one: the war over our minds. And this war is a global and ongoing one. If you wish to save the place you love from the abyss, if you care about your right to know and wish to live your life peacefully and freely, please take this story to heart. This book is served as a warning sign, for those who can still use it.

Between the Li(n)es

'The left-wing media is engaged in a Bolshevik hunt, brainwashing and character assassination against me and my family. It happens every day and night. They produce a flood, there is no other word for it, a flood of fake news ... There has been nothing like it in the history of the state. It's doubtful there was anything similar in the history of any democratic country.'
Israeli prime minister, Benjamin Netanyahu, at a Parliament faction meeting, 2017.

On a chilly evening, late in 2016, Ilana Dayan, one of Israel's most celebrated journalists, found herself uncharacteristically nervous. Nothing in her long career had prepared her for this moment. The fierce investigative reporter was poised to narrate on national television, word-for-word, what amounted to an official smear against her and her work from the most famous and powerful man in the country. When Dayan first became a professional journalist, she could not have imagined that one day she would be standing in front of the nation reporting on air that, according to the country's prime minister Benjamin Netanyahu, she was a traitor.

But that is precisely what Dayan did. For six long minutes, standing in the dark outside Netanyahu's office in Jerusalem, she recited the Israeli prime minister's scathing rebuke of her most recent reporting. Staring directly at the camera, in a red jacket and a polished haircut, Dayan recounted each of Netanyahu's accusations, slowly and deliberately, in her signature deep voice. 'The time has come to unmask Ilana Dayan,' she intoned, dead-serious. She informed her audience that, in Netanyahu's words, she was 'a lefty extremist' working to undermine the Israeli military and harm the country's national security. 'Dayan has a problem not only with me as prime minister,' she continued reading, 'but with the Israeli people.' Despite her poise, her grim expression gave viewers a hint of her inner anguish. To meet the moment and confront her prosecutor, Dayan was running through her own charge sheet, allegation after allegation, on prime-time TV. The dramatic segment quickly went viral, making headlines in Reuters, on CBS and in *The New York Times*. American journalists covering the story did not yet realise how soon they would be stepping into Dayan's shoes, facing chillingly similar challenges.

The very next day, 8th November, 2016, Donald Trump – the chief warrior against America's 'fake news media' – won an improbable election victory to become the 45th president of the United States. The global shock came a few short months after Britain's divisive Brexit referendum saw Nigel Farage, a figurehead of the Leave campaign, casting the BBC as 'the enemy'.[9] One year later, the Czech president Miloš Zeman showed up to a press conference with a gun marked 'for journalists'.[10] The Brazilian president at the time, Jair Bolsonaro, was castigating the 'treacherous' media for engaging in a 'frenzy' against him and 'destroying' the country. In France, Marine Le Pen – whose bodyguards physically attacked French reporters – was running for the presidency for the first time. In Serbia, Aleksandar Vučić – famous for fining critical reporters and banning foreign TV journalists – was elected president, bringing forwards an unprecedented peak in pressures on the media, labelling journalists foreign agents and blocking reporters from official events.[11] In Poland, President Andrzej Duda called for a 're-Polonization' of the supposedly unpatriotic Polish media, and in Hungary, Viktor Orbán and his allies took over most news organisations in the country, inciting violence against the few that maintained remnants of independence. The decade that followed has transformed everything we knew about news.

To my ears, this global smearing trend sounded strikingly familiar from the get-go. Netanyahu, Israel's longest-serving prime minister, had made his war on the free media a cornerstone of his political modus operandi, decades before Trump had turned from a ridiculed reality TV star to the leader of the semi-free world. From his earliest days in politics, Netanyahu found an easy target in journalists, accusing them of everything from 'Bolshevik witch-hunts' to outright treason, weaponising new technology against them as the early-adopter, media-savvy politician he always was. As a journalist in Tel Aviv back then, I was following the developments closely. Today, I can say we were ahead of the global curve: being labelled 'auto-anti-Semites' and bashed as 'traitors' long before it became the go-to protocol for a generation of populist leaders worldwide.

A Cautionary Tale in the Making

While I would have loved to tell this story as some distant dark tale from a godforsaken Middle Eastern nation, a decade later none of this will sound foreign to anyone here in the UK, where I have spent the last decade watching journalists and politicians failing to protect our news. By now, the same tactics have been documented and operationalised across borders, pushing the public conversation further and further to the extreme and overwhelmingly to the right. From the United States, Hungary and Brazil to India, Germany and Argentina, reporters and news presenters face harassment, doxing and malicious abuse online and offline whenever they dare clash with the populist crowd. As always, those who get hit worse tend to come from marginalised and sidelined communities: women, LGBTQ+, people of colour, Jewish, Muslim, disabled and others who fought long and hard to gain their spot in the newsroom.

In my home country, the impact of Netanyahu's war on the media was tangible: by 2017, most of all online hate speech in Israel was directed at – you guessed it – journalists.[12] The following year, almost 40 per cent of all comments on journalists' social media profiles accused them not only of bias or negligence, but *treason*. Leading news hosts who dared to criticise Netanyahu and the populist right have, slowly but surely, started leaving the profession. Old forms of censorship were anything but abandoned – dozens of journalists were killed, injured and arrested in Gaza, the West Bank and mainland Israel during the 2023–2025 war, and reporters' access to the Gaza Strip was blocked almost entirely. But beyond the familiar dangers of war reporting and humanitarian journalism, more insidious forms of censorship enabled the far-right government to tighten its grip on Israel's once relatively free media – and with it, public opinion. The shift was gradual, yet swifter than one might expect. Like democracy itself, journalism is fragile, imperfect and indispensable – its true value is easier to realise once lost.

While in Sweden, crime reporters tend to be the ones facing the most heat, particularly when covering immigration,[13] in South Korea, journalists who cover gender are primary targets.[14] In Israel, political and legal journalists were the main victims of the silencing efforts.[15] In the story told by the populists-in-chief, Israeli journalists are biased against the right and Netanyahu as its leader. The reporters who got the greatest share of online (and offline) harassment were Netanyahu's high-profile targets.[16] At least ten of them had to hire bodyguards due to death threats in recent years.

Why should we care? Journalists are hardly national sweethearts nowadays. Many of us, on the right and the left, have come to despise 'the media' – those privileged elitists who became too comfortable with power and believe they deserve to lead a monopoly over truth and expertise. A few years back, as part of a collaborative project with three excellent scholars, I asked over 1,000 people what they thought were the main traits of journalists in Israel.[17] We got scarily detailed responses, ranging from 'bloodthirsty monsters' to 'lefty Jew-haters'. In India and the Philippines, journalists are regularly called 'presstitutes'. In Germany, the common slur is 'the lying press', and in South Korea reporters are labelled 'pro-Japanese anti-patriots'. In short, hate is in the air.

And yet, we must care. The most consequential outcome of the populist war on the media is not what it means for journalists' daily lives, prestige or mood, but what it means for *our* right to know. The anti-media movement erodes and polarises the public's trust, crushing our ability to debate our shared future based on a minimal set of agreed-upon facts. It transforms journalists and journalism, giving rise to the new censorship (which will be dissected in the following chapters). For all its flaws, we are in desperate need of powerful journalism and fearless reporting, probably more so than ever. The people who hold Trump, Farage, Javier Milei and their copycats accountable cannot be part-time freelancers or bored TikTokers. The issues that journalism is supposed to shield us from are way too grand and their subjects way too powerful for individual users – or even ad-hoc online collectives – to be able to tackle on their own.

The War of the Words

What do you have in mind when you think about censorship? Blackened screens? Redacted paragraphs? Silenced sources? Many of us imagine the 'Deep Throat' version, inspired by the Watergate scandal and its popular Hollywood reenactment *All the President's Men* with young and handsome Robert Redford and Dustin Hoffman in leading roles. But this is not the only – or even primary – type of censorship choking our political conversations today. How about Elon Musk jumping frantically up and down on stage at Trump's 2024 election campaign rallies, speaking highly of free speech and tweeting that 'You are the media now'? Does this sound like censorship to you? I bet it doesn't. But this is precisely how the new censorship operates:

authoritarianism masquerading as democracy, mega-billionaires championing 'the people', loyalty regimes masked as freedom.

It will soon be a decade since Donald Trump mainstreamed the idea that journalists are, in his infamous phrasing, 'enemies of the people' (I know – it feels like both moments *and* ages ago). Over this decade, the MAGA 'fake news' terminology has been replicated and reiterated, with local adaptations, across borders. Demonising any critics, be they political opponents or democratic institutions, has always been a signature move of populist politics. The striking bit is that almost a decade went by and journalists under attack are still unsure what to make of it. A recent study shows how, despite the public confessions and endless commentary about the media's failure to cover the US elections in 2016, little changed in the following election cycle.[18] I doubt that analysing the 2024 elections will bring about more promising revelations.

Authoritarian leaders always work to undermine press freedom. What makes populism different is the sophisticated way in which it weaponises democratic terminology and us, 'the people', to erode it in practice. You could, theoretically, attack the media for criticising the king, who was chosen by God and is therefore above the law. You could hypothetically smear journalists for being too sloppy, for getting things wrong, for boring us to death. In fact, populist media-bashing has become so ubiquitous in vast parts of the world that it is easy to forget it was not always this way. For many years, especially since the introduction of TV, the conservative critique against the media was that it was dumbing us down, inspiring violence among youth by broadcasting too much violence, corrupting good Christians' souls by flooding us with sex, gossip and other blasphemies. This is no longer the main line of attack because it is no longer a *conservative* right, but a populist one.[19] It is wedded to different ideas about politics, media and society.

Importantly, this is not a symmetrical threat: in the 2020s, right-wing populism has transformed how knowledge producers operate, encouraging self-censorship, resignation, surrender to nationalist loyalty tests and a deliberate shift to the right. News anchors, political correspondents and editors-in-chief whom I interviewed over the past decade were somewhat used to old-fashioned state censorship – they were trained to detect and overcome redacted paragraphs, silenced sources and gagged stories. 'Sunlight,' they kept reciting, 'was the best disinfectant.' But what happens when instead of old-school censorship, populists turn to what Trump's long-time adviser turned podcaster Steve Bannon called 'flooding the zone with shit'? What happens when democracy no longer dies in darkness but in broad daylight, and all too often at prime time? What happens when by innocently 'shedding light' you end up amplifying a massive amount of useless, doctored and harmful crap? How is this new type of censorship changing journalism, politics and us?

By weaponising norms like objectivity, impartiality and balance against liberal democracy, the populist right found a way to exercise a more effective and socially acceptable type of censorship, boosted by propaganda operations disguised as news. Instead of banning stories they spread flows of misinformation, which take seconds to come up with and hours, days, sometimes years to debunk. Instead of silencing, they shout louder. Instead of blue-pencilling, they intimidate and dox, employing fake users, bot farms and smear campaigns to dominate the conversation. Heavy-handed state censorship is redundant when one can manipulate people to censor themselves, or simply stop listening. Most importantly, the populist right managed to turn journalism against journalists, using their own professional norms and practices to discredit them. How did they do it?

Free Speech vs Our Right to Know

For decades, the conversations we held around our shared future were immersed in the American obsession with free speech and its step-offspring: freedom of the press. Freedom, in the glittery US vision, is everything, especially among conservatives, Republicans and libertarians, for whom PC and 'wokeness' have become primary villains (although criminalising diversity programmes, banning research terms like 'female' and de-platforming Turkish opposition are apparently just fine). As a result, the heated battles around what should and should not be said in the public sphere have centred on the concept of freedom. Not the freedom to know, but the freedom to express false, dishonest and hateful ideas – and carry no consequences. In 2010, the Supreme Court's Citizens United decision made it evident that the American concept of freedom went overboard: the court's ruling determined that commercial corporations' political donations should not be limited by law, since regulating political donations amounts to restricting the corporations' freedom of speech.[20] In other words, corporations – just like humans – enjoy a birthright to free speech. Their love language: US dollars. As commentators have since pointed out, the court's decision was far-reaching but not necessarily convincing. It affects the political system in the US to this day and may seem perplexing – borderline unbelievable – to those lucky enough to live in countries where regulation of political donations is a standard matter.

Freedom of speech is, of course, truly critical. But the question we must ask first is whose freedom of speech. In the populist imagination, there is only one type of people who deserve free speech: white Christian MAGA supporters in the US, Hindu Modi fans in India, Jewish Netanyahu loyalists in Israel. But more importantly, while focusing exclusively on free speech, we tend to forget about all other basic rights and principles that should instruct us when shaping our public life. This is why I suggest we re-centre our concerns for information around *the public's right to know*. We all have the right to live our lives and determine our positions based on reliable, good-faith information. It is as essential for our lives as any other public-health measure. The implications of polluted, distorted, manipulated public knowledge were particularly evident during the Covid-19 pandemic, the 2020 elections in the US and the 2022 elections in Brazil. However, news is critical not only in crisis times or during election campaigns. We always need 'relatively accurate, accessible, diverse, relevant, and timely independently produced information about public affairs' to keep ourselves safe, to vote, to protest, to flourish, to work.[21] Yet somehow, the public's right to know has been invoked over the years less often than free speech, and mainly in one of two contexts: when paparazzi and tabloids were accused of invading celebrities' privacy, or in battles against government secrecy.

Decades ago, the American economist Joseph E. Stiglitz advocated for the right to know as a basic democratic right that requires greater government transparency.[22] However, with the change in censorship tactics over the years,[23] transparency is no longer enough. Our right to know is not just the opposite of celebrities' right to privacy[24] or governments' right to secrecy.[25] It is, rather, a fundamental epistemic right[26] we all share, without which any struggle for a better future, for equality or for justice will be lost. As media scholar Damian Tambini put it in his book *Media Freedom*, it might be a good idea to shift from the American-inspired negative understanding of media freedom into a more positive and active understanding of what that concept might mean.[27] It is high time that we reclaim our right to know, punish those who make it harder to know and support those who help us know better. After all, what good is free speech when it serves to spread misinformation, incitement and conspiracies? What good is transparency when it is abused to obfuscate and deter?

Can't TikTok Save Us?

For a few good years, to many of us – researchers, reporters and media users – hope looked like Facebook, with Mark Zuckerberg as a poster boy and slogans like 'connecting people' and 'bringing the world closer together'. Can't social media save us from the dirty swamp of media and politics in the 2020s? By now, we are well aware of the privacy problems, mental health and addiction issues, questionable surveillance policies and labour practices, and the many obscure biases which opaque algorithms (re)introduced to the world. And yet, social media allows us all to become active users, sources, witnesses, amplifiers and debaters. It enables us to organise and mobilise, find each other, build counter-narratives and alternative spaces for discussion and action.[28] It is a powerful means of resistance, a shelter for those of us who cannot find themselves elsewhere, who are oppressed in their local communities, who seek to connect, invent new identities, build bridges. Social media is also a wonderful tool for holding the media accountable: to monitor, criticise, encourage and improve it. So why can't algorithms replace journalism altogether?

The truth is, even with Snapchat on one hand and a viral meme on the other, we cannot scrutinise power alone. Yes, the global media industry is flawed on many levels and lets us down regularly; there is no way – or reason – to deny it. In a recent report by the Reuters Institute for the Study of Journalism, the overall cross-national levels of trust in the news media remain terribly low.[29] News avoidance is soaring, and people are actively seeking a way out of what we love thinking of as 'public good'.[30] Too often, consuming news comes hand in hand with stress, anxiety and depression.[31] Various communities feel alienated from the big media organisations, and not without good reasons.[32] This book is not intended to sugarcoat any of these: our media needs to be revolutionised to fulfil its democratic function. And it needs our help to get there.

Despite its viral manifestation online, there would be no #MeToo movement without fierce journalists at *The New York Times* and *The New Yorker* working tirelessly, for years, to provide reliable evidence and put the necessary pressure on decision-makers to make sure film mogul Harvey Weinstein faced the consequences of his serial crimes. There would be no Partygate without the *Guardian* investigation that exposed it, no Cambridge Analytica scandal without *The New York Times* and *The Observer* interviews with an insider whistleblower, no accountability for Jeffrey Epstein, no Windrush scandal, no Watergate, and no on-the-ground reporting from the devastating wars in Ukraine or Gaza without the accumulated and collaborative efforts by reporters, editors, photographers, producers, fixers and newsrooms. No reliable evidence of corruption, war crimes or voter suppression. Even seemingly self-evident matters like 'Who won the last elections?', 'Who started the war in Ukraine?' or 'Does bleach cure Covid-19?' cannot be trusted in the hands of influencers, trolls or AI chatbots. As boring as institutions may sound, they are crucial for accountability, scrutiny and social change. They require some serious fixing, not extinction.

Not only do we need powerful journalism, we need *journalism for everyone*. In recent years, in an environment of disillusionment with the media establishment, many of us turned to niche media in search of better news. After decades of concerns about media and politics that are too 'centrist', hyper-partisan media flourishes across borders – in the US, in the UK, in India, in Israel and beyond. Local media is another substitute hailed by scholars and journalists as a potential alternative to the failures of big news organisations. TikTok, YouTube and X work hard to replace all types of content for young audiences. And yet, as unsexy as it may sound, the time has come to reinvent news for all. The United States has generously offered a stark warning of the dangers of fragmented echo chambers, where communities inhabit vastly different – and sometimes warped – realities. In two words: 6th January. The lesson? It is not enough for MSNBC-watching liberals to know who the next US President is. Certain facts are too basic and essential for public life to leave to the benevolence of Elon Musk or Rupert Murdoch's brawling offspring.

At the next UK elections, will Britons agree on who has won? What about Brazilian voters? And Australians? The answer might seem obvious right now, but very recent history tells us it is not. Our information environment shifts quickly, and if we don't – pardon the Brexit reference – 'take back control' it might slip away faster than expected. The case of Israel demonstrates just how incredible the combination of old and new censorship can be at this moment in our lifetime.

In recent years, many have pointed out the devastating impact of social media platforms and generative-AI technologies on the many ills plaguing society in the 2020s – and often justifiably so.[33] There is ample evidence that algorithmic media facilitates hate speech, radicalises users and misinforms audiences, and new AI capabilities facilitate misinformation and ignorance.[34] But remember: social media was never *supposed* to save us. ChatGPT was not programmed to be a gatekeeper, and Siri wasn't trained to be the one holding those in power accountable. Neither was Snapchat. It is the same old struggling and crumbling journalism that has failed to protect us – or perhaps we, as a society, are the ones who failed to protect it.

Finally, apart from powerful news for all, we are also desperate for *popular* news. If truth hides behind paywalls or subscription fees, if evidence-based commentary and investigative reporting are bound to upper classes, and if the most basic facts and analysis out there are locked away in exclusive newsletters, it simply will not do. We need to find our basic common ground to run society. For that to happen, we need robust and popular news that aims to speak to everyone and empowers democracy rather than hollowing it out.

Lessons from Netanyahu's Israel, and Beyond

This book came out of years of ethnographic research, months of fieldwork, original public opinion surveys, analyses of speeches and literature reviews, and dozens of interviews. It uses the exceptional and explosive case of the Israeli populist right as a cautionary tale against the elusive attempts to dismember our media. The *New York Times* columnist Thomas Friedman, one of the world's most cited commentators on Israel and Palestine, mentioned recently that he 'considers Israeli trends to be a harbinger for wider patterns in Western civilisation'. As someone who studied Benjamin Netanyahu's brand of populism in power against that practised by Narendra Modi in India and Recep Tayyip Erdoğan in Turkey,[35] I can assure you that Israel's trendsetting goes way beyond the West, and is particularly relevant for the new censorship.

Netanyahu himself, Israel's longest-serving prime minister (1996–1999; 2009–2021; 2023 onwards) and the unquestionable leader of the anti-media movement in the country, has always been obsessed with the news. And, as his devout supporters put it, the media has always been obsessed with him. Few remember now that Netanyahu's never-completed PhD dissertation at MIT was supposed to explore how computers – a new and exciting invention at the time – would change political communication forever.[36] You can say many things about Netanyahu, but this was always his game. In the most difficult political times, when struggling to keep his coalition together, he refused to allow anyone to replace him as the Minister of Communications, until Israel's Supreme Court ruled that he could no longer hold the office due to his legal entanglements. His fixation with the media has only grown since.

Netanyahu's rants against journalists include all the washed-out smears, from 'fake news' to 'enemies of the people'.[37] But the populist war on our right to know only begins with words; it quickly extends to bitter legal wars, relentless attempts to crush public broadcasting, hostile media regulation and outright corruption. But let's start with the words that prepare the ground for everything that follows.

In Israel, the populist right's primary claim against the media is that it is 'lefty'. This is the local version of 'the liberal media' accusation in the US and the UK, or 'the lying press' in Germany. As with Trump, Farage, Milei, Modi and the AfD, Netanyahu's targets are not necessarily left-leaning, but rather anyone who dares criticise him – regardless of their ideological inclinations. 'Even when I criticise Netanyahu from the right,' one religious right-leaning reporter told me, 'the backlash I get is still: "You lefty media".' Over the past decade, the populist right in Israel conducted an efficient delegitimisation campaign, portraying the left as anti-Israeli, anti-Zionist and even anti-Semitic. In a survey conducted with my colleagues back in 2021, we exposed how prevalent this perception of Israeli journalists has become, particularly among Netanyahu's voters.[38] As a quintessential populist who focused his political career on media-bashing long before many of his global counterparts,[39] Netanyahu's confrontation with the media can shed light on the sophisticated, long-term mechanism of the new censorship – and, hopefully, how to mitigate it too.

The Israeli case is an intriguing one. Not quite a democracy yet not a full-on autocracy either, not an integral part of the Global North or the Global South, both oppressed and oppressor, Israel's unique geopolitical position and disproportional impact over world politics makes it a particularly compelling testing ground. Israel is all at once a relatively young self-described democracy,[1] a post-socialist society, a bastion of

---

[1] Importantly, Israel can be considered a (flawed) democracy only within its internationally recognised borders. This is not the case in the Occupied Palestinian Territories of the West Bank, where Israel governs through military law as an occupying force, and de facto enforces an apartheid system, applying different legal frameworks to Jewish settlers and Palestinian residents. In Gaza, Israel controls the borders and regulates movement in and out, including goods, but withdrew its settlements and military forces from the Gaza Strip in 2005. There is an ongoing debate about whether Israel should be considered a single entity exercising control from the river to the sea – therefore not a democracy at all – or whether it remains a democracy within its recognised borders while maintaining an occupation beyond them. In this book, I do not take a position on this debate.

Anglo-American culture in the heart of the Middle East, a former British colony turned occupying power, a 'cybernation' and, at least in the West Bank, an apartheid state.[40] A longstanding member of the OECD (the Organisation for Economic Co-operation and Development), a club of primarily wealthy countries, Israel is incredibly powerful militarily, diplomatically and financially. Yet it remains unstable, deeply divided, surrounded by past and present enemies, and shaped as much by a history of prosecution and trauma as by the relative prosperity it currently enjoys.

Israel's democratic backsliding during Netanyahu's time in office – expressed through the delegitimisation of democratic institutions, civil society and political dissent, breaking all existing norms while at it[41] – unfortunately characterises many societies on the democratic spectrum in the 2020s. The occupation of the Palestinian Territories remains a fundamental shadow looming over life in Israel and Palestine. The democratic space in Israel is distributed unequally, excluding Palestinians in Gaza and the West Bank, and to a lesser extent, the Arab Palestinian community in mainland Israel. For Jewish-Israeli citizens, the public sphere narrows over time too. Yet, until recently, there was reasonable space for watchdog journalism, investigative reporting and critical news-making.[42] Amid growing threats that stem from the militarised nature of Israeli society, the ongoing occupation of the Palestinian Territories and recurring cycles of war and bloodshed, the Israeli media also grapples with issues faced by news outlets worldwide: the struggle to adapt to new technologies, deteriorating working conditions, the erosion of professional norms and persistent inequality in newsrooms.[43]

What does the new censorship look like on the ground? During my first round of fieldwork in Israel, in 2017–2018, nearly every journalist I approached was, sooner or later, willing to speak openly. Only a handful requested anonymity, the rest were happy to talk. Just two years later, the landscape has shifted, like moving sands. During my second round of fieldwork (2019–2020), securing interviews with targeted journalists became harder. Nearly all journalists insisted on confidentiality. Some even carried out checks on my background and motives before meeting me. One day, I received a surprising phone call from a former employer whom I had worked for years ago. She informed me, amused, that a popular radio host had contacted her to 'vet' me. I wasn't amused. Why were they being so cautious? Another interviewee questioned two of our mutual acquaintances about me. A senior pundit refused to sign the standard Cambridge University ethics form – required for research involving human participants – out of fear that it might one day reveal he had spoken with me. Was this shift anecdotal? Or merely accidental? I can't rule it out. But it was undeniably chilling.

That slippery-slope reality has led me to question how safe my interviewees are now? Might those who agreed to speak openly in 2018 not have done so in 2020? What if even those willing to expose their identity in 2020 had come to regret it by 2025? And what about 2030? Is it possible to get all the inside information required to understand the new censorship without risking the reputation, well-being and trust that was confided in me by people who don't enjoy living in secure and lovely London, like myself? This is why almost all the quotes in the book you're reading are anonymised. As I am writing these words, no one can guarantee what press freedom will look like in Israel or Palestine in the near future, let alone decades from now. Will it be safer or riskier? Even the names of journalists who initially agreed to speak publicly (some even striving for it!) were anonymised retrospectively. This solution is not ideal, with some great anecdotes left on the editing room floor. But the last thing I would risk is further harm to those who try to practise worthy journalism in one of the most difficult regions in the world.

In times when nationalism is flourishing, hate speech is prospering and media-bashing is effortless – right at the tips of our fingers – journalism has become a 24/7 struggle. To be sure, producing relevant, courageous, reliable news has never been easy: powerful tycoons, political intimidation, unconscious biases and innocent mistakes have always made it difficult to inform the people (who do not always enjoy the information nor cherish the efforts to produce it). Journalists in Mexico and Russia have been struggling to survive for decades. Reporters in Turkey were interrogated and arrested for reporting on Covid-19 in 2020,[44] for downloading an encrypted messaging app in 2017[45] and for supporting the opposition in 2016.[46] Newsrooms were raided. The 'old-school' ways of silencing the media are still alive and kicking – literally – given how in recent years, journalism has become overwhelmingly deadly. The wars in Gaza and Ukraine have cost the lives of photographers, producers, reporters and 'fixers', making 2024 the deadliest year for journalists since the Committee to Protect Journalists started counting 30 years ago.[47] None of these challenges disappeared. But the combination of new infrastructures for censorship and propaganda, surveillance and abuse, alongside rising anti-media movements, has turned journalists' lives upside down – and our information environment with them. The story of the Israeli media is not, unfortunately, unprecedented nor anomalous. The new censorship is everywhere.

The Populist War on Our Right to Know

'Legacy media must die.' *Elon Musk, senior advisor to President Trump, head of the Department of Government Efficiency and wealthiest person in the world, on X, 2024.*[48]

IT WAS 2022 when I stepped anxiously into the German public broadcaster's underwhelming studios at the heart of London, as a young and inexperienced PhD student, invited to give an interview for an ARD documentary. I was excited to find a tower of academic articles – which tend to reach very few readers, and that's an understatement – printed, highlighted with a yellow marker and commented on in what hinted at a very close reading. I was even more chuffed to realise these were *my* articles, about Israeli journalism under attack, that someone in the radio station bothered to read so meticulously. But then there was a pause. Why would German radio hosts find these useful? After the interview, I had to ask. 'We, too, are being targeted,' my interviewer replied, detailing the relentless assault by the AfD party on legacy media in Germany, which ranged from banning journalists from covering the party's rallies to smearing the public radio station as part of the 'lying press', a term associated with the label the Nazi regime popularised early in the 20th century.[49] 'And we're not coping much better,' he sighed. What made the new censorship so difficult to handle, particularly in a country with a comparatively strong and independent news environment? 'Honestly,' he said, 'I'm not sure.' I left the studios more confused than when I entered.

How does the new censorship actually work? What makes it so tricky to handle? The following sections outline the many facets of the populist war on the media: what populism means, why it clashes with journalism and truth-telling, and which conditions help it spread as fast as an Elon Musk post on an Elon Musk-owned platform.

Enemies of the People, The Making of

Populism might be the most overused term in political theory and public debate at present. It is therefore worth taking a (very brief) moment to define it, just to make sure we don't confuse it with overlapping concepts like demagogy or charismatic leadership. The unquestioned rock star of populism studies today, Dutch scholar Cas Mudde, has become the leading resource for academics and reporters who struggle to write on this topic. Mudde defines populism as a 'thin' ideology, that divides society into two homogenous groups: 'the real people' and 'the corrupt elites' who conspire against them.[50] It is 'thin' because unlike 'thick' ideologies such as conservatism or communism, populism is not committed to a specific set of solutions or values. Populism doesn't offer you a set of policies in all areas of life. You could be a socialist, environmentalist or libertarian and still be a populist so long as you believe that only your supporters and allies are 'the real people' or 'the authentic people', and everyone else is part of the conspiratorial and corrupt elite that is intentionally destroying the nation.

Political theorist Jan-Werner Müller emphasises that populists are not anti-elitists as much as they are anti-pluralists – only one way of thinking is allowed.[51] Since they claim to exclusively and eternally embody 'the real people' against 'the enemies of the people', populists defy any legitimate claim for opposition or checks and balances. We are no longer debating this economic policy or that immigration reform. Instead, it has become a moral struggle between the wholly righteous and the utterly evil. There is no room for concessions, deliberations or compromises, only 'real people' and 'vile enemies'. This anti-pluralist perspective ensures that the populist worldview comes into direct confrontation with journalism. Populists demand that journalists serve the public by representing the uniform stance of 'the people' and any criticism of such would be tantamount to betrayal. But who *are* 'the people'? They are defined, of course, by the populist. And what do they have in common? They are those who do not question the populist-in-chief. Any criticism of the populist leader is therefore seen as an illegitimate attempt to undermine the will of the people.[52]

This is not a new idea or way of leading: in 1665, King Louis XIV famously declared: '*L'État, c'est moi*' ('I am the state'). A Trumpian adaptation of this absolutist conceit might be: '*Le peuple, c'est moi*' ('I am the people'). The populist media-bashing sets a unique challenge for journalists in the 2020s. In line with the populist logic, which divides society into the 'authentic' people and its enemies, the populist claim attributes the media's alleged bias and blind spots not to innocent errors or mere negligence but to a malign conspiracy against 'the people'. Journalists are thus required not only to defend their reputation as credible professionals but also as legit members of society. It is a very different type of allegation, with very different implications.

Understanding the inherent clash between populism and democracy is vital, since the attempt to delegitimise journalism – and not merely criticise it, which is generally desirable – is the defining feature of anti-media populism. In the populist mind, good journalists are those who are unequivocally loyal to 'the people', namely, to the populists themselves as the representatives of the people. For populists in power – like Netanyahu, Trump, Milei, Modi or Orbán – the media is expected to side with the government. For populists in opposition – think Farage, Le Pen, AfD or Bolsonaro – the media is condemned as an ally of the 'ruling elites'. Apparently, anti-media populists are just fine with the media, as long as *they* are the media.

In the last UK election campaign, Nigel Farage exemplified this dynamic when his long-time tabloid cheerleader – the *Daily Mail* – accused him of being too sympathetic to Putin. In a single headline, the *Mail* went from being one of Farage's staunchest allies to, in his view, conspiring with the Kremlin.[53] This minuscule Kremlin-gate demonstrates that populism is not really about anti-elitism – it is about loyalty. It is therefore not surprising that more often than not, populist leaders – while riling people against 'corrupt elites' – are themselves the very epitome of privilege: the pampered sons of billionaires, daughters of nationally recognised politicians or privately educated Oxbridge alumni.

When Bad News is Good News

Classic accounts of journalist–politician relations delineate a 'tango dance' or 'tug of war':[54] an ever-shifting give-and-take, a push-and-pull with politicians desperate for media exposure and journalists seeking stories, leaks and sources. Both sides had things to gain and things to lose by engaging in this complicated and often-gone-wrong love-hate relationship. But what happens when 'the fake news media' becomes a rallying cry?

Anti-media populists are less dependent on positive media coverage, as both positive and negative attention serve their campaigns. By framing journalists in the public mind as biased 'enemies', any future negative coverage becomes an asset that 'confirms' the media's alleged resentment towards the populists and their supporters. Journalists who fear the potential effects on the public's trust are then trapped in a lose-lose situation: either they don't criticise the media-bashing, arguably against their professional interest, or they do criticise it, thereby confirming the populist accusations. For decades, the conventional belief was that journalists *need* politicians to gain information, and politicians *need* journalists to gain attention.[55] They were getting too cosy.[56] Now, populist politics and the endless alternative sources for news challenge this seemingly trivial *quid pro quo*.

Many in the media have come to the realisation that their chances of winning the debate with the populists are slim. 'It's a cruel war,' one of them said, defeated, 'and I don't think we can win it. Netanyahu managed to push us into this position of "the lefty media". It's a win-win situation for him. Each criticism is seen as our revenge for him turning against us. Then there's self-censorship. Journalists say, "Wait, they will say I'm going after him, that I'm part of the campaign." Even our fiercest investigation turns into an asset. Each negative item "proves" the media's alleged hostility.' This dynamic poses journalism at a clear disadvantage in its confrontation with authoritarian leaders, who manage to turn even corruption scandals and embarrassing investigative revelations into fuel for conspiracy theories against the media, the legal system and the deep state that allegedly runs them both.

Compounding the challenges, the current wave of media-bashing catches journalism at a fragile moment. In the next section, I lay out the conditions that made the populist war on the media so impactful: social media and the rise of the broligarchy; the collapse of the traditional business model for news; and a forgiving approach to corruption in the newsroom.

Conditions for Hate

Whenever I give lectures on journalism under attack, there is always someone in the room who takes the opportunity to tell me off, with the claim that – in the words of the popular Spider-Man meme – 'it always has been': nothing is new, journalism has always been under attack and always will be.

In one instance, in a room filled with legal scholars, an elderly professor recounted how, in the 1980s, a journalist neighbour had found an angry note left on his car windscreen about his reporting. To the professor, this anecdote proved that nothing has changed: people hate journalists, and journalists have to suck it in – nothing to see here. To me, it was quite the opposite – a fantastic example of the massive change in scale, spread and impact of media hate. A single note left on a car can be unsettling or irritating, but today, as journalists around the world can testify, the 'notes' are everywhere. You couldn't escape them if you tried.

It has become a cliché to even note that one of the most groundbreaking changes to our lives in the past decades – during which the populist campaign against the media took over the public conversation – is the emergence of social media. But it is true. Consider this: Elon Musk could, theoretically, decide that as of tomorrow we shall only get tweets from Donald Trump, the Proud Boys or Nigel Farage on our X feeds. There is no mechanism in place that could stop him. Frankly, it might take us some time to even realise or prove it had happened.

But let's start from the beginning. In the 2010s, with the introduction of personalised newsfeeds and micro-targeting techniques, social networks captured the advertising revenues that funded modern journalism for about a century.[57] This trend is detrimental to journalism, and not just because of the money. Apart from eating away digital ad revenues, social networks – applauded in the early 2000s as free and democratic alternatives to institutional media – provided politicians with a new and exciting platform for media-bashing.[58] After all, it is much easier to smear reporters behind their backs, and, more crucially, when you are not entirely dependent on them to reach your potential voters.

For populists, who tend to excel in the divisive and simplistic content that works well online, TikTok, YouTube and the rest of them were particularly beneficial.[59] Algorithmic media incentivises toxic discourses, turning them into a constant presence in the daily lives of journalists (and to varying degrees, of all of us). The digital sphere – which many of us hoped would help us break existing hierarchies and inequalities – allows abusive messages to travel quicker and further, with vocal users able to easily and freely express offensive language, baseless slander, disinformation, hate speech and conspiracy theories that they would scarcely resort to face-to-face – rarely with any consequences at all.[60]

In a recent study, a rising star in political psychology – and my former Gates-Cambridge colleague – Steve Rathje, set out with his colleagues to check why Twitter (also known as X) rewards content that most people disapprove of.[61] According to their findings, later replicated by others, social media *misrepresents* public opinion. Instead of reflecting what we all think, it represents the preferences of a minority of vocal extremists. This won't sound like news to any of us with access to Twitter, but American senators' tweets which dismissed their opponents earned 2–4 times more likes and retweets than their non-divisive tweets. A representative sample of ordinary people had the opposite inclination: they actually preferred the non-divisive tweets. Another team of researchers offered two possible explanations for this phenomenon. The first is that a small share of Americans (6–7 per cent), who are more ideological and extremist than their fellow citizens, provide most of the engagement and buzz to US senators' tweets.[62] The second explanation is that the silent majority of Americans, who attest to disproving dismissive tweets, rarely or never interact online.

At the same time, the popular allure of social media platforms became another unconventional weapon in the populist war against the media. The underdog image of social media, the common perception of Facebook's algorithm as 'unmediated', 'direct' and 'authentic' – unlike evil TV producers – was just what the populist campaigns were striving for. A culture of anti-expertise, 'the cult of the amateur' that came about in the early days of social media,[63] fit like a glove to the populist hand.

Ultimately, social media became an unleashed breeding ground of incitement and conspiracies. One of the leading media sociologists of our time, Silvio Waisbord, termed what came next as 'mob censorship': unprecedented levels of online abuse and violence, aimed at disciplining and silencing journalists. The early utopian hopes that social media would lead to enhanced dialogue and audience engagement in news production have been soured by the grim reality of cyberbullying, doxing and abuse.[64] In the past, targeting a journalist required significant effort: tracking down their address, identifying their car and leaving a note (seen only by the journalist) without getting caught. Today, however, any statement made on air, or a single tweet on X, can expose journalists to a barrage of low-cost, easily accessible attacks, ranging from trolling and spamming to doxing and intimidation – threats they are often ill-prepared to handle. What was once an occasional note on a windscreen from a grumpy neighbour has evolved into mass harassment campaigns and constant nuisance, following reporters 24/7 no matter where they are.[65] It is one thing – surely unpleasant – to get a death threat once every few years when you break an explosive story. It is a different matter altogether to know that any criticism of a populist figure or movement could spark a coordinated hate campaign, with thousands of vilifying posts – and sometimes even incitement to violence – delivered instantly to the device we are all addicted to, now seemingly an extension of our very selves: our smartphone.

The online war against critical journalists could be considered a mere continuation of offline forms of silencing techniques.[66] However, the change in circumstances is significant for two pivotal reasons: the current nature of online communication, and the spread and speed of circulation. Due to these very technical, almost random developments, the public's ability to affect journalists' lives and work has grown exponentially. Bad faith actors were quick to capitalise on that. Why yell at the telly when you could share the anger with someone else, say, the presenter? So far, this new proximity of audiences and news producers has generally not had the democratising effect many were expecting and hoping for. Some researchers call it 'dark participation'[67] – the unintended outcome of believing that social media and mobile phones would democratise journalism, dismantle hierarchies and foster an egalitarian news ecosystem.[68] Instead, we've ended up with multiplying bot farms, conspiracy theories and death threats.

To this, we should add another factor distorting public opinion on social media – what we once referred to in real life as fraud. Fake users, bot farms and campaign workers pretending to be voters have all become powerful tools in any political toolkit. Former Brazilian president Jair Bolsonaro was aided by online advocates known as 'Bolsonaristas'.[69] They were organised by a supporters group called, flagrantly, 'The Office of Hate'. These Bolsonaro fans set up fake accounts on social media as a tool for supporting their leader and targeting his adversaries, including journalists. If a politician were to pay thousands of people from overseas to travel to their country and pretend to be local voters, this might sound ludicrous. But this is what online political campaigning looks like every day. Buying likes, shares and comments, purchasing existing profiles, fabricating new ones, faking support and spreading anonymous smears are all the outcomes of an unregulated, algorithm-based, surveillance-oriented, commercially driven media sphere. It's far easier – and cheaper – to buy likes from Indonesia than to pay demonstrators to appear enthusiastic on the streets. Faking public opinion online has become remarkably simple – and this is yet another factor enabling the rise of the new censorship.

However, hate and lies – and even fake users – are not some innate or inevitable features of the internet. The current generation of populists turned the online world into a secret weapon, but the first US president to use social media to bypass White House reporters was Barack Obama.[70] There is nothing essentially right-wing or conservative about these man-made algorithms, and nothing inherently cruel or chaotic. There is a parallel universe where the internet became a liberal, or at least democratic, heaven. It is not 'the invisible hand' nor 'human nature' that makes algorithms so prone to highlighting hateful, racist, divisive conversations. This is the outcome of how social media CEOs and programmers built and trained their algorithms for years. How we allowed them to shape our conversations. What they hoped would boost their gains ended up boosting our losses – and the price journalists are paying is merely one example of the harm done to our information environment.

Expensive Truths, Cheap Lies

Another convenient condition for the populist assault on the truth stems from the difficulty of funding journalism today. But before we get into the weeds of stats, let's figure out what it feels like, in the shrinking world of newsrooms.

For someone who was working as a journalist, I have always been spectacularly bad at confrontations. I hate them, and to this day I am willing to go to great lengths to avoid them. For that reason, I remember particularly well one day over a decade ago, a rather heated argument with the head of the commercial department at a Tel Aviv magazine over our weekly cover. That week, I wanted the cover to feature our story about the thousands of Sudanese refugees who were being pushed by Netanyahu's government – yes, he was already in charge – to leave Israel for unspecified and likely unsafe destinations. This was, in fact, an early version of Rishi Sunak's 'Rwanda Plan' – sending asylum seekers to allegedly safe third countries instead of processing their claims and granting asylum to those in need, as required under the 1951 Refugee Convention (a convention spearheaded by the state of Israel at the time as a response to the lessons of the Holocaust). That week in 2014, the Israeli home office sent over a thousand Sudanese asylum seekers to the so-called 'safe' third countries of Uganda and Rwanda. Within a year, a report came out documenting the horrors these asylum seekers had faced in this so-called 'safe' journey.[71] But that week, all we knew was that families of asylum seekers were being put on buses to the unknown, in the heart of Tel Aviv. I was determined to have their stories on the cover.

The head of the magazine's commercial department – a generally affable and strong-minded lady – insisted that with summer approaching the cover just *had* to feature popsicles. I am neither joking nor exaggerating: this was a refugees vs popsicles situation. Advertisers were pushing for a lighter, more colourful cover to complement their campaigns, and for the commercial department that was the priority; refugees had very little to offer when it came to ad campaigns. For the editorial staff, popsicles were not a priority. To my surprise, after hours of fighting, shouting and, if I'm not mistaken, even a few tears – I won that particular mini-battle. I was in a senior editing position in this section of the newspaper at the time, and I managed to fend off the push for a colourful frozen treats cover, at least that week when terrified refugees were being sent on perilous journeys from our city to hostile countries.

Sounds like a relatively happy ending, right? Except that a few months later, my colleagues and I were summoned to a meeting with a senior commercial executive. 'We are shutting down your magazine,' he said. 'It is not profitable enough.' Dozens of people lost their jobs. The popsicle projects found their way to other sections. The refugees? Not so much.

This story is far from unique, and the conflict between journalism and commercial interests is nothing new. But it is getting worse. Over the past two decades, at least 2,500 newspapers in the US shut down, resulting in the loss of over 40,000 jobs. This decline created vast 'news deserts', with millions of Americans living in areas with limited access to local news.[72] In the UK, over 300 local newspapers shut down since 2005.[73] When Covid-19 hit, the general trend of newsroom closures turned into a global tsunami. Newsroom layoffs and cuts took over Mexico, Germany, Brazil, Nigeria, South Africa, the Philippines and beyond.[74]

But while the pandemic had finally ended, a vaccine for the collapse of the business model for news has not yet been found. At least 8,000 journalism jobs were cut in the UK, the US and Canada only in 2023.[75] The Canadian Broadcasting Corporation (CBC) alone announced it was cutting 600 positions that year. In 2024, the BBC announced budget cuts totalling £24 million, leading to a loss of 155 jobs – including 130 journalism roles.[76] The same year in New Zealand, Warner Bros. Discovery chose to close all its news operations, resulting in 350 more journalists losing their jobs.[77] As of 2025, after Trump's second administration decided to stop all federal funding to USAID, independent media organisations in the Global South – from Ukraine to Afghanistan – who were supported by USAID were being forced to lay off staff or shut down.[78]

The conflict between financial considerations and valuable journalism has always been there, long before I was fighting with the marketing department over popsicles and refugees. But the highly unstable state of the news industry in the 2020s makes reporters and news organisations an easy target for authoritarian-wannabes. While we can all recognise its social value, journalism tends not to be profitable – particularly not since we got used to getting it for free.

Original and bold reporting is expensive, particularly the valuable, serious, expertise-based investigative type. And our willingness to pay for good journalism, as a public, is still scarce. Lies, however, are incredibly cheap. They are easy and quick to produce, and easy to spread. They tackle the algorithms the right way, thus gaining much organic reach. Fact-checking is important when populists gain power, but it requires human resources that most news organisations no longer have. Moreover, it takes time. This is what the populist machine is counting on: by the time reporters figure out how best to refute the daily lie by the populist in chief the lie has already become an axiom, and ten others were spread online and in the populist echo chamber in the meantime. This is not a fair fight. That's what makes 'shit-flooding' so tantalising. In the zero-sum game of money, attention and time, the populist lies are enjoying a freeride.

50 Shades of Media Corruption

And when the money is scarce, corruption is ubiquitous. Back in 2006, as a young and hopeful – if not particularly studious – student eager to break into the news industry, an old friend discreetly handed me a wrinkled, cryptic note. On it was a familiar name and a phone number. 'You should call him,' the friend said, 'he knows who you are.' My friend had contacts at the Likud party (which Netanyahu has been leading for decades). Scribbled on the note was the phone number of a close associate of Netanyahu – someone, I was surprised to learn, who could secure me a promising job in the national media. Just like that

I didn't take the offer (an easy decision in your early 20s, when idealism runs high and you're vain enough to believe you can make it on your own). Others, however, have probably found their way to the news industry through similar wrinkled notes bearing confidential phone numbers, or, in later years, a simple text message. This was not an anomaly, but a routine example of the entrenched corruption that has shaped and plagued Israeli media over time. With a handful of powerful owners controlling the industry and little accountability, regulation or transparency, the country's news landscape has long been vulnerable to political influence – whoever holds power. Astute politicians quickly learned to exploit this reality. None have mastered this art better than the most influential Israeli leader in the 21st century: Benjamin Netanyahu.

But this is not a story about Netanyahu. It is also about a global and evolving set of tactics designed to bring the media to heel. It is part of an emerging playbook for shaping public opinion – one that blends old and new forms of censorship, both mass and personalised media. Even countries that see themselves as havens of free speech and free press, like the UK or the US, suffer from variants of very similar maladies.

Could some Tory operative get me a job in Rupert Murdoch's media empire? Could Nigel Farage offer a gig on GB News? Media corruption, and corruption more generally, has always been a severe matter, more pervasive than those of us in 'safe' and wealthy societies are willing to acknowledge. Its affinity with the populist right is not incidental. The populist worldview – where you could be either with us or against us, where democratic institutions trying to hold power to account should be denounced, and where loyalty is everything – is an excellent fit for depraving corruption. Media corruption has thus become the fertiliser of the new censorship – an enabler and primary beneficiary.

The Stories We Tell Ourselves

Since democracy has been the main source of legitimacy for journalism in modern societies,[79] it is unsurprising that it stands at the core of the populist media-bashing. The kind of democracy that journalism and populism are striving for are, however, entirely incompatible. When going after the press, authoritarian populists establish a very specific notion of democracy: direct, majoritarian, expressive democracy. It is sceptical – if not antagonistic – towards establishments, representatives and gatekeepers, and disregards minority rights.[80] Direct democracy means that journalism – as a democratic institution, part of the system of checks and balances, and essentially a mediating institution – is unnecessary. Both politics and the media are required, in this 'democratic' universe, to serve as mirrors to 'the will of the people'.

The populist story about democracy emphasises its majoritarian aspect. Democratic institutions, the argument goes, are undermining the rule of the majority in favour of privileged elites and the minorities they promote. Sociologist Paul Starr would classify this narrative as part of the 'minimalist' approach to democracy.[81] In minimalist democracies, the main criterion is competitive elections. Other scholars call it 'procedural democracy' or 'illiberal democracy' – societies where elections are held regularly, but the liberal spirit at the core of modern democracy is ignored. Think, for instance, of elections in Hungary. They keep taking place, but the conditions guarantee that the ruling Fidesz party will win. It is therefore a pretty generous reading to call these societies 'illiberal democracies', and it is no wonder that Orbán himself was quick to embrace the term.

Political theorists like Jan-Werner Müller and William Galston insist that 'illiberal democracy' is not a democracy at all – despite its fixation with majority rule and self-governance.[82] In fact, the populist story about democracy should be understood as 'anti-democratic'. In the populist narrative, the media is seen as a pipe – a platform for the free expression of 'the people' (certainly not a watchdog, fourth estate or holding power accountable). Journalists' role as monitoring the powerful or giving voice to the weak is mocked and ridiculed, dismissed as gossip or scolded as rude. Instead, missions like representing the 'real' people and allowing the far right's free speech are heralded.

The story journalism tells us about democracy is more complicated, dynamic and varied. Every political universe is distinct, and different types of democracy require distinct forms of journalism.[83] The dominant narrative around media and democracy, however, is deeply rooted in liberal ideals and liberal democracy as the climax of human progression. Most of the established roles of the press – informing, gatekeeping, watchdog of democracy – require the intervention of professional reporters in the free expression and public opinion of the majority. Journalists are the ones to decide what people should be informed of before elections and to criticise their elected representatives once they assume office. The fact they won elections does not make journalistic scrutiny redundant; quite the opposite. This journalistic narrative about democracy is both institutional and pluralistic. It expresses belief in democratic institutions as mechanisms to monitor power and defend minorities from the tyranny of the majority.

The populist narrative assigns a pretty passive role to the press: journalists should simply transmit the people's will, as represented by their leaders' will. To some extent, journalism becomes unnecessary when social media is around. The journalistic story assigns the media an active role: gatekeeping, investigating and scrutinising. Those roles are being demonised by populists as corrupt, arrogant and detached. The inevitable act of 'filtering' information before 'transmitting' it to the people is portrayed as a cult-like censoring act. The very act of mediation is disputed.

At some crucial points, the stories populists tell us about democracy coincide with another influential narrative of our times: the utopian vision of social media and technology as potential saviours of humanity. This powerful narrative originated in Silicon Valley but travelled everywhere in the 2000s. Its dominance has prepared the ground for the populist agenda to resonate. And the Musks of the world know it.

Netanyahu, Javier Milei and Geert Wilders regularly praise the sacred impact of social media on democracy. Marine Le Pen thanks her 'internet militants on social media', Donald Trump, after his 2016 electoral victory, attributed it to 'Facebook, Twitter and Instagram',[84] as has Narendra Modi,[85] and the surging YouTuber, TikToker and right-wing populist, 24-year-old Fidias Panayiotou, who won a surprising EU seat for Cyprus in 2024, called social media 'my biggest weapon'.[86] In Hungary, a pro-Orbán organisation named Megafon offers free four-day training for those who wish to become 'right-wing digital freedom fighters'.[87] The symbiosis is evident.

In the early 2020s, many writers championed social networks as the embodiment of democracy, a tool for improving citizens' engagement in the political debate – the ultimate realisation of free speech. Prolific writer Clay Shirky, one of the earliest commentators on all things internet, celebrated the sharing culture of the internet, the global flow of free information and how it facilitates collective actions.[88] Influential sociologist Manuel Castells claimed social networks shook up the political system, undermining established hegemonies and threatening authoritarian regimes.[89] Others shared his optimistic vision, predicting a generation of informed citizens, collapsing hierarchies and a new tolerant society.[90] 'A whole new world,' it was said, has been rising right before our eyes, 'unlimited by the constraints of time and space, appearance and prejudice, gender and power.'[91] In retrospect, it hasn't quite worked out this way.

Like populism itself, social media was believed to be 'fixing' the illnesses of modern democracy.[92] It was considered a potential cure for journalism's failings too: an alternative, exciting, compelling, inclusive and decentralised platform for public debate.[93] Despite being harshly criticised since,[94] the optimistic story we told ourselves about social media and democracy still holds.

Apart from seeing social media as a democratising force, the conceptions behind this Silicon Valley-style techno-optimism sit well with the populist argument. Rejecting any restrictions on free speech, which is seen as the paramount ideal of democracy, aligns with the populist rationale that celebrates social media as a liberating technology. It relies on the glorification of direct democracy rather than institutional democracy, which makes democratic institutions like traditional media futile and unnecessary. Authoritarian populists manipulate the no-filters, no-gatekeeping sentiment to spread majoritarian ideas that contrast with liberal democratic values.[95] Just read this hyperbolic bit by the secret star of this book, Benjamin Netanyahu, in one of his attempts to establish his own TV channel on Facebook:

'The characteristic of North Korea is that when you switch to channel 11, 12, 13, all of them, you always hear the same thing, the same line, the line of the Left. And it is hard for [journalists] to digest that we don't live in North Korea, because we have something that North Korea doesn't.'

Interviewer: 'What?'

Netanyahu: 'Facebook. Social media. It is hard for them to acknowledge that you can express different voices, the voice of the Likud, the voice of the Right, without going through their filters – it drives them crazy! So they call it North Korea. No, they are North Korea!'

For those advocating for democracy in its modern, liberal form, the populist and techno-utopian approaches – both of which push forwards ideals of 'direct' and majoritarian democracy – endanger the freedom of speech and democracy rather than enhancing them. In the words of Austrian-British philosopher and public intellectual, Karl Popper: 'If we extend unlimited tolerance even to those who are intolerant, if we are not prepared to defend a tolerant society against the onslaught of the intolerant, then the tolerant will be destroyed, and tolerance with them'.

The romantic idealisation of direct democracy unites the populists and the broligarchs in their hostility towards expertise, the celebration of the 'ordinary people' and common sense. Andrew Keen, one of the most controversial and influential commentators on the internet, observed as early as 2008 that user-generated media and social networks promote a culture of 'noble amateurs' vs the 'dictatorship of experts'.[96] With amateur journalism lauded as the saviour against the media's oppressive experts, you can see why populists love the tech-utopia. The title of Dan Gillmor's 2006 book captures this sentiment: *We the Media: Grassroots Journalism by the People, for the People.*[97] The innuendo? Professional journalists are, apparently, not part of 'the people' nor working for them.

The anti-expertise sentiment – which you probably remember well from the Brexit days – stems from the obsession with *direct* and *majoritarian* democracy. So, importantly, social media has not only hurt journalism financially, but also in the narratives it pushed to the fore, advancing the smooth adoption of widespread anti-elitism, anti-expertise, anti-hierarchies, anti-mediation and pro-majoritarianism.

The next chapter digs deeper into how the populist playbook capitalises on these fruitful conditions.

The Playbook: Choose Your Weapon

'You know why I do it? I do it to discredit you all and demean you all so that when you write negative stories about me no one will believe you.'
US President Donald Trump to 60 Minutes *journalist Lesley Stahl, 2018.*[98]

THE POPULIST PLAYBOOK to crush our right to know takes different forms in different countries and cultures. As Austrian linguist Ruth Wodak pointed out, dog whistles only work when one is familiar with the overtones.[99] But whether decrying 'presstitutes' or 'fake news', 'urban Naxals' or 'the lying press', the populist playbook has a common rationale, and a common repertoire of tactics, adapted to the local settings. To fight it, the playbook needs to be identified and demystified.

Old techniques to limit what the public gets to know are still very much with us: killings and arrests of journalists continue, as do raids and closures of news organisations. But in many cases – particularly where democracy feels relatively 'safe' – these tactics have become redundant. No one needs to bleed for the news to die. Censorships – old and new – join forces to transform our information environment, amplifying, enabling and boosting each other.

The new censorship is needed for the type of regime that populists in power seek to establish: 'hollow democracies'.[100] In such regimes, the courts keep working (but always rule with the authorities), elections take place (but always end up with the victory of the leader), and importantly, the media keeps broadcasting (but makes sure not to enrage the authorities). In short, the democratic façade remains, but the free society disappears. One of the features that makes populism so difficult to recognise and resist is its manipulative use of the terminology of democracy to achieve its authoritarian goals. The gradual shift from a functioning (even if flawed) democracy into a hollow democracy is facilitated by the language of democracy – and those tasked with safeguarding it. The capture of the media is explained as attempts to 'fix', 'diversify', 'balance', 'democratise', give 'the real people' what they want. Attempts to reject the media takeover are framed as 'censorship', 'bias', 'corruption' and 'treason'. This mirroring trick makes it extremely difficult for journalists, public servants, academics and other knowledge producers to protest the populist assault. If Netanyahu, Trump, Modi, Milei and Farage are the ones speaking for 'the people', shouldn't we all align with them? Ignoring or dismissing them would be detached and elitist. Even illiberal! Isn't serving 'the people' what democracy is all about?

Kim Lane Scheppele, Professor of Sociology and International Affairs at Princeton University, has long been the sharpest analyst of what she calls 'legal authoritarianism', and the best guide to help us detect the populist takeover of the media. Back in the 1990s, Scheppele worked in Hungary, where she met Hungarian PM Viktor Orbán. 'What we have witnessed is a new generation of leaders, trained under this new democratic resurgence, who began to realise that they could compromise democratic governments while still leaving the shell of them intact,' she wrote. Maintaining this shell is one of the most effective tools in the populist war on our right to know.

Scheppele outlines three strategies which legal authoritarians are using to subjugate the media: (1) starting newspapers and TV channels that operate as propaganda channels; (2) using regulation to weaken news outlets which refuse to align with the authoritarian leadership; (3) constant campaigning against free press and critical journalists. These three strategies have evolved and expanded since, with new technologies and logic incorporated into the fight:

(1) The Online War

When Emilia Șercan, an established Romanian investigative reporter, published a story revealing that the then-prime minister, Nicolae Ciucă, had allegedly plagiarised his doctoral thesis, she surely expected some flak. And indeed, the flood of threats was immediate.[101] But Șercan could not have possibly seen what was coming next. On her Facebook Messenger she found a message from a complete stranger, with personal photos of her taken 20 years earlier by her then-partner. Creeped out, concerned that her phone might have been hacked and her photos stolen, Șercan called the police.

The next day, she found out that the screenshot she shared with the Romanian cops was somehow posted on a Moldovan website. From there, the intimate photos have spread elsewhere, including foreign adult websites. It was, she said, a clear attempt to intimidate her.[102] Suspicious articles on ghost-media websites, tarnishing her reputation, were promoted on Facebook and then strangely deleted. Emilia has reasons to believe the ruling party had a hand in the online abuse she was suffering at the time. To this day, Şercan is fighting to hold her smearers accountable: the first investigation into the case was dismissed quickly, drawing public resistance and protests. It has since been re-opened and awaits a decision to this day.

The rhetorical war might sound like uncivil yet harmless insults to journalists and that they should 'toughen up and suck it up'. But its impact is undeniable. It opens the path for populists to use all the other weapons in their toolkit – the delegitimisation and dehumanisation of reporters releases the safety catch. 'You don't always have the emotional momentum to deal with 700 messages attacking, insulting and threatening you', explains Lucas Fauno Gutiérrez, a queer, HIV-positive activist and journalist who was subject to thousands of hate messages from Argentinian President Javier Milei's army of trolls.[103] 'Once they've installed that hate speech, we think twice before saying things'.

Many reporters I spoke to over the years believed that the best way forward was to not let it get to them and wait till Trump, Netanyahu or Modi are over. This is indeed what many journalists – particularly women – are being told, or come to believe, when targeted by the populist right. However, years of empirical research make clear that the verbal war is the infrastructure of the new censorship. Without it, nothing else makes sense: the rhetorical war is what enables authoritarians to weaponise democracy against us. The hateful rhetoric towards journalists and journalism – expressed in campaign appearances, televised debates, social media accounts, public speeches, media interviews, and spread by multiplying fake users and bots – justifies all else. Without it, no one would join the war against the media. If journalists are 'anti-Slovaks', 'Israel-haters' or 'Brazilian anti-patriots', perhaps they should indeed be restricted by new governmental regulations, replaced or fired.

In the rhetorical battlefield, the populist media plays an indispensable role. In Serbia, populist president Aleksandar Vučić has outsourced much of his campaign to discredit unfriendly media outlets to the pro-government tabloid *Informer*.[104] Instead of smearing the media all by himself, the Serbian tabloid repeated the government's talking points, accusing critical journalists of mafia ties and collusion with foreign intelligence agencies. As will later be explored in more detail, the populist media, or anti-media media, is an unparalleled amplifier of the populist war against our right to know. It allows populist leadership to adhere to dog whistles and hints, wink-winking their way to media-bashing and fearmongering. They can count on the loyalist media to do the interpreting for the audience: preparing them for the lies to come, ingraining the seeds of conspiracy theories in their minds, and establishing racist, hateful connotations and associations. TV channels and websites like OANN and Breitbart in the US make sure that when Donald Trump speaks incoherently about people eating pets in Ohio his base will know what the hell he is rambling about. They come prepared. GB News might play a similar role in the UK, as does Channel 14 in Israel. But words are just the beginning, to be followed by bills, lawsuits, cyberbullying and actual violence.

(2) The Legal War

A dear friend called me a few weeks back, sobbing, inconsolable. 'What happened?' I asked, praying everyone we know is alive and safe. These were times of war, after all. 'I am being sued,' she said, still weeping. In her shivering voice, I heard the notes of both anger and humiliation. 'Do they have a case against you?' I asked, trying to keep my cool. 'Of course not,' she said. I really didn't need to ask – she has always been the most meticulous, cautious and reliable source of information. 'Why are you crying, then?' I started losing my patience. 'Because I can't afford a lawyer now,' she whispered. This little moment, nothing heroic, no big deal, no public scandal – just a short warning letter from a giant lawyer's office – was enough to make my feisty young friend fearful for her future, her hard-built reputation and foremost, her overdraft.

The UN called the legal war on journalism 'judicial harassment'. What people often forget about the legal warfare against the media is that one does not need to win in court for the silencing lawsuit to work. Take British journalist Carole Cadwalladr, a decades-long contributor to *The Observer*, one of the first to break the Facebook–Cambridge Analytica scandal in 2018, and a much higher-profile investigative reporter than my poor friend. Ever since the exceptional journalist was sued by Arron Banks – a British businessman, co-founder of the Leave.EU campaign, and a donor to Nigel Farage and his then-UKIP Party – she had to spend endless time, energy and resources on clearing her name, hiring lawyers and testifying instead of reporting about the shady links between tech companies and political campaigns. Cadwalladr ended up founding an NGO, dedicated to protecting investigative journalists against SLAPPs, so they can keep asking the tough questions for us.

Between 2015 and 2021, 187 lawsuits or SLAPPs (strategic lawsuits against public participation) were filed against independent media and journalists in Poland, alongside 58 criminal cases – many of them for allegedly 'slandering' a public figure.[105] In Brazil, nearly 50 lawsuits were filed against five reporters who revealed the suspiciously high earnings of judges in Paraná State. The lawsuits used similar language and seemed orchestrated, but strangely, they were spread out very broadly geographically, taking place in courtrooms across Brazil. Why? To set a price tag. The geographic spread forced targeted journalists to spend precious money, time and effort travelling between courts instead of investing these scarce resources in independent, rigorous, investigative reporting. News audiences I talk to often think, 'Well, if what journalists reported was true, they'll be fine.' That is very far from what the legal warfare on the media looks like on the ground.

(3) The Legislative War

And once populists gain power, the toolkit grows. A recent report by the Committee to Protect Journalists portrays a grim picture of the legislative trench battle against journalists across borders.[106] In Hungary, a new law, masked behind the seemingly innocent title 'National Sovereignty Protection Act', allows courts to deem media outlets as foreign agents if they dare collaborate with organisations outside of Hungary.[107] In the Middle East, journalists find themselves accused or convicted of a range of crimes, including blasphemy, supporting terrorism and insulting the regime.[108] Dozens of countries – from Russia to Singapore – passed laws against 'fake news' and misinformation, which were intended to use the moral panic around social media to prosecute independent journalists.[109] Russia was particularly effective in turning the public's fake news concerns into excuses to arrest journalists who refuse to align with the Kremlin.[110] In 2024, Argentinian President Milei shut down the country's largest public news agency for spreading 'propaganda'. 'Public television has become a propaganda mechanism,' he declared in his first interview as president on Radio Mitre, 'it must be privatised.' 'Privatisation', like 'pluralism', 'competition' and 'efficiency' are other hashtags populist leaders invoke in their cry to shut down public-funded media. Unfortunately, it works.

But make no mistake, the legislative war is far from a Global South problem or one reserved for fully authoritarian dictatorships. While this specific form of war on the media has not yet reached full swing in the UK, it is expected to flourish in the US during Trump's second administration. According to *Rolling Stone*, 'he's begun occasionally soliciting ideas from conservative allies for how the US government and Justice Department could go about turning his desires – for brutally imprisoning significant numbers of reporters – into reality.'[111]

Another critical aspect of the legislative war is the attempts to take control over the media regulators to make sure they do not have the appetite to push back against media capture. These efforts were documented vastly in countries like Israel, Argentina and the US. This is not unique to populists, nor is it new; but in the new populist playground, taking over regulators – as well as statistics officers, rating measurements and anyone who might tell the public something they don't like – makes populists' lives much easier.

(4) The Physical War

Ultimately, the orchestrated online and offline hate spills into the streets in the form of physical violence. The Committee to Protect Journalists documents a clear rise in violence directed against reporters, but apart from the killings and arrests, most journalists encounter much more mundane, constant forms of violence – from being spat at to receiving elaborate death threats. Protesters regularly attacked journalists in Germany and Hungary,[112] while in the Netherlands, newsrooms were forced to hire safety personnel to accompany reporters to demonstrations. In Slovakia, protesters aggressively attacked TV cameramen, as have many in the US since Trump's MAGA movement took off. In Israel, some reporters told me they simply stopped covering pro-government protests and right-wing rallies, knowing they might be easy prey.

Right-wing activists have been using online forums, Facebook groups and WhatsApp chats to plan their own raids on Israeli newsrooms. One post called for citizens to gather around the television studios of News 12 – the leading Israeli newscast – stating: 'Today we burn the place down. Today we show the traitors what we really think of them'.[113] Following a steep increase in digital harassment, Israeli news organisations approached Facebook and Twitter, demanding that the companies end the incitement on their platforms.[114] A similar demand from the leaders of this campaign – those sitting in the PM's office – has never been clearly articulated. No response was recorded by Facebook or Twitter.

The number of journalists who burst into tears when talking to me about the threats they received, the humiliation, the stress, is telling. Harassment has real-world consequences, on reporters' mental health and well-being, their everyday lives and the kind of people who choose to enter the profession to become the journalists of the future – and therefore, a massive, unaccounted-for impact on all of us. The range of assaults and threats varies considerably between regions, but the trajectory appears to be clear. Countries where journalists used to feel safe to tell us the truth are facing an informational climate change.

(5) The Access War

Access has always been a powerful tool to manipulate and direct news. But populist politicians, and particularly populists in power, make excessive use of this resource. Take our central case study: Benjamin Netanyahu. Since 2021, the Israeli PM has not given *any* interviews to Israeli journalists, after past interviews were far too adversarial for his delicate taste. Instead, Netanyahu gave rare 'interviews' for his local propaganda outlets, which pretend to be journalistic entities but are loyal to Netanyahu's political ambitions rather than the public's right to know. Even after 7th October, for over a year of war in Israel, Gaza, Lebanon and beyond, Netanyahu gave almost 30 interviews for international news outlets but hasn't sat for a single interview with an actual Israeli reporter.[115]

Ignoring journalists, however, is only one munition in the access war against the media. Remember when Trump tried to ban access to briefings for the BBC, CNN, *NYT* and the *Guardian* reporters back in 2017?[116] Two years later, Trump revoked critical journalists' press passes to the White House, and most recently, in 2024, reporters from the *Washington Post*, *Axios* and *Vanity Fair* were denied access to his presidential campaign as revenge for their damning reporting. Geert Wilders, the leader of the Islamophobe right in the Netherlands, is another fan of the access war, as are Marine Le Pen in France and Narendra Modi in India. In Slovakia, Prime Minister Robert Fico refused to answer questions from the biggest independent dailies, and his party refused to participate in pre-election debates, attacking the TV networks' objectivity and impartiality. Sounds familiar? That's what the playbook looks like. You might remember how, before the last UK elections, Nigel Farage was kind enough to attend the BBC's *Question Time*. It was not an easy ride – Farage was asked difficult questions by many of the Britons in the room, who didn't seem to be impressed with his answers. Will it happen again in the next elections? Farage was quick to accuse the BBC of picking a 'biased' audience – not part of 'the people', apparently – and called for a boycott of the public broadcaster. It won't come as a shock if he chooses to use access as his weapon of choice in the war against the UK media in the future.

The access war ranges from preventing reporters from accessing press conferences to blocking them from professional WhatsApp groups, threatening their sources, or trying to cancel the legal protections for whistleblowers. The goal remains the same: punishing and rewarding. Carrots for loyalist media, sticks for critical reporting.

(6) The Financial War

While many leaders led a financial battle against the media over the past decade, Hungarian PM Victor Orbán had probably outdone them all. Bringing back 'Hungarian ownership' to the media industry – the local version of 'take back control' – was the dog whistle the government used to shift media ownership to the hands of Orbán's associates. Tailored taxes, governmental advertising budgets and pressures on private advertisers to pull out of independent news organisations were all weaponised to capture the media. By 2018, the last independent newspaper in Hungary was closed.[117]

The financial war against the media can be divided into two targets: publicly owned media and privately owned media. Trying to take over the public broadcaster includes, for instance, threatening to cancel the licence fees – as the Tory

Party threatened to do to the BBC time and again. Another tactic is threatening to privatise or shut down the public broadcaster altogether – as Netanyahu's governments did regularly over the past decade. With privately owned media, the path is different, but the goal remains. Trying to capture commercial media means, for instance, ensuring that the PM's wealthy friends get government loans to buy out independent media outlets. Commercial media owners might find themselves subject to surprising tax investigations, or new legal requirements that take them out of business. Another tactic adopted by Orbán was banning TV stations from broadcasting political ads. The damage, in this case, is dual: both for the news industry, which lost a substantial source of funding, and for potential political rivals, who lost a valuable platform to approach voters.

But importantly, these multilayered and concurrent weapons of war, from lawfare to financial intimidation, are not hitting journalists evenly. The new censorship hits some of us quicker, harder and earlier than others. The next section delves into the deep entanglement of the populist war and inequality.

The Quiet Un-Equaliser

The story of Aisha, which is not her real name, is a difficult one to tell. I met her a few years ago in Jaffa: a young and talented Palestinian woman, who tried to make it in the Israeli news industry. As much as I would love to tell you everything about her – what she looks like, the way she dresses, where she worked and what it was that drove her out of journalism – I am very cautious of how easily this book might make her, once again, a target for right-wing thugs and bullies. It is difficult to tell Aisha's story without her name, gleaming eyes and detailed experience of chasing her dream to become a leading reporter. She was the one who opened my eyes to how the war on the media not only changes what we get and don't get to know about the world, but also who gets to tell it. With all her charisma, ambition and talent, after one orchestrated attack – led by extremist politicians, hostile media and right-wing activists – Aisha found herself out of the newsroom (which was not packed with Palestinian women to begin with).

It had only been years after my first round of interviews with journalists under attack that I realised that I had been missing something this entire time. Something important. Apart from self-censorship and strategic bias, another form of 'grey' resignation was creeping under the radar, unacknowledged and underreported. Journalists under attack were leaving the profession, and they were not doing so at equal rates or pace. Many stopped using social media the way they used to due to the constant toxicity they met online. Some chose to no longer cover 'hardcore' topics, or Likud party rallies. But when I looked back at all my interviewees who were bashed by the populist right and ended up quitting their positions in the media industry, they were all women, with no exception. One of them was Aisha. After her name was smeared, her bosses were pressured, and she was summoned to a hearing and advised to take back a controversial statement she made on social media – Aisha was let go.

Another four influential women left the profession around the same time. These were quiet resignations, not celebrated ones, but they were meaningful. In 2023, women comprise only 32 per cent of the broadcast journalists in Israel and only 12 per cent of the broadcast commentators during the Israel–Gaza war.[118] According to a Reuters Institute report, which sampled 240 news outlets in 12 different countries, only 24 per cent of the top editors were women.[119] Senior journalists who leave the profession are, therefore, a massive deal.

By now there is enough evidence to confirm that attacks on the press always hit women and minority groups harder. In the United States, the UK, Germany, Nepal, Pakistan, Sweden, Turkey, India, South America,[120] the assault on female reporters was found to be harsher, more frequent, more sexualised and more consequential. It matters, not just because it makes life harder for journalists from disadvantaged backgrounds and marginalised communities but also because when targeted journalists choose to leave the profession it has a troubling effect on gender, racial and ethnic inequality that shapes our future knowledge and power.

A global UNESCO study from 2020 surveyed women journalists in 15 countries, including Brazil, Poland, the UK, South Africa, Mexico, Sweden, Sri Lanka and the United States.[121] Nearly three in four women journalists (73 per cent) reported they had experienced online violence. Threats of physical violence (25 per cent) were followed by sexual violence (18 per cent). One in five women journalists (20 per cent) was attacked or abused offline following online incitement. Twelve per cent of the respondents mentioned seeking medical or psychological help consequently. Almost half of the women (!) reported being harassed with unwanted private messages. It is notable that 'political actors' were *the second most frequent sources of attacks and abuse of women journalists.*

But women were not only most targeted, but also – like Aisha – most likely to leave. The journalists surveyed by UNESCO most frequently responded to online violence by self-censoring on social media (30 per cent). One-fifth withdrew from all online interaction, and 18 per cent specifically avoided audience engagement. Online violence significantly impacts the employment and productivity of the women respondents. 11 per cent reported missing work, 38 per cent retreated from visibility (e.g. by asking to be taken off air or hiding behind pseudonyms online), 4 per cent quit their jobs, and 2 per cent abandoned journalism altogether. To me, Aisha became the face of the corrosive effect of populist media-bashing over equality in the newsroom – and therefore, in the news.

In the context of Israel, the hierarchy is clear: Israeli journalists are suffering from the new censorship, facing increasing threats, intimidation, lawsuits, smear campaigns and online harassment. Palestinian journalists in Israel are suffering from all of the above, but also from abuse and sheer violence by the state authorities – the military, the police, as well as raging far-right Jewish settlers and falangists. Palestinian journalists in Gaza and the West Bank are suffering from all of the above, but also from the risks of war reporting in a region that does not respect the 'Press' vests. Palestinian sources claim journalists in Gaza were targeted intentionally during this war;[122] Israeli sources claim that they were simply caught in the crossfire when the military was fighting Hamas terrorists. Nevertheless, the death toll is harrowing. As of July 2024, the Committee to

Protect Journalists (CPF) reported the killing of 108 journalists and media workers in the Israel–Gaza war, 103 of them Palestinians, two Israelis and three Lebanese. Others were injured, captured, hurt. This has, by no means, started in October 2023: Shireen Abu-Akleh, a beloved Palestinian journalist for Al Jazeera, was shot by an Israeli soldier back in 2022, stirring much grief and resentment among her admiring audience. Whether due to intentional targeting or inexcusable negligence, journalists have paid an unacceptable price for the war in Israel, the West Bank, and particularly Gaza.

This is why it is so important to stress that the new censorship is not distributed evenly. Not only do populists limit the scope of the news we get, as journalists silence themselves and intentionally tilt to the right, they also limit the scope of who gets to produce and spread the news. These trends are now detected, to varying degrees, in numerous news industries worldwide.

Newsrooms have never been lighthouses for diversity or equity but numerous, Sisyphean efforts have been taken over the past decade to promote diversity and equality in newsrooms. Journalism, as a profession, is still to reckon with its histories of exclusion and inequality.[123] American scholars have done extraordinary work uncovering the difficult histories of news and racism in the United States. This type of self-reflective work is by no means completed, in the US or elsewhere. But the efforts are there, and they matter.

The point is, inequality in the newsroom is a problem not just for those excluded from it. Underrepresentation and misrepresentation affect underrepresented communities' trust in the media.[124] It reduces the scope and quality of information we all get by incorporating fewer perceptions, considering a limited range of sources, covering certain stories and ignoring others. We all need more diverse and equal newsrooms to get better news. So many people have been working tirelessly for this purpose for years; however, these blessed efforts might be quickly erased if populist media-bashing continues pushing some of us out of the newsroom. The loss is all ours.

The following chapters reveal how the populist playbook plays out in the news – what it does to journalists, journalism and, eventually, to news audiences, determining what we get to know about the world.

The Nigel Farage Effect: Mainstreaming the Far Right

'Hey, leftwing media, elite, intelligence services and justice system: Listen carefully! Whatever you do, it will only make the PVV and me stronger! Bye.'
Geert Wilders on Twitter, December, 2016.

IN NOVEMBER 2023, after eating penis-shaped pizza and showing off his naked arse, Nigel Farage – the former leader of the UKIP party, the current leader of Reform, the recently elected MP for Clacton and the driving force behind Brexit – revealed his strategy for competing on *I'm a Celebrity . . . Get Me Out of Here!* In an episode of this VIP version of *Survivor*, Farage admitted he aimed to take part in trials – which contenders are supposed to avoid – to get more airtime. 'If you do the challenges, it's 25 per cent of the airtime,' he was caught explaining to a fellow contestant on camera, 'I'm looking at reaching a whole new audience.'

This tiny telling TV moment is a wonderful analogy for the rise of the far right today: as traditional politicians and old-school reporters are playing by the rules, the Nigel Farages of the world are manipulating the playing field to execute an entirely different game. Even if Farage didn't win the TV reality game, he had the potential to win what he was really after – attention, celebrity fame and new audiences (and, of course, the 1.5 million pounds he was reportedly paid by ITV to join the show).[125] Similarly, current US President and indicted criminal Donald Trump could formally lose his countless legal trials and still gain points where it truly matters: his resentful, conspiracy-fed base. The Nigel Farages of the world – and their multiplying copycats – are playing a different game.

When he is not nude sunbathing on air alongside other British celebrities, Nigel Farage is also one of the politicians with the highest number of appearances in the history of the BBC's prestigious *Question Time* programme, with no fewer than 36 appearances over 24 years, even though he is not a member of either of the main parties in the UK (as of yet). That hasn't stopped him from declaring, after his most recent appearance on the show – where he was pressed on a series of racist remarks made by Reform party candidates – that he is now boycotting the BBC.

The same was true for Trump in the US, who got more airtime than any other Republican contender in the 2015 primaries and twice the earned media coverage of his then-opponent Hillary Clinton in the 2016 elections.[126] In the lead-up to the 2017 presidential elections in Serbia, nationalist populist Aleksandar Vučić got ten times more airtime on national broadcasters than all other candidates combined.[127] In the Netherlands, proud Islamophobe and relentless media-basher Geert Wilders enjoyed similarly obsessive media attention.[128] This requires some explaining. We know that granting attention to the extreme right grants their views attention, legitimacy and traction – even if challenged on air.[129] So how has the extremist politician who has one of the highest rates of public dislike in Britain, lost in seven elections to the House of Commons before becoming Reform MP for Clacton, and repeatedly bashed the BBC as liars and anti-patriots become the public broadcaster's sweetheart? And what does it have to do with the new censorship?

Who Gets to Be Extreme?

For a clearer perspective, let's turn our gaze many miles away, from Nigel Farage to his Middle Eastern version: Itamar Ben-Gvir. A Jewish supremacist and religious nationalist, Ben-Gvir first emerged in Israel's public life in the 1990s. He was famously videoed after vandalising then-prime minister Yitzhak Rabin's car, saying proudly to the camera: 'We got to his car, and we'll get to him too'.[130] Two weeks later, Rabin was assassinated by a religious right-wing extremist for leading the Oslo peace talks with the Palestinians.

For decades following this national trauma, Ben-Gvir was cast as a *persona non grata*. The IDF refused to recruit him to military service due to his support of Kach, a Jewish terrorist organisation. Ben-Gvir, whose hero was Baruch Goldstein – a Jewish terrorist who shot dozens of Muslims in their backs as they were praying in a mosque – was indicted again and again for incitement, racism and violence, and was clearly out of touch with the Israeli mainstream. He was considered deranged, dangerous, unhinged. For years, he served as the loyal lawyer and advocate of Jewish terrorists who attacked Palestinians in the West Bank. But in 2022, Ben-Gvir was appointed Israel's Minister of National Security, which oversees the Israeli police force. How have we gotten to this point? How does a criminal *persona non grata*, rejected from the military and subject to numerous police interrogations, get appointed to a prime role in the Israeli government?

As a former journalist, I am embarrassed to say that one answer to this question stands out: the media. Not Facebook, Instagram or TikTok. Not deepfakes or Russian troll farms. In 2019, Ben-Gvir ranked as the fourth most interviewed politician in Israel's *mainstream media*.[131] You could always catch glimpses of his fiery Jewish supremacy on TV, patronising Palestinian reporters, bashing news hosts, threatening investigative reporters. At this point, Ben-Gvir was leading a fringe radical party called Jewish Power, which had not come anywhere near the voting threshold in Israel. In fact, in the 2020 elections, Ben-Gvir's party got fewer than 20,000 votes nationally, out of millions of Israeli voters. In other words, Ben-Gvir's party was still extremely unpopular. And yet, Ben-Gvir was everywhere: live TV, live radio, live anything. This was not a one-off glitch: the following year, defeated Ben-Gvir received more than 100 hours of airtime on Israeli mainstream TV channels – more than any other parliament member in the country. By 2022, he'd become the second most quoted, heard and interviewed politician in the Israeli media, second only to then-prime minister Naftali Bennett. It was not 'the people' who had propelled him to prominence – at least, not yet.

So why did the news media embrace such a hateful and violent character? It was hardly a matter of direct support. While Israel's mainstream media has never been as left-leaning as Netanyahu and his allies claim, nor has it been aligned with the far right. Journalists' ideological leanings are difficult to quantify and vary across cultures, but if they lean anywhere, it is typically towards some imagined centre. Privately, many reporters likely despised Ben-Gvir, perhaps even feared him. And yet, the numbers are striking. Why did journalists grant this dangerous figure endless airtime and a national platform?

In October, 2022, a moment of drama played out in one of Israel's leading TV studios when one senior journalist decided to ask that question. In a rare moment of on-camera reflection, Nadav Eyal, a veteran political commentator, challenged his colleagues.[132] 'Itamar Ben-Gvir enjoys more airtime than the top politicians in the country,' he said. 'It didn't start last year nor the year before. I say it with sadness, but here too, on the same screen as me, Itamar Ben-Gvir has been normalised. And as a result, he became "the new normal". And whoever gets loads of media exposure will be considered by people as more reasonable'. The lead broadcaster in the studio was visibly uncomfortable with the direct *mea culpa*. 'I must say, if we go behind the scenes, he simply always comes when we call him,' she murmured apologetically, trying to brush it off, 'unlike other politicians, with whom you have to negotiate. He is simply a "filler".'

Sound familiar? The 'he always shows up' line of defence has also been common among UK media outlets trying to justify their obsession with Nigel Farage, long before he became an electoral success. The same was said about Geert Wilders, the far-right provocateur who slowly but surely paved his way to the frontline of Dutch politics, and Donald Trump when he was still an obsessive businessman calling any reporter who was willing to listen to his self-congratulatory mumblings wrapped in falsehoods. As Eyal poignantly replied to his colleague on air, while that might be true – some politicians are more willing to show up than others – this should probably not be the only criterion. Surely, there should be some higher bar for granting one of the most precious resources in modern societies: the public's attention.

When accused of mainstreaming the far right, media organisations worldwide have developed an impressive arsenal of excuses. Apart from 'they always pick up the phone', high on the list are 'it's all about the ratings' and 'that's what the people want'. Let's challenge these popular assumptions. Is it truly about ratings? If so, why don't we see extremist lefties drawing similar traction? Moreover, is it 'what the people want'? And who decides what people 'want', or who are considered 'the people' to begin with?

Is It All About the Ratings?

If the mainstreaming of the populist right was only a matter of ratings, as much writing on populism and media seems to imply,[133] it would not be as relevant for public-funded media, right? Journalists who work for non-commercial media, and therefore less enslaved to ratings and traffic measurement, should be free from the far-right frenzy. In my research, however, I found that the public media in Israel was similarly obsessed with Ben-Gvir, and that journalists discussed this issue similarly, regardless of the business model funding their newsroom. But perhaps most importantly, if the increased airtime for right-wing extremists was purely due to the outrageousness and provocation that drew audiences, surely we would expect to see as many radical extreme lefties swarming the TV studios? This is not what has happened in Israel over a decade of anti-media populism, nor in other countries overcome by a populist wave. Quite the opposite: left-wing voices, opposition voices, and in the Israeli context, particularly Palestinian voices, found themselves vanishing from the media representation of the Israeli society. So it can't really be purely about ratings. There must be another explanation for the media's fixation with Ben-Gvir, Farage and Wilders.

One finding, replicated in many countries yet rarely highlighted, tells us that political elites tend to over-estimate how right-wing or conservative the public actually is.[134] Based on original surveys of 3,765 politicians' perceptions of constituency opinion on nine issues, for instance, political scientists established that state legislative politicians in the US – from both parties – dramatically overestimated their constituents' support for conservative policies. This overestimation, they wrote, may arise from biases stemming from who contacts politicians, since in recent years, Republicans were more likely to contact legislators than Democrats. Their findings, they say, suggest that 'a novel force can operate in elections and legislatures: Politicians can systematically misperceive what their constituents want.' In a follow-up study, a group of researchers tested whether this finding holds beyond the United States. Do politicians elsewhere overestimate how conservative their voters are? Based on their research in Belgium, Canada, Germany and Switzerland, and despite the significantly different political systems in these countries, they found a strong and persistent conservative bias in how most of their 866 elite interviewees estimated public opinion.[135]

Does the media, too, overestimate how right-wing public opinion is? Unfortunately, we only have preliminary findings on this issue. A pioneering study conducted in Belgium and published in 2018 combined quantitative surveys and qualitative interviews to test the accuracy of journalists' perceptions of public opinion. 'Journalists in our sample have a systematic right-wing bias in their perceptions of public opinion,' they found. 'Journalists systematically think the public is more conservative than it in reality is.'[136] Against the researchers' expectations, the right-leaning reporters in their sample were actually better at assessing public opinion. Left-leaning and centrist journalists, they explain, 'seem to "over-correct"', and therefore overestimate how right-wing the public is. Hopmann and Schuck found similar findings in Germany in the 1990s and 2000s.[137] Their work indicates that German journalists misjudge their audiences' views to be more right-leaning than the audience reports. When interviewing journalists under attack in Israel, the US and the UK, I can attest that rarely have they mentioned 'the people' when referring to the left or centre. 'The people', more often than not, and regardless of empirical electoral votes, were overwhelmingly associated with the populist supporters and the right-wing base.

We can speculate over why politicians, and apparently journalists, believe that people are more conservative than they actually are, but unfortunately, there is not enough empirical data to determine for sure. One plausible explanation suggested by political scientists is the asymmetrical sphere of activism that has developed in various countries over the years. Broockman and Skovron, for instance, note that the bias in politicians' perceptions might be the outcome of bias in activism: those more vocal are perceived to be more numerous. In my own research, I found similar balances and asymmetries. In a couple of public opinion surveys I led with a team of dedicated colleagues, we asked citizens in Israel whether they had contacted journalists in the past, and if so, for which purpose (praising them, criticising them, inquiring about their reporting). The results were clear: the populist right is being more vocal and active about its grievances, and contacts journalists more often to complain about their reporting. Aside from the fact that this is just chilling in itself, it can also explain the potential bias in journalists' perceptions of public opinion. If you constantly hear from the most extremist voices in society, you might end up overestimating their popularity and reach. As the ones holding the mic, journalists' reporting might then turn into a self-fulfilling prophecy.

The X Argument

What if it was social media which normalised and popularised the far right all along? This question leads us to another popular excuse used by those in charge of saving democracy: 'It's not us who normalised him – it's TikTok!' However, while research shows that big tech platforms matter, and that exposure to far-right content online can radicalise and promote hateful views,[138] there is ample evidence that mainstream media and social media operate differently when it comes to public trust and moral cues.

The toxic discourse online, as we have all come to experience first-hand, is not necessarily representative of the views of the broader public. Rather, it is often led by hardcore partisans, hateful provocateurs, not to mention fake profiles and bots paid for by political actors. Therefore, journalists – who tend to live on social media 24/7 – might get the distorted impression that a vocal minority of anti-press activists somehow reflect public opinion. Previous research confirms that online discourse shapes journalists' perception of their audience.[139] But it also means that people don't take their Facebook feed as seriously as they take the evening news.

The Reuters Institute, based at Oxford University, termed this phenomenon 'the trust gap'. After surveying people across four countries (India, the UK, the US and Brazil), the institute's researchers found that audiences simply trust platforms less, particularly when it comes to news content.[140] Across all four countries, public trust in news on social media, search engines and messaging apps consistently lagged behind trust in traditional news outlets. The scepticism was especially pronounced when it came to political news, with social media platforms viewed as particularly unreliable. These findings align with previous research showing that established, reputable news organisations exert greater influence over public opinion than partisan or alternative media.[141] Hence, by platforming the far right, the mainstream media attributes 'legitimacy and authority' to the far right, dispelling potential doubts about their relevance and electability.[142]

With all due respect to Ben-Gvir's significant following on TikTok and Instagram, the level of damage he could gain from being normalised in the mainstream media is a whole different story. It is one thing to have millions of (real and bought) 12-year-olds following your TikTok challenges, but it's a whole other thing to lead the national conversation in the most renowned newsrooms, which are followed closely by national and global elites and decision-makers. Life on social media seems to have convinced us it's all about the numbers, but truth is, it isn't. Even today, the type of prestige and gravitas attributed to political commentators on the evening news, compared to the kind of capital they can gain in a platform packed with millions of Swifties, ambitious make-up influencers and campy fail videos, is incomparable.

Moreover, as noted earlier but seems to slip from our minds too often, social media platforms were created to help Ivy League students date each other, not to save democracy. Journalists and newsrooms cannot cry 'press freedom!' and pride themselves on being essential for democracy, but blame it on TikTok whenever democracy goes rogue. If reporters wish to be praised and protected as watchdogs, some watchdogging might be warranted.

Boycott? Normalise? Contain?

But what can journalists do? Ignoring populists is difficult: their provocations coincide with both traditional news values and commercial incentives – they tend to be infuriating, outrageous and fun.[143] When populists gain power, they enjoy a double privilege: they generate drama and conflict like all populists while also capitalising on their position as part of the ruling elite.[144] In certain European countries, journalists, following the steps of the mainstream political parties at the time, applied a distinct approach to the populist right: the *cordon sanitaire*. The *cordon sanitaire* (literally, 'sanitary cordon') is a strategy which refuses to give the far right the platform they so desperately seek. The concept was introduced centuries ago, as a way to describe the blockade of movement between nations, intended to block the spread of historic plagues and infectious diseases – something like the Covid-19-days quarantine. Over time, the term was embraced by politicians and political scientists to denote a strategy aimed at isolating extremist and populist parties, stopping their harm from spreading.[145] To this day, there are many disputes over the effectiveness of the *cordon sanitaire*.[146] Does it help to ignore populists before they gain power? Or does it merely fuel their self-victimisation narrative? What would be the pro-democracy way to handle these parties? What should we expect and demand from our watchdogs?

Based on a study conducted two decades ago in Belgium, France, Denmark and Norway, extremism researcher Willian M. Downs concluded that the *cordon sanitaire* approach might be counterproductive.[147] In fact, he suggested, constructive engagement with the populist right might be a better strategy than ignoring it altogether. 'Erecting a *cordon sanitaire* around a far-right party may be politically correct, may adhere to the advice of most anti-racism groups, and may give mainstream politicians the ability to present their clean hands to the voters,' he wrote in 2002, 'but "doing the right thing" often yields unintended and undesired consequences.' However, these were very different times in terms of media, long before Facebook and chatbots changed the public conversation. A lot has changed since, both within the populist movement, its opposition and the battlefield where they grapple with each other. Recent research from Spain indicates that audiences are uncomfortable about mainstream parties boycotting far-right populist parties, and prefer that they would be treated like any other party.[148]

Based on all this data, it would seem that the best way of tackling the populist right is 'business as usual' – treating them like any other political actor. The question remains, what does 'business as usual' even mean when it comes to Trump, Le Pen, Milei or Modi? How to cover a party that does not accept the premise of democracy, 'like any other party'? How can journalists make sure that exclusionary, racist, mean and xenophobic voices are not using the media's fixation with drama to gain public traction? And is there a way to avoid the *cordon sanitaire* yet cover the populist right without it setting the agenda?

The 'Trump Bump' Myth

After Trump's first electoral victory in the US 2016 election, a new catchphrase started spreading, whispered among political operatives and insiders, finally slipping into the public domain:

'The Trump bump'. The US media, the know-alls explained, was publicly bashed by the American incoming president, but at the same time, quietly benefited from his outrageous, divisive smear, which turned out to attract enormous percentages of Americans to their screens and news subscriptions. CBS CEO at the time, Leslie Moonves, was infamously quoted saying that Trump 'may not be good for America, but it's damn good for CBS . . . The money's rolling in and this is fun.' There is some truth to the Trump Bump analysis – since populists free themselves in advance from many of the limitations and restrictions other politicians adhere to, they are in a great position to attract the gold rush of the 2020s: eyeballs. Commercial media has a lot to benefit from populists' ability to attract uninterested audiences to consume more news, whether because they are scared by the rise in Trumpism or elated by it.

And so, the Trump Bump anecdote gained traction. It made the US media seem like Trump's happy accomplices in crime – battered publicly but cashing in behind closed doors. For people who enjoy conspiracy theories, or simply dislike both Trump and the media, it was a particularly appealing narrative. However, evidence shows that the Trump Bump was not only temporary but also extremely limited in scope. Yes, the biggest papers of record, *The New York Times* and *Washington Post*, had an incredible run of exceptional journalism and a sharp rise in subscriptions. So have a few other powerful newsrooms across the US. But implying that this somehow made Trump good for journalism is misleading and shortsighted. Trust in the media sunk across the board, journalists were beaten up, their equipment destroyed, their online profiles hacked. Even worse, once Trump became president again, he – like Netanyahu and Orbán before him – made elaborate efforts to capture the media using their executive power.[149]

Let the Trump Bump myth be the carrier of the following advice for journalists and audiences everywhere: think long-term, not short-term. Autocratic provocateurs might increase your ratings or traffic tonight – your bit might even go viral! – but are also likely to annihilate the freedom of the press once they get into office, thanks to the disproportionate media attention they get. This is not just about saving democracy or truth. In the long-term, it is also about saving your profession, industry and workplace.

The Great Normaliser

The Nigel Farages, Geert Wilders and Itamar Ben-Gvirs of the world have always been there. Each culture has its own extremist voices in the margins, be they anti-Semitic, Islamophobic, transphobic, misogynist or any other type of racism, supremacy, fundamentalism or incitement to violence. Eradicating these ideas might be implausible. However, by now, there is solid empirical evidence tracing the process of mainstreamisation of the darkest forces in society. The question as to whether society survives such hateful politicians will not be determined by the extremist far right, but rather by the mainstream and the media, and how well they cope with the challenge the populists bring to their doorstep. Here, again, journalism can be our life ring – or the fatal millstone that drags us under.

In the past, most research into the normalisation of the far right focused on the political sphere: the participation of radical right-wing parties in parliament, different voting systems and election results. In an experimental study from 2020 titled 'From Extreme to Mainstream', three American political economists show how Donald Trump's rise in popularity, and eventual victory, increased individuals' willingness to publicly express xenophobic views. After being shown data suggesting that Trump's election was certain in their state, Americans were more likely to donate to anti-immigration causes. Even individuals who were less likely to agree with xenophobic behaviour sanctioned it less when they learned that it was more popular in their community than they expected. 'Social norms . . . can change quickly when new public information arrives, such as a surprising election outcome,' write Leonardo Bursztyn, Georgy Egorov and Stefano Fiorin. 'People may become more inclined to express views or take actions previously perceived as stigmatised and may judge others less negatively for doing so'.

In other words, it's not like suddenly, one morning, entire societies wake up racist. Such victories change how people perceive their own communities, what can be said and what might be sanctioned. Another study, conducted in the UK, shows how when the far right enters parliament, voters feel safer to express support for it, as the once stigmatised radical right has been normalised.[150] A similar effect was detected around the rise of the AfD – a party declared by the German domestic intelligence agency to be a 'proven right-wing extremist' and anti-constitutional organisation in three out of sixteen federal states, and also, since February 2025, the second-largest party in the country.[151] Concerned about the rise of the party, which has Nazi roots, the German Journalists Association (DJV) suggested that media outlets should use clear warning labels in all their articles about the AfD, similar to health-risk warnings on cigarette packets.[152] This is not necessarily a bad idea; however, the effectiveness of such warning labels is yet to be proven. Clearly, the political establishment has a critical role in defining the acceptable within any culture, and when the mainstream embraces the far right – for either electoral, opportunist or any other reason – the result is the legitimisation of those initially marginal voices.

We do not yet have a similarly rich body of literature about the media's role in normalising the populist right. Much research indicates that right-wing media drives support for right-wing candidates, but it is often difficult to discern causation. And what about the rest of the media? Recently, experiment-based research conducted simultaneously in Australia and the UK exposed just how powerful the media can be in churning support for the populist right. Not the populist media which genuinely and openly supports the populist right as it stands for similar values. No: the amplification of the populist right happens via all news outlets – populist, anti-populist and anywhere in between. In this pioneering study, political scientists Diane Bolet and Florian Foos show that 'exposure to uncritical interviews on TV channels like Sky News, or on online platforms like YouTube, increases agreement with extreme right statements, and perceptions that a larger share of the population shares these views'. This data suggests that the overamplification of right-wing populists, particularly when they are not yet popular among broader publics, is extremely consequential. 'Unchallenged interviews with extreme right actors fuel extreme right attitudes,' the scholars report, 'and foster the belief that a larger share of the public support the extreme right actors' statements.'[153] The media has a lot to answer for. Uncritical platforming spreads and normalises extreme-right views. When interviewers strongly challenged the extreme-right interviewee, the benefits to the provocateur were cut. Even critical interviews did not seem to have the power to decrease support for the extreme right, but at least they could mitigate the drift towards them. In other words, journalists matter – and we need them to do better.

Strategic Bias: How Our News Universe Shifts to the Right

'There is a great deal of parliamentary activity ... about the BBC being all left-wing. Until the matter is cleared up, I would be grateful if you would keep off leftist speakers as much as possible.'
Secret memo by the then-BBC director general Sir Cecil Graves to BBC controllers, 1942.[154]

IN JULY 2022, I found an unexpected message in my Twitter DMs. It was from Emily Maitlis, the distinguished BBC reporter and presenter who has won awards for reporting on UK and world politics, and – most famously – her 2019 interview with Prince Andrew. Maitlis, who ran into my research on journalism in Israel, was horrified to realise how much it resonated with her own experience here at the seemingly safe and free press democracy of Britain. The following month, in a packed venue at the Edinburgh TV Festival, Maitlis gave a speech that instantly sent ripples across the UK media pond. 'I remember – to my shame – interviewing the Trump acolyte, Sebastian Gorka, on *Newsnight* in the early days of the Trump victory,' she said. 'Gorka would use up most of the interview time screaming abuse at the BBC. He didn't have any problem with the BBC. He quite liked the BBC. He was always happy to say yes to the interview. But he used our time on air as an effective conduit to sell a key populist message – that the mainstream media could be dismissed as "fake".'

Gorka was merely following the populist playbook. But Maitlis wasn't sure how to handle it. 'Once you understand how this works, it seems so obvious,' she reflects, 'but in those days, I didn't. As a journalist, I was mortified. I would spend half our allotted interview time trying to defend our objectivity, and the rest bending over backwards to reconcile his strangled version of the truth, just to prove his criticism of me wrong.' After speaking to so many of them for decades, I can safely say that journalists rarely express self-criticism – certainly not in public. It was, therefore, remarkable that Emily chose to hold her public *mea culpa* on the most visible stage possible, knowing it would get significant media coverage and fury.

She tried to explain, in real time, what drove her to expose her professional faults on stage. 'I looked back at an interview I did with Gorka, and I was horrified. In my opening question, I say, "Dr Gorka, I know in our previous encounters we have spent a lot of time analysing whether *Newsnight* itself is fake news. So just for the sake of our viewers and moving the story on, why don't we agree to recognise that's how you view things".' Laughing, she continued: 'It is insane. We didn't spend "a lot of time analysing" anything. He levelled the accusation to get social media traction. And I allowed it to become a viable debate. Either way, Gorka won. The BBC lost.'

Maitlis is a powerful figure, with all the cultural and social resources most journalists hope one day to attain. Yet, for her, her colleagues and competitors, the question remained unsolved: how to cover the populist campaign against you, your workplace, your profession? If journalists choose to report the baseless 'fake news media' claims, they end up promoting people who build their careers by undermining the role of journalism in society. But if they choose not to cover the allegations against them, they are bashed once again for 'censoring' their critics. The media's helplessness when facing populist aggression too often leads them to grant massive exposure to the populist smear. In fact, most people who are exposed to the worst conspiracy theories against the media – find out about it through 'the media'.

Special Treatment for Media-Bashers

The first dilemma journalists face when bashed by a populist leader or movement is whether to cover it at all. Is it newsworthy that someone called your reporter 'a scumbag'? Or has it become an easy, cost-free way to dominate the news cycle? Is ignoring a reasonable response to openly brazen lies? And what to do when verbal attacks turn into action?

The political economy behind this mechanism cannot be overlooked: at times when many news outlets struggle financially and operate with limited resources, airing Trump's speeches, Netanyahu's replies or Nigel Farage's tweets is easier than dedicating time and resources to produce original content, and likely to attract viewers, users and readers. On top of these practical considerations, the journalists I interviewed over the years repeatedly mentioned the weaponisation of journalistic professional norms as preventing them from simply ignoring the bashing. Let's take, for example, the right of reply.

When Netanyahu used his right of reply to bash the media, journalists I spoke to felt obliged to cover it, to keep their 'impartial' façade. 'When Netanyahu sends us a vilifying five-paragraph reply, journalistic guidelines force us to publish it,' explained a committed print editor. 'Otherwise, we have just handed him a great excuse to bash us once again for censoring his reply. But if we publish his reply word-for-word, we have just given massive exposure to our own defamation in our own newspaper'. A TV reporter regularly targeted by Netanyahu's government had similar feelings. 'You amplify their media-bashing – you don't have a choice, really,' he said. 'Because if you don't read the full reply, you will allegedly prove that you are censoring him, and they'll go: "You see, they slander us, and then they don't even read our replies."'

These quotes demonstrate a quite broad interpretation of the prime minister's right of reply. Historically, the right to reply allows people who feel misrepresented or smeared the right to have their response published by the same news outlet where the original report aired.[155] Its legal status varies between countries, from Brazil, where the right to reply is considered a constitutional right, to Sweden, where the right to reply is a matter of self-regulation.[156] In Israel, the right to reply is not enforced by law but is broadly accepted as a professional convention.[157] Essentially, the right to reply is aimed at protecting 'ordinary persons who would not otherwise be able to access media sphere'.[158] This is clearly not the case for Benjamin Netanyahu, or any other politician in power, who have immense – if not excessive – access to the public conversation. And yet, for many of my interviewees, the prime minister's right to reply trumped many other criteria, norms and journalistic considerations, like the veracity of his claims, their relevance to the matter at hand or their public value. 'When Netanyahu's trial began, he started sending us replies that were utter, transparent lies,' a young news editor recalled. 'I said to myself, "How can this person be our prime minister? I know for a fact that none of this is true."' When asked whether she published his bogus replies, she answered, unblinking: 'Of course I did.'

When Populists Go Live

The right to reply is a prime example of how the new censorship flips democratic norms and practices on their heads. Instead of protecting the voiceless against unwarranted slander, under Netanyahu, the right to reply turned into a means to slander critical journalists in their own studios. But it is merely one example. The next norm to be manipulated by Netanyahu might remind you of Trump's media coverage in 2016: live speeches.

Netanyahu's speeches, always timed for the evening newscasts, were another factor journalists saw as narrowing their freedom to determine what counts as news. Netanyahu's friend (turned enemy turned friend again), Donald Trump, was performing a similar stunt back in his first national election campaign. CNN's president at the time, Jeff Zucker, later apologised for the unlimited airtime his network granted Trump's campaign of lies and hate. 'If we made any mistake last year, it's that we probably did put on too many of his campaign rallies in those early months and let them run,' Zucker said.[159] And yet, preliminary findings show that live speeches and rallies continue serving the populist right to gain massive unmediated, unchecked attention two election cycles later. Why?

The combination of a populist leader's high-ranking status and the drama of live broadcasting prompted a media event that journalists could not resist. 'It must air live,' TV political correspondents insisted. Very few of the reporters and editors I talked to contended that Netanyahu's attack on the media should not be covered. Ignoring it, they thought, might only frame them as biased. And so, journalists under attack repeated their concerns that any divergence from 'ordinary' journalistic routines and practices would confirm their bias against the prime minister and 'the people'.

No Defence Is the Best Defence?

Empirical research repeatedly shows that spreading populist rhetoric 'as is' risks discrediting and demonising the media.[160] And yet, journalists keep spreading the word, oftentimes without bothering to debunk it. Most reporters I spoke to were reluctant to directly refute the accusations voiced against them, their newsrooms or the media. A similar tendency was found among Australian journalists, who avoided responding to populist politicians calling them 'fake news'.[161] When targeted, journalists – whose normal professional instinct would be (or should be) to counter false and defamatory claims – came to believe that exercising their own right of reply would hurt their impartial image too. They cited three distinct but interrelated reasons. First, defending themselves would invite accusations that they are using their media power to benefit themselves. Second, it might confirm that they were indeed the populist's adversaries, rather than professionals covering him impartially. Finally, they held that refuting the allegations against them would make them part of the story, undercutting their neutrality as outsiders simply observing and reporting the news.

'We are very cautious not to harness the screen to protect our own interests,' one leading TV commentator told me. 'There is something in our DNA as journalists that says we're not the story,' agreed another online reporter. This sentiment aligns with what American journalist Craig Crawford expressed in his pioneering book about journalists' experience of political attacks. 'We are trained to avoid making ourselves the story,' he wrote. 'When politicians make us the story, we aren't sure how to handle it. Instead of defending ourselves against attacks from politicians, the news media reports the attacks to viewers, readers and listeners who naturally believe the criticism because they seldom get the other side.'[162]

Others were concerned that confronting the populist accusations would reinforce their portrayal as part of 'the opposition party' – a concern expressed by US journalists when confronted with Donald Trump's 'fake news' commotion, as well as Israeli journalists when covering Netanyahu's fact-free rage.[163] 'Responding to his lies only serves Netanyahu's campaign, which delineates a war between him and the media,' a senior journalist noted. And, to be fair, what would an effective debunking actually look like? 'What kind of an argument could we have theoretically voiced that would work?' asked a leading news editor. 'Because when a journalist is attacked for being "a lefty traitor" and their response is, "No, I'm actually not a lefty", what kind of an argument is that?!' 'It's a real "catch-22",' summarised a popular TV host. 'So for a very long time, we did nothing. No one acted. We kept doing our work the way we always had done, hoping that someone would eventually return to their senses or that the public would understand what's going on. I'm not sure what we were thinking. But we did nothing. There was this vanity, as if we were above it all – we won't go low, we won't be dragged into this catfight.'

Notably, the right of reply – which was considered a significant factor when journalists chose to air Netanyahu's smearing comments – was not invoked by journalists as a reason to reply to his false claims against the media. Some interviewees went as far as to argue that not only journalists but also politicians should avoid defending the media when under attack. 'When you defend journalists, it only hurts them,' said a radio correspondent, as he was sipping his coffee in the parliament's café. 'Each defence is dismissed as politically motivated. For journalists, there is no better response than saying nothing.' Of course, opinions varied, and some journalists recognised over time that their reluctance to debunk baseless accusations might take a toll on their public image. 'People might get the false impression that we really *are* all biased lefties,' sighed one young and successful commentator. 'But what else can you do?'

STRATEGIC BIAS: HOW OUR NEWS UNIVERSE SHIFTS TO THE RIGHT

Luckily, academic research demonstrates that there are, in fact, some things that could be done differently. Attacks on the media, broadcast on the media, have the power to affect public trust in the media, especially when expressed by political elites.[164] Preliminary evidence also suggests that counterarguments in favour of the media are crucial for maintaining the public's trust – as is critical interviewing, debunking lies and fact-checking.[165] By shying away from replying to populists' provocative accusations, journalists become *de facto* complicit in undermining their own status and authority. Ironically, their attempts to protect their objective façade contribute to the public's belief that they are biased.

As always, there were outliers, like the reporter and commentator who argued in favour of a pro-media defence campaign in response to anti-media populism. 'Our arguments are not being heard loudly enough, if at all,' a prime target of Netanyahu's intimidation told me, frustrated. 'When Netanyahu claims that he is being unfairly persecuted, the media should remind the people how critically we covered previous administrations. We have the means to do it. We have the evidence. There's no other way – we must run a counter-campaign, but we don't know how.' Based on the data and research collected so far, I tend to agree. Journalists will have to do more to educate and engage with their audiences, and that includes advocating for journalism and its role in society. Counting on the education system to explain the basics of democracy, checks and balances, and press freedom – particularly in countries when the populist right is in power – is no longer a plausible expectation in many regions worldwide.

The Double Standard

But it's not just about the media bashing. What I realised over time was that, simply put, the populist leader receives special treatment in the news industry. Some interviewees acknowledged that Netanyahu's campaign against the media fostered excessive caution, leading to a different set of professional standards applied when covering him. At times, they admitted, they went as far as burying stories. This was not driven purely by fear of Netanyahu or his potential retribution, but by a deeper concern: losing 'the people', their attention and their trust – this is the defining feature of the strategic bias. 'If there is a story about Netanyahu's wife, I guess its chances of getting published are ... well, the holes in the filter are smaller,' reflected a parliamentary correspondent. 'We won't publish it unless we're 100 per cent confident that any rational viewer would go: "Wow! This is outrageous!" We are more careful there.' Netanyahu's third wife, Sara Netanyahu, a prominent and controversial figure in Israeli politics, was involved in several corruption scandals herself, and reportedly has a say on the highest appointments in the country's national security establishment, despite lacking the necessary security clearance.[166] Covering her is, therefore, essential. An investigative reporter who has long been targeted by the Netanyahus had a concrete example. 'Ever since this confrontation began, I've made many adjustments to maintain the public's trust and attention,' he told me. 'There were stories that I didn't run, and if I hadn't been branded as Netanyahu's enemy, I would have. I had, for example, documentation of Netanyahu's bank accounts abroad. It wasn't outright illegal, but it was ethically questionable. I figured that if I published it, it might seem petty. Netanyahu's fans would say, "See, you're really going after him; you mistreat him." So I didn't run this story.' This is what the new censorship is all about.

Actual violence – while still prevalent, targeting mainly Palestinian reporters in the Israeli context – is unnecessary for the new censorship to transform the news. Protecting their professional façade has encouraged journalists under attack to practise the ultimate journalistic failure: self-censorship. Journalists with the best intentions at heart choose to practise self-censorship rather than self-defence, or, perhaps, self-censorship *as* self-defence. In Israel, journalists' self-censorship when covering Netanyahu adds another layer to the existing state-censorship concerning national security.[167]

Journalists' desperate hope to prove they were *not* Netanyahu-haters was evident during our meetings too: many of them tried to convince me – as an imagined audience of one – of their utter impartiality by finding reasons to compliment Netanyahu or criticise his opponents. 'My dad always voted Likud,' or 'When it comes to foreign affairs, Bibi is a genius,' were examples of my interviewees' attempts to demonstrate that they were not – by any stretch of the imagination – Bibi-haters. I could trace similar veins among British journalists who tried to emphasise they were not as anti-Brexit as Farage contends, and American reporters trying to signal they were, against all expectations, not anti-MAGA.

By delivering the populist message unchallenged, journalists under attack have adopted a naïve, somewhat anachronistic conception of objectivity, striving to present themselves as mere 'flies-on-the-wall',[168] who happen to cover someone smearing that miserable fly. In their mission to maintain an impartial image, they sought to appear neutral even when it meant spreading their own slander or burying otherwise valuable news stories. This approach emphasises the media's role as pipelines connecting citizens to their leaders rather than gatekeepers who facilitate a political debate or watchdogs who scrutinise those in power. By refusing to perform greater agency, Israeli journalists were hoping to quietly signal to their audience – and particularly Netanyahu's sympathisers – that there was no media bias against him, his party or his supporters. While powerful in transforming our information environment, this strategy has never proven itself useful over time.

Objectivity as Censorship

While journalistic objectivity has been understood for decades as a means to protect the media against criticism, political pressures and even legal lawsuits,[169] journalists' adherence to what they believe their audience would *interpret* as objectivity currently limits their professional autonomy rather than boost it. The most serious biases, American political scientist W. Lance Bennett observed years ago, 'occur not when journalists abandon their professional standards, but when they cling most closely to the ideal of objectivity.'[170] The populist war on the media should be understood as a form of sophisticated censorship: a mechanism which uses journalists' audiences as a lever to turn their professional norms against them. By framing journalists as biased 'enemies', any future negative coverage becomes an asset which 'confirms' the media's alleged hostility towards the populist and 'the people'. Journalists, who fear the potential impact of such allegations on the public's perceptions, are then trapped in a lose-lose situation: amplifying the 'enemies of the people' allegations against their interest or criticising it publicly, thereby risking confirming the populist accusations. This chilling mechanism operates in two stages: first, populists address the public directly to erode, or at least polarise, the trust in journalism. Next, journalists adjust their professional decision-making in light of the impact the populist rhetoric has over their audiences. The shift from the first step to the second is facilitated by journalists' desire to project impartiality. Ironically, journalists' devotion to objectivity is thus used to erode the public's trust in that very same objectivity.

However, covering populist media-bashing is just the tip of the toxic iceberg that is journalism under attack. How to cover politics at all when one party incites against you, demonises you, strives to silence you? How to interview politicians who claim you 'need to get your head examined'? How to convince the public that these allegations are baseless, without seeming partisan and revengeful?

Balancing Unbalanced Realities

In May 2014, John Oliver ran a sketch that has since achieved cult status, amassing over nine million views on YouTube alone. Titled 'Climate Change Debate', the skit features Oliver hosting a televised debate about climate change, as many news hosts have been doing before and since. Oliver's twist? His debate was *statistically representative*. After inviting one speaker to explain the risks of climate change and one to deny climate change, into the studio marched 96 more scientists and two more climate denialists to represent the actual consensus over climate change in the scientific community. The result was a sharp indictment of the standard 'climate change: yes or no?' format, which falsely implied an evenly split debate in the name of formal balance. 'I can't hear you over the weight of scientific evidence,' Oliver quipped by the end of the sketch, 'this debate should not have happened!'

Although the witty sketch went viral in the UK and the US an entire decade ago, this type of false equivalence has never gone out of fashion – quite the contrary. The rise of populism, denialism and media-bashing has made 'bothsides-ism' extremely popular. Professor Jay Rosen from New York University, the founding father of the Public Journalism movement which encourages journalists to centre their attention on the public's wants and needs, was the first to popularise the term.[171] 'Bothsides /bōTH//sīdz/ (verb),' he writes, is 'the act of distorting a news report by taking an asymmetrical situation and putting it in symmetrical terms, falsely suggesting there are two equal and opposing sides in normal conflict with one another.'[172]

And climate change was only one unfortunate casualty. 'Let me take you to early 2016,' said Emily Maitlis in her explosive MacTaggart Lecture in 2022. 'The UK is beginning to debate the big questions around Britain's potential exit from the EU. It is complicated stuff: we are trying to offer our viewers both sides of a fiendishly difficult debate. And that intention was right. But we still got it wrong . . . It might take our producers five minutes to find 60 economists who feared Brexit, and five hours to find a sole voice who espoused it. But by the time we went on air, we simply had one of each. We presented this unequal effort to our audience as "balance". It wasn't.' In the Brexit case, it was our old friend from previous chapters, Brexiteer-in-chief Nigel Farage, who capitalised on the two-sides-at-all-costs approach embraced by TV hosts. Farage was the fourth most interviewed person on TV in the lead-up to the 2016 referendum – although he was not an official member of either the Vote Leave or Leave. EU campaigns.[173] Conservatives were not suffering either: 73 per cent of the most interviewed politicians on TV in the run-up to the referendum were Tories, evenly split between Leavers and Remainers – quite an interesting interpretation of balance.

Lani Watson, a philosopher based at Oxford University, makes the case that the British media reporting on immigration around Brexit illustrates 'the widespread and systematic violation of epistemic rights'.[174] Epistemic rights, she explains, include our rights to 'information, knowledge, understanding and truth'. Or, in short, our right to know. We have the right to get accurate details about our medical condition when we see our GP or take a blood test, and just as much, we have an epistemic right to reasonably accurate details about our elected officials when we turn on the news. However, bothsides-ism deeply undermine our right to truth.

Balanced or True?

'I must be doing something right if both sides are slamming me!' You might have heard this axiom if you had ever talked to journalists before. During my fieldwork this was one sentence I kept hearing, in varying wording, over and over again across countries. It was like an informal journalistic mantra. Admittedly, there is something soothing about being 'in the middle'. It feels right. It sits well with both the liberal temperament of moderation, the century-old Western ethos of journalism which prioritises impartiality and balance. And what could be more balanced than the very middle?!

There are only three problems with that popular intuition, which leads journalists and other opinion leaders to force balance on unbalanced realities. The first is empirical: in reality, piling up criticism is a very poor litmus test for quality journalism – or anything else, really. You could easily be bashed from all sides, and still be incredibly wrong. What if, just theoretically, one of your critics is blabbering, but the other one is spot on? Or what if – God forbid – both are right? The fact that someone called you 'nasty Tory' and someone else called you 'liberal lefty' does not make your reporting balanced. On certain factual issues – like who won the elections, or how many words are in this sentence – there is no need for balance, but for accuracy. Reality, or scientific evidence, can be pretty one-sided sometimes.

The second problem is that, more often than not, the cardinal debates for our shared lives as a society have far more than two perspectives to them. There are so many different angles and approaches when discussing our future, economy, immigration, social justice or foreign policy that bringing two 'sides' to an orchestrated circus, hoping they somehow balance out each other, is a terrible way to set a discussion. A better strategy to cover such complex issues would be to seek as many valuable, innovative, fact-based ideas, and make sure they are being heard. On some issues, there might be only one founded, useful, relevant perspective; on others, there might be six. The one-on-one formula is limiting, rather than enriching our understanding of the world. Too many communities are often left out of this he said, she said type of reporting – they are not considered part of the balancing act.

The third problem goes deeper. That mantra, 'I'm pissing off everyone, so I must be doing something right', demonstrates the toxic appeal of the middle ground. It assumes that there is such a thing as a safe and stable middle ground, where one could seek refuge from hyper-partisanship, polarisation and extremism that threatens to drown us. That if only one secures their position between the two big parties or political camps, they would be safe from the horrors of bias. The bad news? There is no such *place* as the middle ground. In real life, the world is rarely symmetrical. Politics certainly isn't.[175] The centre is hence relational, dynamic and constantly shifting. What happens to those 'in the middle' when one party drifts further and further to the right? Which concessions are made to maintain the cushioned position at the centre? And at what point do news presenters, politicians and opinion leaders say 'enough is enough'?

False Centrism

There is nothing newsworthy, or journalistic, about the centre. It has nothing to do with truth-seeking, informing or scrutinising power. The evolving histories of the Democratic and Republican parties in the US are a great case in point. When one party supported abolishing slavery and the other went to war to keep it, what would be the ideal position of the press? 'Somewhere in the middle'? 'Half-slavery'? 'Good people on both sides'? How about the suffragettes' movement? How should a serious British reporter in the 1910s approach the fight to grant women the right to vote? Measure where the Conservatives and Liberals are and position themselves somewhere in-between?

The deceptive appeal of the middle ground is something we – citizens, journalists, activists – must learn to recognise and reject. If you stand for anything at all, be it democracy, equality, freedom or truth, you will inevitably find yourself closer to certain parties, politicians and movements, and further from others, at any given moment in time. Sticking to the middle, between two dynamic parties, essentially means disarming from your values. Remember the 'birther' conspiracy theory? When Obama was running for president, then-failing businessman Trump was among the super-spreaders of the clear-cut lie that Obama was not born in the US and therefore could not run for president. The news coverage of the Obama 'birther' conspiracy was a remarkable demonstration of the balance trap. As few radical Republicans raised the issue, the media discussed it as news – debating whether Obama was indeed born in the US or not.[176] Similarly, climate change deniers, anti-vaxxers and Big Lie supporters are quoted as the balancing counteract to the rest of the factual world. This is how radical, offensive views get attention and legitimacy in the name of balance and impartiality. And that's even before they get overshared due to opaque, profit-oriented algorithms.

To make things worse, journalists often avoid determining who is right, as each deviation from their neutral stance is considered unprofessional or partisan. Since facts seldom speak for themselves, as proponents of objective journalism often – quite naïvely – assume,[177] the audience remains confused. It might be safer for the messengers, but certainly worse for those on the receiving end.

As populists abuse the situation to mislead us, certain scholars suggest that under exceptional circumstances, journalistic objectivity should be abandoned altogether.[178] What does objective reporting mean when covering racism, for instance? Or when reporting war crimes, or infectious pandemics? Should populist media bashing be considered one of these scenarios, where impartiality should simply be dropped?

Instead of renouncing objectivity altogether – as journalism has not yet established an ideal alternative – journalists could reinterpret it in ways that align with our normative expectations from them. They could use their own right to reply to counter populist attacks on the media. This does not require abandoning the right to reply; rather, it means applying it more wisely. They could also insist on correcting falsehoods, setting the news agenda rather than surrendering to the new shiny object that populists keep popping out of their sleeves, and explaining the role of news in our daily lives. They could apply more cautious consideration when broadcasting populist media-bashing and hate speech, keeping in mind that providing valuable and truthful information for the public is as important as their impartial façade. By airing smearing speeches live, journalists give up on substantial editorial independence; recording the speeches and airing the valuable parts later would be wiser if one is to avoid spreading lies, conspiracy theories and incitement. Similarly, approaching any tweet and post by any leader as immediate news turns them – *de facto* – into your editors-in-chief.

One could easily imagine a world where impartiality does not translate into a passive surrender of editorial control. Where balance is not interpreted as forcing symmetry on unbalanced realities. Where fairness is expected in the media's approach to each story, not in how balanced the outcome may be. The most critical takeaway, I would say, is that objectivity and balance are means for a cause, not a sacred goal themselves. The cause is truthtelling, informing, revealing. When we witness journalists both-siding, flik-flaking, hiding or censoring what they understand to be true – in the name of balance or impartiality – we should play a 'game over' sound in our minds. The means defeated the cause. Time to recalculate route.

What is Strategic Bias?

Strategic bias is a defence mechanism, where journalists knowingly slant the news to favour one candidate, party or political camp – regardless of their personal beliefs and without informing their audience – as a response to populist challenges to their public credibility and legitimacy.[179] Strategic bias differs significantly from other forms of more familiar ideological biases in two main ways.[180] First, unlike unconscious bias, where journalists slant the news in line with their political preferences, strategic bias is exercised intentionally and does not necessarily reflect journalists' personal views. In fact, journalists often turn to strategic bias for noble reasons: to maintain the public's trust during impossible times or to prevent future attacks on the press.

Second, unlike partisan bias, where news outlets openly slant the news in alignment with their ideological beliefs, the strategic bias is not publicly declared. This makes strategic bias even more risky: when you watch Fox News in the United States, M1 TV in Hungary, Channel 14 in Israel or GB News in the UK, you probably know what you're in for. The strategic bias, exercised by journalists in all news organisations, is far more difficult to detect. It requires talking openly to those who make the calls. The more the attacks against the press intensify, the more journalists turn to strategic bias in a vain attempt to shed their image as 'enemies of the people'.

Simply put, Israeli journalists and media outlets, when trying to counter Netanyahu's bad-faith accusations and reinforce public trust in their reporting, have intentionally tilted their political reporting rightwards. This might not sound like a typical form of censorship, as it does not necessarily include direct silencing; rather, it often is reflected in journalists' choices to speak differently or disingenuously, invite different interviewees, pick their topics cautiously. The implications, however, remain the same: shrinking boundaries of legitimate discourse and taming of journalistic scrutiny.[181] The toll on the public's right to know is clear. To me, the 2023–2025 war in Israel and Palestine became the most striking example of strategic bias and the infectious silences it reinforced.

Does Bias Still Matter?

Although competing journalistic norms have risen and dissolved over the years,[182] and younger news audiences in several countries attest to being more open to news platforms that don't commit to objectivity,[183] the notion of 'bias' has remained associated with the worst sin of the mainstream media, in Israel and various other journalistic cultures inspired by the Anglo-American tradition of news. The media has undeniably been going through a process of reckoning in recent years, with broadcasters and researchers rethinking concepts like objectivity, truth-seeking, lies, exclusion and inequality.[184] For instance, should adopting an anti-racist approach to news be considered journalistic bias? How about embracing a pro-democracy point of view when reporting on politics? Is it 'unprofessional' for sexual assault survivors to cover rape?[185] Scholars, journalists and activists are currently struggling with such questions. Despite the many considerations and question marks, based on my research and others', the role of bias in the media's confrontation with hostile populists is still immense. In my interviewees' accounts, bias was a powerful, motivating and ultimately destructive force. In a large-scale survey I led with communication scholars Yariv Tsfati and Yossi David and political scientists Noam Gidron and Lior Sheffer, we found that overall, audiences in Israel were as obsessed with objectivity and bias as journalists were.

Bias, however, is a slippery concept, difficult to define and even harder to study. According to the *Oxford Dictionary of Media and Communication*, bias is 'the conscious or unconscious interpretation or representation of a phenomenon in a way that (typically recurrently) favours (or is perceived as favouring) one particular point of view rather than another. In journalism, bias is defined as a personal or institutional stance that is perceived to be reflected in factual reporting (e.g., a news report, overall news coverage of a topic, an interview, or a documentary) – especially in its apparent pattern of selectivity; a professional lapse in the journalistic goals of impartiality, objectivity, and/or balance (regardless of intention).'[186]

It is important to contextualise the bias question and highlight that the ethos of objectivity has never been the only format of journalism (as media historian, Michael Schudson, describes in his seminal book *Discovering the News: A Social History of American Newspapers*).[187] Since the middle of the 20th century, the climax of trust in rational and unbiased media began to wane, and media scholars started questioning the necessity of objectivity in journalism.[188] Several movements contested the value of traditional objectivity, from post-modernism to gender and queer theory,[189] suggesting that objectivity limits human thought by enforcing one dominant, exclusive and often elitist narrative. Advocates of peace journalism repudiated the concept of neutral reporting at times of war, arguing that the alleged impartiality masks journalists' bias towards militarism and conflicts.[190] Journalists then cover wars as horse races, misinform the public and even incite violence. These criticisms were generally rejected by the news industry, and generations of reporters adhere to their neutral position or the attempts to pursue its optics. So do many news consumers.[191]

What objectivity looks like, in practice, was scrutinised as much as the abstract ideal itself.[192] Critical scholars noted that the real-world manifestation of objectivity has become, on many occasions, nothing more than a symbolic and empty ritual.[193] Radical critiques added that neutral reporting ended up reinforcing the media's already-problematic leaning towards the elites, and that the bias in favour of powerful figures is concealed behind the impartial and detached tone.[194] Journalists were accused of utilising objectivity as a rhetoric strategy to self-legitimise their position and authority in society, and to manufacture a false impression of accountability.[195] When that happens, objectivity no longer serves the public nor allows different groups in society to agree on facts. And yet, no alternative to the ethos of non-bias succeeded in taking over the hearts and minds of news producers and news consumers in most countries. And so, even news organisations which are committed to certain ideologies, policies or parties try keeping a non-biased face. While a few alternatives were suggested and practised – from transparency to fairness – none of them managed to sideline the dominance of balance, impartiality and bias in the public conversation.

Over the years, scholars detected multiple sources of media bias, from journalists' ideological inclinations to the commercial interests of media owners and advertisers.[196] Communication scholar Robert Entman usefully distinguishes between two different types of bias: content biases, namely, 'consistent patterns in the framing of mediated communication that promote the influence of one side in conflicts'; and decision-making biases, which 'operate within the minds of individual journalists [...] and influence the framing of media texts.'[197] While content bias refers to the outcome of bias – namely, slanted news items – decision-making bias refers to the *production* of slanted news: 'the motivations and mindsets of journalists who allegedly produce the biased content.'[198] This is what strategic bias is all about: what happens in the heads of those in charge of delivering the news to us when they are being consistently delegitimised, looking at the mirror and seeing enemies of the people staring back at them.

The Pro-Populist Bias

The media's efforts to stick even more strongly to 'the rules of the game' were intended to prove that journalists were not biased against the populist leader, the right and 'the people'. 'Even if I thought we should open up to new theories about the profession, like "Let's report from our personal perspectives" and all that, now is not the right time for it,' stated a TV host. 'Now we must go back to basics. Journalism focused on bringing the facts hasn't got the luxury of adopting trends and fashions like these. I find it unacceptable. And if it makes me old-school, anachronistic, rigid – but so be it.' Another print editor had a similar take: 'There is no appropriate media response to the slander against us,' he said. 'The only strategy is to return to objectivity, at least for now.'

Researchers found similar perceptions among journalists in the United States and Germany.[199] When examining how American journalists defend themselves against Trump's attacks, Michael and his colleagues concluded that the media defends 'the institutional myth' of journalism by emphasising ideals like objectivity and even-handedness[200]. Analysing media coverage from the German press, Benjamin Krämer and Klara Langmann demonstrate how reporters double down on objectivity and balance when facing right-wing populism.[201] Krämer, a pioneering scholar of media and populism, suspected that 'objectivity' and 'balance' might result in journalists normalising right-wing populists to prove the allegations were false.[202] My findings from a decade of anti-media populism in Israel demonstrate that his concerns were warranted. Feedback from journalists in the UK, the US, Australia and beyond confirm this is not a unique case. While striving to perform balance, journalists under attack were drawn to practise pro-populist bias, as their daily lives were increasingly disrupted, their well-being harmed, offensive graffiti drawn on their homes and their children getting bullied at school.

As media commentators Patrick Barwise and Peter York summarise it in their book *The War Against the BBC* – and despite the wild and consistent accusations against the British public broadcaster – 'the academic research reveals a consistent pattern: the BBC's political coverage is dominated by representatives of the two main political parties, especially whichever is in power, but with a bias towards *conservative* voices and issues.'[203] This was true for the sources used, the think tanks quoted, media coverage of immigration, the EU, elections coverage and religion.

The 'Business as usual' motto I heard from leading newsmakers in Israel was their version of 'We're at Work, Not at War', the famous catchphrase coined by Marty Baron, then editor-in-chief of the *Washington Post* in 2016. What he meant by it was, 'it's not for us to defeat Trump – we just cover him'. It was only when we dove into the details of everyday reporting that it turned out journalists were actually employing a strategy that directly clashed with their abstract commitment to objectivity and balance.

Strategic bias has not necessarily reflected journalists' approval of the populist argument: even journalists who insisted that the media was balanced – or, in fact, biased to the right – admitted to leaning rightwards to distance themselves from the left, as a strategic move aimed to pre-empt and refute populist attacks. In other words, leaning to the right was not meant to correct an actual media bias but rather to perform a 'correction' to the supposed bias journalists believed their audience attributed to them following Netanyahu's accusations.

'It feels like we are constantly trying to prove that we're OK', explained one commentator, who later chose to leave the profession. 'Instead of saying, "You can attack us as much as you want; we'll keep doing our job", we keep apologising. We have added more right-wing hosts to the panels, for instance.' This particular technique reminded me of the anonymous BBC journalists' reports that right-wing Brexit supporters were recruited to positions of power in the corporation, or the chase to hire Trump sycophants in the US.[204] The attempts to appease and obey in advance are visible. But they do not seem to work.

While in other societies the left–right division is often determined by economic positions, in Israel the dominant partisan cleavage reflects voters' stances towards the Israeli–Palestinian conflict.[1] The hawkish right traditionally advocates

---

[1] Nevertheless, Israeli politics has increasingly come to revolve around the 'values' cleavage and the attendant 'culture wars'. See Hirsch-Hoefler and Mudde, 2020.

for the annexation of the Occupied Palestinian Territories and more militant responses to Palestinian violence, with the dovish left traditionally supporting a peaceful agreement between the nations.[205] Netanyahu's leader-centred populism has given rise to another fissure between his supporters and opponents, which has become increasingly dominant over the past decade. These two sets of distinctions – right vs left and pro-Netanyahu vs anti-Netanyahu – largely, but not entirely, overlap. When journalists admitted to applying strategic bias, they referred to both levels: they were hoping to flee their affiliation with the 'anti-Netanyahu' camp, as well as to distance themselves from left-wing stances on the Palestinian question out of fear of being labelled 'leftists', 'Arab-lovers' or simply 'traitors'. In the UK, strategic bias might translate into Brexit, Nigel Farage or far-right rioters getting their special treatment. In Germany or Poland, the coverage of immigrants is often the most affected. The crucial point is that the populist right is the one marking out the boundaries; the media – competing with platforms like X and TikTok all the way to the bottom – are following their lead. And so, the entire information environment drifts further and further to the right.

When the War on the Media Meets War

'If liberty means anything at all, it means the right to tell people things they do not want to hear.'
George Orwell, written in 1945, published in 1972.

THE 7TH OF OCTOBER was a heartbreaking day, to be followed by many others. As an Israeli based in London, I spent the day glued to my phone, TV and laptop, watching the news and frantically calling my loved ones. In the utter chaos of the day, it took time to figure out that my friend's parents were slaughtered in their homes, that my friend's cousins were kidnapped while dancing at a music festival, some tortured, others maimed. For a few good months, everyone I knew was broken and shocked, somehow affected by the vicious attack launched by Hamas terrorists against children and babies, men and women, many of whom were peace activists for decades, dedicating their lives to ending the Israeli occupation of the Palestinian territories. For a moment, it seemed like things could not have been worse. But then started the long, harrowing war in Gaza, led by Israel's most far-right coalition in history. The atrocities and horrors accumulated by the day: while the declared war goals were targeting Hamas terrorists, on the ground, dozens of thousands of Palestinian men, women, children and babies were killed in their masses, buried under the rubble, bombed in their refugee tents, hungry, sick, freezing to death. The numbers were unfathomable. Entire families were erased, millions were displaced. My TikTok account exploded with bleeding, dying newborns. But in Israel, Gaza disappeared.

My mind was in a 'split-screen mode': with one eye on Israeli News 12, and another on the BBC, I quickly felt like I was either going blind, or mad. The epistemological rift between the two realities was irreconcilable. On the one hand, I saw my compatriots murdered, tortured, held hostage. It was easy for me to believe because I knew these people and their families (contrary to its massive global resonance, Israel is a *very* small place). On the other hand, I saw people in my professional milieu and social circles in the UK refusing to recognise Hamas's unjustifiable violence against civilian Israelis and Palestinians, or in fact, to acknowledge any Israeli grief at all. For some of my friends, we became indefensible. As time went by, and the death toll in Gaza reached an unbelievable scale, I found – to my disappointment and heartbreak – the same denialism, blindness and conspiratorial thinking spreading fast among my community back home. This felt, above all, incredibly lonely.

If you have been exposed to the horrific footage coming out of Gaza, on global media or social platforms, you might have seen captions and hashtags reiterating the idea that 'This time, we can't say we didn't know'. In a clear reference to the Holocaust's main takeaway – 'Never Again' – protesters worldwide felt that this time they could not keep silent, as the atrocities in Gaza were unfolding in front of our eyes. As a granddaughter to four Holocaust survivors, each of whom arrived in Israel after World War II as the sole, broken remains of what was once a big happy family, the 'never again' sentiment resonated strongly with me. The visuals of hungry children and destroyed neighbourhoods coming out of Gaza shook me to the core, as have the testimonies from the 7th October attack before them. However, not everyone was watching. I quickly realised I was no longer on the same ground as my homeland community. They were not watching what I, and millions around the world, were watching.

Born and raised in a grey city near Tel Aviv, I grew up in a politically split family. While my mom has always been a staunch humanist, a secular, liberal and progressive educator, the rest of our family has voted for parties ranging from the centre right to the far right. As political tensions in Israel soured, I learned – like many of us – not to discuss politics at the dinner table. In her fantastic book, *Democracy Lives in Darkness*, Emily Van Duyn describes how Americans stopped sharing their political views with those who disagree post-2016.[206] I, too, stopped discussing politics with the people I love and care for most; it was too taxing, frustrating and seemingly futile. But my mom had always remained a political ally, a passionate conversationalist and a partner for demonstrations and protests that became increasingly heated and violent over the years. This is why my red flags were in full swing when the war in Gaza broke out, as I realised that my mom and I were no longer political allies in the way we used to be. In fact, we were no longer sharing the same universe of very basic truths at all.

This experience might resonate with some of you. In her book *Messengers of the Right*, American historian Nicole Hemmer tells the story of the rise of conservative talk radio in the US, and how it created a rift in her close relationship with her Southener father.[207] But to me, this came as a surprise: my mom did not become addicted to some wacko conservative radio station with Covid deniers spreading bad faith nonsense. She was not following the pro-government propaganda Channel 14 or any of the far-right influencers or podcasters. In fact, she did not change her news habits at all. If anything, since the horrors of 7th October she had become an even more consistent and devoted news consumer, glued to the mainstream media like most of my Israeli friends and acquaintances, always alert to the possibility that another rocket was on its way to Tel Aviv, another siren going off, or another terror attack unfolding. Quickly, it became clear that unlike Hemmer's father, what changed was not my mom's sources of information. It was the same journalists she always trusted, who no longer presented her with a reasonably representative picture of the unfolding events. These were the same reporters who did phenomenal work investigating Hamas atrocities, but failed to do the same when covering the following war in Gaza. But why?

To me, the 2023–2025 war became the most striking example of the new censorship and the infectious silences and blind spots it forces. The mainstream media was blinding us instead of letting us see what was, evidently, too painful – yet real. It was an exemplar of what happens when a crisis hits after years of compromising our right to know.

How the Occupation Disappeared

To understand the setting in which this war broke, let's rewind, years back, to Israeli summer, 2018. In the middle of a busy bar in Tel Aviv, what started as a fun and chill research interview with a charismatic prominent TV journalist ended with her bursting into tears. After too many questions and a fair share of drinks, my interviewee – an inspiring and successful TV correspondent – found the courage to confide in me her experience auditioning for a new news programme. She had never told the story before. Following a successful pilot, she was told she had gotten the job. She was thrilled, but the excitement turned sour as her new bosses politely insisted that she stop bringing up the military occupation of the West Bank and Gaza in the programme because it sounded 'too Tel Avivian'. Like many other big cities worldwide, Tel Aviv is more liberal than the average Israeli city. As such, it is often portrayed by the populist right as a detached, elitist, lefty stronghold filled with spoiled artists and vegan anarchists. 'Too Tel Avivian', in other words, means 'too left-wing', as my sobbing interviewee quickly understood. Her emotional breakdown at the bustling pub had to do with my follow-up question. It was: 'And have you ever said "occupation" on air since?' She had not.

'At any given moment there is an orthodoxy, a body of ideas which it is assumed that all right-thinking people will accept without question,' Orwell wrote in a later-discovered introduction to the 1972 edition of *Animal Farm*. 'It is not exactly forbidden to say this, that or the other but it is "not done" to say it, just as in mid-Victorian times it was "not done" to mention trousers in the presence of a lady.' In the very non-Victorian times of the 2020s in Israel, after decades of Netanyahu's leadership, the occupation was the primary casualty – the trousers not to be mentioned in front of a lady. After all, why bother mentioning the most burning question that will determine the future, life and death of both Palestinians and Israelis between the river and the sea?

As my conversations with journalists worldwide revealed, this is – unfortunately – not an Israeli phenomenon. In different cultures, other topics were vanishing from sight as strategic bias spread across society. In Turkey, it might be the Armenian genocide which disappeared from the public eye. In Germany, immigrants' and refugees' voices are sidelined. Certain words fade away, some claims dissipate, and specific interviewees dissolve. As news consumers – and more crucially, as citizens – we are the ones paying the price, with topics and figures labelled too 'liberal', 'metropolitan' or 'globalist' disappearing from the horizon. The entire political imagination and public debate is shifting, slowly but surely, further and further to the right, pushing more and more ideas, topics and agendas away from sight.

How could the Israeli occupation of the West Bank and Gaza disappear from the Israeli public debate? Why were reporters willing to drop this term, despite it being, in their minds, the most accurate way to describe the situation? After all, there was nothing more important for Israelis and Palestinians to discuss, regardless of their political views on what the potential solutions to this national conflict may be. It was a difficult conversation that was critical for us to have.

The real-world materials that great journalism is made of. And yet, following years of populist media-bashing, strategic bias has come to dominate the public sphere. It became a journalistic – and then public – no-go-zone. Lord Voldemort of the Middle East.

'I've been a journalist for 30 years now, and I have always tried to be fair and balanced,' explained one feisty and charismatic TV broadcaster. 'I've never even told my family who I vote for! But now, if you're not on the right, you're labelled a "lefty". Journalists distance themselves from the left, and honestly, I did too. I really didn't want this label.' This is, in essence, what strategic bias sounds like in the inner dialogue journalists hold among themselves after years of threats and defamation. A print editor put it slightly differently: Netanyahu, he told me, 'convinced everyone that the media is lefty, and now newspapers – including mine – try hard to prove otherwise.' A passionate veteran radio journalist explained what this meant in practice. 'We must balance any item that might be perceived as "lefty",' he said. 'But radical right-wing content is just fine.'

The Israeli occupation of the Palestinian Territories, where millions of Palestinians live, was the single most popular example mentioned by Israeli reporters as a topic which has become extremely difficult for them to address in the new hostile environment (the second was pro-Netanyahu rallies). Even when I have not brought it up directly, journalists noted they would no longer use the term 'occupation' in their reporting – even if it best describes the situation in their view – since the word has been labelled by the populist right a 'radical lefty' term.

For context, the right-wing camp in Israel – led by the religious settlers' movement – fears that merely acknowledging the occupation might advance those seeking to end it. Referring to 'the occupation' has become associated with the left; the right prefers the biblical term 'Judea and Samaria' to describe the West Bank, as it alludes to Israel's religious ties to the land rather than the Israeli control over millions of Palestinians. In such discursive wars, the mainstream media has a decisive role, marking and signalling what is legitimate, debatable and illegitimate through the question of what is considered objective reporting and what requires a balancing act.[208] In the fight between the 'occupation' and 'Judea and Samaria', the latter has come out on top.

How did this happen? The first way was more explicit, as in the incident described above when a journalist was directly asked to drop the word. Interestingly, other interviewees mentioned their hesitance when using the term as well, although no direct instruction was given to them by their bosses or superiors. 'It is always on your mind,' said a radio host, 'the far right is legitimate, but God forbid if you mention the occupation.' A political correspondent for a big news website had a similar experience. 'When I use the word "occupation", I do so very carefully. Just because I feel like it will trigger all this antagonism, that nobody listens to what you're saying anymore, just for the fact that you have used the word. It's crazy how sensitive this word has become. So that's something that I'm often cautious about.' 'Frankly, I think twice,' added another TV presenter. 'Sometimes I prefer to spare myself the evil comments ... To tell you I'm proud of that? Of course not. But this is the trickle-down effect of the incitement against us.'

None of these journalists had a parallel example for a word that they had stopped using because it was labelled as 'too right-wing' or 'too hawkish'. Their understanding of 'good journalism' and how their audiences perceive it has driven them to tilt the entire political debate in favour of the same political figures who express ongoing disrespect towards press freedom. On a personal level, interviewees expressed hope that their behaviour might spare them further attacks by Netanyahu and his allies. On the professional level, they believed that strategic bias would help them to protect their professional façade and thus their public authority, credibility and legitimacy.

Even before Netanyahu's war on the media, right-wing politicians and pressure groups were using military conflicts to denounce Israeli journalists as 'leftist mafia',[209] although research consistently refutes that Israel's news was indeed biased to the left or anywhere near pro-Palestinian.[210] In fact, 'the Israeli media has been repeatedly shown to be "patriotic" by constructing news frames that reflect and reinforce the belief that Israel is virtuous and victimised',[211] with military conflicts drawing it even closer to Israel's official policy. This background has prepared public opinion for Netanyahu and his allies to frame journalists as 'enemies of the people', equating them to Hezbollah leaders and Hamas terrorists. It demonstrates how polarised, traumatised and hurting societies – particularly those haunted by national conflicts – provide fertile ground for the demonisation of the media, through its association with the nation's perceived enemies from outside as well as from within.[212]

Journalists' avoidance of using the word 'occupation' demonstrates how consequential the strategic bias may be for one of the most burning life-and-death issues in the region. Classic sociological theories, like the Spiral of Silence,[213] describe the mechanism through which the media's intentional leaning rightwards may further narrow the scope of ideas that can be freely expressed in public in the future. It erases the voices of Palestinians in the West Bank and Gaza, but also of anyone in Israel who opposes the occupation or the right-wing framing of it. And this is just one focal point of the populist storm; any criticism of Netanyahu himself was quickly stained as part of the same alleged anti-Israeli or anti-Semitic plot.

In their wish to maintain what they believe could rescue their status as authoritative professionals and legitimate members of 'the people', journalists thus participate in the campaign to shift left-wing ideas and terminology from 'the sphere of legitimate controversy' (where political controversy is acceptable) to 'the sphere of diversion' (where political actors and views are rejected and censored as 'unworthy of being heard').[214] Although declaredly purported to defend journalism, strategic bias may undermine journalism in the long term, as well as the required conditions for a healthy public conversation. By slanting the news to the right, journalists both serve their populist adversaries at present and narrow the spectrum of legitimate controversy in the future.

How to Hide a War

In times of war, fear and rage – and even revenge – are to be expected, and empathy for losses and casualties on the other side of the border is rarely a major news story. Israel is not unique here either; few in the US and UK news industry – or the public, for that matter – shed tears over the hundreds of thousands of Iraqi and Afghan casualties during the early 2000s. As was documented at length in previous rounds of violence worldwide, our care for the death of others is extremely limited as violence proceeds. Research analysing the US media coverage of the Iraq war in 2002–2003, including ABC, CBS and NBC, found that the Bush administration officials were the most frequently quoted sources, the voices of anti-war groups and opposition Democrats were barely audible, and generally, all TV channels promoted a pro-war perspective.[215] Civilian casualties on the other side of the border hardly make it above the fold.

And yet, even during previous military operations and full-on wars in the Middle East, there was always *some* visibility of innocent civilian lives taken on the Palestinian side. I still remember the shock and tears in my mom's living room, in front of the TV back in 2009, when Israeli reporter Shlomi Eldar was live on the phone with his friend, Palestinian physician Dr Abu al-Aish, who had just found out the IDF had bombed his young daughters. Both were crying, as were we. Not this time around. Stories like al-Aish's were, unfortunately, ubiquitous in this war. But they left no mark on Israeli TV screens. There were several reasons for this change: the national trauma of 7th October, the ongoing fear of further escalation in the northern and southern borders of Israel, and the fact that millions of Israelis were directly affected, displaced and scared. But the other reason, which must not be ignored, was that for over a decade the Israeli media has been threatened and intimidated, redesigned, crippled and silenced.

During the first six months of this bloody war, I had two determined coders watching the most popular TV newscast in Israel, News 12. They diligently coded every item in our sample covering the war. The findings scared us. Only 4 of over 700 hundred items mentioned any civilian Palestinian casualties in Gaza at all. Only two of these included footage from Gaza showing human suffering, death, blood, hunger. If you remember what the visuals looked like on the BBC at the time – and it's hard to forget – you probably realise how ghastly the gap is. Even when visuals from Gaza were broadcast on the Israeli newscast, they were sterilised of the pain and loss inflicted on Palestinian children, covering mostly evacuated empty ruins of buildings. No footage of anything that might raise the suspicion that what the IDF is doing in Gaza merits scrutiny – only our brave soldiers fighting invisible and inhumane Nazi-like enemies.

Not only has the human suffering of Palestinians in Gaza disappeared from the screens, as they were haunting those living anywhere else, but so have Palestinians themselves. Not just those living in Gaza or the West Bank, but even those with Israeli citizenship, within the acknowledged borders of Israel. For those unfamiliar with the stats, around a fifth of all Israeli citizens are Palestinians who self-identify as Palestinian citizens of Israel or Israeli Arabs. As the war broke, they disappeared from the Israeli media almost overnight. According to a study led by media watchdog The Seventh Eye, during the first half of 2024 only 1.3 per cent of the interviewees and pundits on

TV were Israeli Arabs – although their share of the population is closer to 20 per cent.[216] Opposition voices, both Jewish and Palestinian, were hardly heard during the first year of the war. In January 2025, Arad Nir, a foreign news editor on News 12, revealed that he had lost his spot on the TV network's leading weekly show after calling to end the war.[217]

Whatever your position on Israel and Palestine, whatever your position on objectivity and impartiality, whatever you think about war, hiding big truths from your audience means betraying journalism (and in my view, patriotism too). This is the heavy toll that strategic bias and fake balance take on the public's right to know. One cannot make wise, informed decisions about the future without knowing what is happening at present, one hour's drive away from home. Ignoring the human suffering on the other side of the wall is incredibly offensive towards the Palestinians in Gaza, but it is also unbelievably harmful to those shutting their eyes.

The Israeli case is an extreme one, but far from a one-off. As news consumers in Hungary, Poland and India know well, the populist war on the media is in full force. The silences are growing. It is hard to go back once backsliding sneaks in, and it is certainly harder when the next crisis hits – be it a pandemic, a natural disaster or war.

Deride and Conquer: The Populist Crackdown on Solidarity

'When these criminals with microphones provide joint statements, by joining together they form a collusion.' *President of Argentina, Javier Milei, about Argentinian reporters who dare criticise his administration, 2024.*[218]

IN MARCH 2024, a little history was made on American cable news. In a series of fiery on-air monologues, high-profile NBC talents – including Chuck Todd, Joe Scarborough and Mika Brzezinski – publicly condemned the network's decision to hire a staunch Trump loyalist as a political pundit. The televised rebellion took place after the network reportedly hired Ronna McDaniel, the former chair of the Republican National Committee and a collaborator in Trump's attempts to overturn the 2020 elections, as a paid contributor. 'You wouldn't hire a mobster to work at a district attorney's office, right?' MSNBC star Rachel Maddow asked her millions of viewers as she burst into laughter. At the end of her monologue, she acknowledged how inconvenient this entire situation was. 'We are contending with something we never had to contend with before,' she said, 'and our country needs us to be strong right now.' It took NBC leadership less than one week to drop McDaniel's appointment in response.

The message was clear: no collaborators of the Big Lie – the attempt to overturn the 2020 US elections – should be granted the legitimacy, fame and prestige of a regular NBC commentator. It was a small win, overshadowed by many losses. But it shows us what happens when journalists are willing to join forces and use their power to make sure we all get better news. The Ronna McDaniel case was exceptional but by no means unprecedented. On 21st October, 2019, Australians awoke to an unusual sight: the front pages of every major daily newspaper were blacked out. The coordinated protest was a response to new laws and police raids that threatened press freedom in the country. It was a creative and bold collaborative move. In the last national elections in India, President Modi won by much smaller margins than originally predicted. Some commentators attributed this hopeful development to the newly founded coalition of independent journalists, joining forces to push back against Modi's powerful and loyalist media (what became known as 'Godi media' in India).[219] In Hong Kong, journalists collaborated – among themselves and with their audiences – to download and archive entire news websites the Chinese government had been trying to shut down since 2019.

Curiously, the journalists I met in small cafés across Israel between 2017 and 2020 – those directly targeted by the populist assault on the media – did not feel emboldened or united by the experience. Instead, the strongest impression they left was one of overwhelming loneliness. To be honest, this was not what I expected. I approached these famous, renowned journalists as part of an extremely powerful cultural elite. They had the resources, reputation, skills and everything that goes with it. As a nerdy PhD student, I trained myself to conduct what sociologists call 'elite interviews', namely, interviews with powerful individuals.[220] Yet interviewing elite figures under attack in times of democratic backsliding is a different matter. The emotionally charged, at times tearful, discussions with senior reporters and presenters revealed they had become quite a vulnerable elite. They still wielded significant influence over the national conversation, yet that very position had made them acutely exposed. As media gatekeepers they enjoyed the privileges of massive social media followings, substantial salaries and institutional authority. But they also bore the consequences of being cast by authoritarian leaders as 'the enemy'. While some were forced to hire bodyguards, others scrubbed graffiti from their homes, only to step back into the studio and decide what Israelis would learn about the war in Gaza.

After several interviews, I realised nobody mentioned collaborative efforts as a means to counter the populist war on the media. I was puzzled. How come this did not come up? I started asking journalists, directly, if they ever considered collaborating or working together to better cope with the orchestrated campaign against the media. If they ever held newsroom meetings brainstorming how to fight back.

They cracked up laughing.

But this was not always the case. Three decades ago, when Netanyahu was first elected prime minister, the two national

TV networks in Israel – one public, the other commercial – were forced to confront a novel dilemma. The young, fresh-faced and charismatic Netanyahu refused to submit to the established method of dealing with reporters by answering their questions in televised media gaggles. Instead, the new prime minister scheduled pseudo-press conferences: podium addresses that corresponded with the evening newscasts, thus hoping to 'force' the TV networks to air his remarks live, leaving them no space to ask questions and no time to edit his statements. Back in the 1990s, Netanyahu was already working to bypass journalists' editorial considerations, speaking above their heads straight to the Israeli people, who were watching the evening news obsessively – decades before the rise of social media platforms.

At the first of these no-questions-allowed 'press conferences', the TV networks took the bait and broadcasted PM Netanyahu's remarks live. But when the CEOs of both channels realised that Netanyahu was playing a crafty game to narrow their editorial freedom, they did something exceptional: they decided they would no longer broadcast his speeches live, at least unless reporters were allowed to ask questions. This was not a quiet agreement behind closed doors: in an unusual public appearance, the two CEOs announced their decision to the Israeli people, explaining that surrendering to Netanyahu's PR tactic would violate the foundations of journalism.

It was not a one-time historical incident of solidarity among journalists in the region. In his fascinating article on the collegial relations between Palestinian and Israeli journalists back in the 1980s, Orayb A. Najjar describes how – despite the deep animosity between the nations – some Israeli and Palestinian journalists had managed to collaborate and support one another, becoming colleagues rather than enemies. Najjar detailed how several forms of collaboration developed between Israeli and Palestinian journalists in the West Bank, going back as far back as 1980 (which, by then, Israel had already occupied for over a decade). Israeli journalists, Najjar wrote, 'increasingly turned to Palestinians for their news about the occupied territories,' establishing a form of working relationship.[221] In 1982, when three Palestinian editors were under town arrest, Israeli journalists paid a visit. A few years later, the Jerusalem branch of the Israeli Journalists' Association protested against the planned expulsion of Akram Haniyeh, then head of the Association of Arab Journalists.

But for the Israeli journalists I spoke to in the 2020s, three decades after the national TV networks teamed up against the populist attempts to manipulate the news, collective action sounded like science fiction. Not even a reasonable path of action which, after consideration, they chose not to follow – but more of a joke. Two competing newsrooms collaborating? Journalists expressing collegiality? Joining forces against powerful politicians? Clearly, something – or rather, a few things – had changed since the dominant newsrooms in the country decided to stand up to a young prime minister who tried to obstruct their work and escape public scrutiny. What was it that had changed? What precisely was stopping journalists from collaborating when subject to an intensifying political campaign aimed at discrediting them, undermining their profession and sabotaging their work? What would it take for them to get together and fight back?

When They Go Low, We Drift Apart

Apparently, the populist media-bashing has another brilliant advantage – it discourages journalists from collaborating. On an emotional level, it had to do with the fear of attracting further smears if they were to stand in solidarity with their colleagues. This sort of fear, experienced by journalists worldwide,[222] was often accompanied by fatigue and burnout: an attempt to spare oneself the extra emotional labour that defending other journalists entails. On the strategic level, Israeli journalists came to see any form of collaboration as a risk of proving the populist argument against them.

Clearly, collaboration was never the first word that comes to mind when thinking about journalism or news. Collective action among journalists and news outlets is rare, as journalism has long been framed – particularly in the US and the UK – as a highly competitive profession, with journalists and newsrooms routinely fighting over scoops, exclusive stories, leaks, sources, subscribers and attention.[223]

While combing through the dusty wooden shelves of the university library for my doctoral research, I was struck by how little attention had been given to the notion of solidarity in journalism and its role in safeguarding the public's right to know. Recent studies have examined solidarity between journalists and the marginalised communities they operate within, and a growing body of research is shedding much-needed light on global collaborations between investigative journalists, especially around the publication of explosive materials like the Panama Papers or the Pegasus scandal.[224] But little thought was granted to the role solidarity can play as a tool to empower journalism, boost public knowledge and shield democracy in hostile times. It's about time that we did – for more than one reason.

First, solidarity – and the lack thereof – has been a determinant factor in the well-being and professional lives of targeted journalists around the globe. This has been particularly true when physical threats are involved. In Venezuela, for instance, in the late 2010s, journalists reported experiencing 'an all-time high' in solidarity after violent pressures from the authorities.[225] This sense of solidarity, they report, has helped them to fight side by side against the powerful pressures from the government. In some regions of Mexico, journalists started working as collectives to minimise the physical and sometimes deadly threats to their safety and independence, mainly by local mafias[226]. In Pakistan, journalists found themselves relying on each other when facing death threats and state violence.[227] Investigative journalists in China – always in a complicated position vis-à-vis the ruling party – have formed informal networks to share information, help one another to access sources, provide support in times of trouble and discuss professional dilemmas.[228] When journalists have been attacked, harassed, falsely accused or detained, their fellow journalists have signed petitions, published critical editorials and held protests in the streets. In Finland, a much safer haven for free press, journalists considered collegiality in the newsroom among the most helpful practices against anti-press harassment – it provided targeted journalists with much-needed emotional support, they explained.[229] So, there is nothing inherent that makes journalists incapable of working together to protect us (and them) against the new censorship. The template exists. One beautiful example was journalists going through their colleagues' online profiles to erase and report any abusive comments or toxic threats. This tactic might reflect true friendship, but this is surely not their job.

In other regions, journalists under pressure have complained about the *lack* of solidarity with their colleagues. In research conducted for the Reuters Institute, journalists in Central and Eastern Europe defined the lack of collaboration and solidarity as one of the main threats to press freedom in the region.[230] In a cross-country study from 2021, journalists under attack in Pakistan, India, Bulgaria and even the Democratic Republic of Congo have similarly considered the lack of solidarity and weakness of professional unions as leading contributors to their feelings of isolation, vulnerability and helplessness.[231] It is perhaps not surprising that references to journalistic solidarity and collaboration are easier to find in countries like Venezuela, Mexico and Pakistan, despite the limited attention that these countries occupy in journalism studies. Journalists' work, freedom and lives tend to be intimidated in these countries in ways rarely found in the United States or Western Europe: more sheer violence, less soft censorship. Therefore, the need for defensive collaborations becomes a crucial matter of life and death rather than well-being, credibility or prestige. When journalists' lives or freedom are under such tangible threat, other considerations are pushed into the background.

Second, solidarity should be expected when journalists are under attack. The prolific research on the psychology of group identification shows that external threats generally increase in-group solidarity and unity.[232] In other words, nothing bonds people like having a mutual adversary. Perceived threats to your group trigger a greater sense of belonging, as well as increased hostility towards others. One would imagine, therefore, that being called 'lefty traitors' and 'Hamas terrorists' by the same leader again and again might bring journalists together.

So, both strategically and emotionally, I would expect that when the news industry is scathed, the threat will push its members, who I know so well, closer together – or at least encourage them to consider collaboration as a coping strategy. As media scholar David Karpf put it when Trump first rose to power: 'It is time for American press organisations to take their shared social role and responsibility seriously, and to act collectively to defend it ... Journalists will need to abandon their prideful resistance to collective action. They will need to stand together if they want to avoid falling apart.'[233] Have American journalists been listening? The NBC tale that opened this chapter might suggest they have. That would be a significant stretch, though.

The Kidney Tale

None of this coming together effect was felt when the political attacks against Israeli journalists skyrocketed in the 2010s and 2020s. To my surprise, one investigative journalist explained to me, entertained, that, 'It's quite the contrary – there is no solidarity whatsoever. None. It's frustrating, because we could have had so much power together. And these struggles weaken us all.' I couldn't hold myself from asking: Why *don't* you collaborate, then?

Those who found the lack of solidarity to be a problem, often blamed it on others – their colleagues or competitors (an act that expresses little solidarity in itself). But interestingly, not all have mourned the lack of solidarity, and in fact, many have carried it as a badge of honour, or at least seemed fairly amused by it all. For me, the turning point was 'the kidney tale'. I was sitting for an interview with an influential and famously targeted journalist, a vocal critic of Netanyahu. 'There is no cooperation at all,' he told me, noisily sipping his drink. 'Whenever people say, "the media", I find it really amusing. Because if there's a profession where there's no team spirit whatsoever, it's our profession! It's a very independent profession, built of an assemblage of soloists. You are willing to lose a kidney, if it means your competitor will lose both kidneys.' So many journalists I spoke to seemed proud of how viciously competitive and self-interested their profession has become. That didn't strike me as a brilliant long-term strategy. Journalists still hold incredible power in society. They hold the mic, or laptop, they sit in the studios, they have massive followings online. Together, they could make a difference.

This self-declared lack of solidarity was supported by the fact that most journalists I talked to expressed unprompted, piercing criticisms of their competitors. In most cases, it was during the segments of the interview that the journalists asked to be kept confidential in which they had levelled their poignant critiques. In other words, the most secretive moments in those interviews were not the ones in which reporters confessed to be practising self-censorship, but rather those where they were trash-talking their colleagues.

Since collective action seems to be a reasonable strategy, which may have emboldened journalists' power to fight the new censorship, it is unclear why it has not become a viable possibility in their minds. Their testimonies point to several changes to our information environment that might explain their refusal to work together to safeguard democracy, or at least press freedom.

The first was the increasing affective polarisation in Israel – the hostility between people who support different political parties – which penetrated the newsroom and divided journalists into two antagonistic groups, triggering their contrasting partisan identities rather than their common professional identity.[234] The second was the financial constraints forced on news outlets. This unfavourable environment, which has made journalists' working conditions more precarious and unstable, sharpened the competition among news outlets and individual journalists.[235] The third is journalists' criticisms of their colleagues in the news industry. This critique is often very different to the populist one: they thought their colleagues were not professional enough, or too sloppy. Not enemies of the people. And yet, despite the significant discrepancy between the critiques, journalists' eagerness to support their colleagues was compromised by their frustration with the deteriorating professional standards they witnessed around them.

The individualistic, competitive and isolated approach to handling media-bashing was evident during the interviews I held with journalists. While prestigious and well-connected, my interviewees seemed very isolated when it came to coping with the hostile environment that surrounds them. During our conversations, a few mentioned that they had never discussed these matters before. This was remarkable given that most of them expressed deep concerns and even distress around the issue, with one breaking down into tears and five others describing their experiences in terms of 'trauma'. Keeping their thoughts and feelings to themselves, in other words, was not the outcome of indifference or carelessness. They were hurt, concerned, suffering. By the end of our conversations, quite a few uttered phrases like: 'Boy, it feels good to talk about it,' or, 'It is such a relief to unload this.' When I asked whether they had anyone else to discuss these issues with, journalists explained that they did not want to worry their families at home, and that the competitive nature of the industry discouraged them from discussing it with their co-workers.

It was not technically impossible: at least within newsrooms, regular meetings did take place but these rarely led to substantial debates. 'Before each general election, we have a meeting within our network,' one TV host told me, 'but it always deteriorates very quickly into questions like, "Where should we screen the exit polls?" or, "What colour should the election studio be?" So, it's not like journalists are not thinking strategically about the attacks on the press. They do – but individually, privately.'

This lack of a comfortable environment in which journalists could share professional pressures was also palpable when journalists continued our dialogue for months and sometimes years, sending me links, print screens and text messages like, 'I thought about our conversation, and ...' or, 'I ran into that story and realised that ...' sometimes years after our initial interaction took place. There are other reasons, of course, to stay in touch: studying in a fancy UK university comes with certain social capital that could make our conversation valuable. And yet, my overall impression was that in most news organisations, loneliness was a real part of journalists' daily lives. The majority of my interviewees were therefore eager to talk with someone who knows their way around the newsroom. After building a sufficient level of trust, this loneliness made my work as a researcher slightly easier; but it also surprised me, as I expected these busy people to be stingy with their time.

In some cases, interviews with targeted journalists felt like therapy sessions. It was a bit of a worrying realisation: as kind and sensitive as I hope I am, I am certainly not trained to treat anyone, especially when the term 'trauma' is involved.

'We Are No Elders of Zion!'

It took me a while to get my head around this, until finally, a senior TV news editor explained how it worked behind the scenes. 'It's a problem,' he said. 'We hold regular meetings where all the editors and reporters sit down together, and once in a while, someone asks what we should do about [Netanyahu's bashing]. At the peak of Netanyahu's attack against our own newscast, someone raised the question: "What do you think we should do? Should we launch a campaign? Should we debunk his lies?" And there were no conclusions. Because if the media goes on a campaign to defend itself, it won't go down well. It might miss the point and fan the flames. Because it labels us as those who want to topple the government.'

'There are no "Protocols of the Elders of the Lefty Media"; there's no such animal,' a prominent and opinionated news presenter insisted. A particularly frank and courageous woman, both on air and in real life, her words hit me: 'Everyone competes against everyone else; there is no orchestrated effort to work together.' The implicit assumption was that any joint effort to battle hostile populism would somehow confirm the infamous anti-Semitic conspiracy theory regarding the Jewish plot to take over the world. In other words, by collaborating with other journalists, certain journalists believed they would be seen as a 'cartel', a 'junta', a 'closed elite' or a conspiratorial 'Elders of Zion' – just like the populist right claimed they were. According to another reporter, this was the motive behind the inaction of the Union of Journalists in Israel when Netanyahu's government kept punching the press. 'They, too, were attacked more than once, labelled as illegitimate forces who try to safeguard "the guild",' she said, and therefore were cautious not to respond as a group.

By accusing journalists of collaborating, conspiring and plotting, Netanyahu and his global copycats discourage journalists from acting together. The populist right smeared the Israelis as a 'cartel' with a 'monopoly' over public opinion, secretly colluding to leave the public in the dark and manipulate it for ideological, self-serving purposes. This idea has apparently percolated deep into journalists' consciousness. As my wise colleague and dear friend Yonatan Levi always says: 'Netanyahu's greatest achievement is the little Netanyahu he managed to plant in his opponents' minds.' When asked about a potential collaboration with her colleagues, a veteran presenter and pundit told me, slightly annoyed, that: 'There were no meetings to discuss this issue, and I'm proud of it! We should not bring about policies to counter populist media-bashing. We are not a junta.' The use of the term 'junta' in this context is, I think, telling. It reflects the populist rhetoric, associating any collaboration between journalists – and even any discussion of such collaborations – with anti-democratic, exclusionary and illegal practices of a small and oppressive elite. Collaboration equals conspiracy. Solidarity is collusion.

The reality is that journalism is inherently collaborative. The strength of institutional media is precisely what makes it indispensable. This is why TikTok influencers, while often effective, are no substitute. Holding power to account requires robust journalism, and for journalism to be powerful, journalists *must* work together rather than tearing out each other's metaphorical kidneys.

The Politics Problem

The deride-and-conquer strategy has thrived under a specific set of conditions that made it particularly successful. The

Israeli news industry – like many others around the world – has gone through an extraordinary transformation since the 1990s. The proliferation of new news outlets, first offline and then online, followed by the rise of social media in a society of early adopters, has fragmented a media environment that used to be hyper-centralised and mainstream-oriented. In the 2000s, a third TV channel was introduced, as well as regional radio stations, the first satellite TV service and multiple news websites and mobile news apps.[236] This fragmentation and multitude gave Israelis many more choices, but also made it difficult to collaborate across newsrooms. On the practical level, while in the 1990s it was enough for two powerful TV newscasts to agree on a joint declaration for them to make an impactful public move, nowadays, such an effort would have to include many more newsrooms, with varied routines, resentments and priorities.

But it was not only the technical structural fragmentation that made it difficult for newsrooms to join forces against Netanyahu's threats. Since the 2000s, various right-wing news outlets *à la* Fox News and GB News were launched in Israel, making any kind of collective action far more complex. In 2007, the late Sheldon Adelson – then Netanyahu's most generous donor and a prolific campaign contributor to the US Republican Party – founded *Israel Today*, a free daily paper that supported Netanyahu unabashedly, for years, to the extent that it was accused of carrying out unlawful election advertising in breach of the campaign finance laws, and was found by researchers to have shifted votes in the general elections in favour of Netanyahu's Likud party.[237] By 2014, the *Israel Today* group took over another newspaper, *Makor Rishon*, which was associated with the right-wing Jewish settler movement. The same year, Yitzhak Mirilashvili, the son of a Georgian billionaire with questionable ties to Netanyahu, established a new TV channel, Channel 20 (today Channel 14), that grants Netanyahu and his supporters' incredibly sympathetic media coverage.[238] A decade later, Netanyahu's supporters are reportedly taking over another new TV channel in Israel: i24 News.

Why am I only telling you about the partisan media on the right? Well, there isn't much happening on the left. *Haaretz*, the left-leaning high-brow newspaper I've been working for over many years, keeps serving the liberal elites in Israel. But no one on the left invested similar resources in reshaping the media environment in Israel, pushing forwards reliable reporting or liberal ideas. Like in the US, the UK, Hong Kong and beyond, the media sphere in Israel is incredibly asymmetrical.

The establishment of new right-wing media outlets, which prioritise partisan inclination over professional practices, expressing greater loyalty to political figures than to abstract ideals like truth or norms like fairness, made it difficult for reporters to build a support network for news. 'The media is now divided into camps,' one insider explained. 'There is right-wing media that is decent and a genuine partner for dialogue, and there is right-wing "journalism" that never discusses factual evidence in good faith. So no, it doesn't feel like solidarity has increased over the past few years.' 'Organising the Israeli media today would be impossible,' one of Netanyahu's frequent targets explained to me as we were sipping coffee in a leafy garden at the heart of Tel Aviv. 'Bringing together *Israel Today* [the free daily established by Netanyahu's biggest donor], News 13 [a leading TV newscast featuring some of Netanyahu's greatest critics], and *Yedioth Ahronoth* [a popular mainstream newspaper] all together – it just wouldn't work. There is no forum for journalists who try to deliberate together about anything.'

Even worse, these partisan media outlets, like their global equivalents, gleefully join – and sometimes lead – the public campaign against 'the leftist media'. In India, the US and Eastern Europe, what we refer to as 'partisan media' or 'alternative media' often operates, *de facto*, as spearheads of the campaign against journalism.[239] Naturally, these media outlets do not share their colleagues' concerns regarding the surge in media-bashing – quite the contrary, they are leading the war against journalism. Moreover, some supporters of the populist anti-media movement were integrated into the mainstream media, voicing their opposition to it from within. 'When editors-in-chief don't take the side of journalism, but rather the side of the attackers, then the forces that seek to undermine the trust in what we broadcast have infiltrated our newsrooms,' observed one news editor. Why is this happening? Why was Ronna McDaniel invited to join NBC to begin with? Wasn't it clear to NBC CEOs that she had nothing to do with news? Couldn't they see it was a Trojan Horse they were inviting into their already shaken newsroom?

Surely, there are ratings considerations. And there is strategic bias. On top of these, some journalists genuinely believed that incorporating such anti-media figures into the mainstream media would reduce the impact of these hostile voices or blunt their critique. It is difficult to assess how effective this strategy was; so far, it does not seem to have worked. Associates and supporters of the populist right continue to echo the top-down propaganda about the 'lying media', using the airtime granted to them to amplify their evidence-free attacks.

The penetration of anti-media figures into the mainstream media has created a situation of 'us' vs 'them' within the newsroom. Regardless of the impact this has had on the audience, it has generated a particularly toxic working environment for journalists, which certainly has not encouraged any kind of collective action. The important lesson from the Israeli case here is that political polarisation doesn't stop at the doorstep of the newsroom. The rise in partisan hate is often discussed as a distinct social phenomenon that is only covered or exacerbated by the media. But when political polarisation rises across society, it does so among journalists too. The same is true to courts, public service, universities and any other target of the populist campaign. When partisan hate penetrates the institutions that are established on a traditional ethos of fairness, balance and impartiality, solidarity and collaboration are the first scapegoats to be thrown out of the window.

The Money Problem

Has anyone begged for you to pay for news recently? Since the internet convinced us that news is for free, media organisations, entrepreneurs and researchers have tried anything and everything to get us paying for journalism again. The budget cuts and layoffs – which began long before social media took over but accelerated ever since – created an unstable and under-resourced work environment, which have made journalists' working conditions precarious and shaky. Communication researchers Yariv Tsfati and Oren Meyers found back in 2012 that most Israeli journalists report on lower wages, unstable employment and growing gaps between a thin tier of well-paid journalists and the rest.[240] The same trend was documented virtually everywhere. In the US, 2023 marked the worst year for job cuts in journalism since Covid-19, with thousands of jobs eliminated, and the upcoming years are predicted to be worse. *Press Gazette* tracked at least 8,000 jobs lost in the UK, US and Canada journalism sector in 2023,[241] and more than 500 US journalists were laid off during January, 2024 alone.[242] Local media is oftentimes hit worse, but even the most established, resourceful and well-known news organisations, like *The New York Times* and *Washington Post*, have seen massive cuts. With no new business model in sight, this is incredibly bad news for the public's right to know.

The hype around generative AI and the unleashed power of the broligarchy further aggravated the situation. The competition between newsrooms has grown even fiercer. Since the Israeli media market is relatively small, the existential threat to journalists' careers and news outlets' survival is particularly palpable, but similar trends were felt elsewhere, making collective action even less likely. 'The entire industry has been weakened for 20 years now – it's a war of attrition,' an experienced print journalist reflected on his past two decades in political reporting.

'The media's immune system is compromised, and all our capabilities are undermined. Each of us is fighting to just hang on to our own job.' A famous radio host gave a similar account, saying: 'Everyone is now fighting their little ratings wars, instead of fighting the big war.' The big war, in this metaphor, is the war for the sake of journalism. 'It's a profession of assholes,' summarised another reporter in a classic Israeli chutzpah. 'So instead of increasing solidarity, these attacks have the contrary effect. Each person smells their colleagues' blood, thinking how they can use it to take over their jobs.' 'When do you get strong alliances? When news outlets are powerful,' one senior news editor claimed. 'In vulnerable organisations, the survival instincts, ego issues and existential fears prevent us from forging an alliance'.

These feelings of precariousness and instability in the news industry are not unrelated to the populist anti-media movement. As documented at length by Netanyahu's biographers, one of his primary goals as prime minister has been to weaken the major news outlets he perceived as hostile, both public and commercial. He therefore led a regulatory process of splitting the most popular TV channel in two, as well as shutting down and redesigning the public broadcasting corporation. Similar processes took place in Hungary, Poland and even the US during the first, and now second, Trump administration. Perceiving power as a prerequisite for solidarity, however, is problematic. If news outlets must be powerful to express solidarity and unite, then solidarity is least available when it is needed most – precisely when external threats endanger fragile institutions. Once again, the public bears the cost.

Some journalists see the deteriorating working conditions as bolstering the de-professionalisation of newsrooms across the country. They had some harsh criticism for their colleagues, which seemed to allow them to distance themselves from the populist criticism, placing themselves on the side of 'the people' rather than 'the media', but also made it harder to imagine any form of collective action against media capture. 'Ethically, shit happens all the time,' said a young and thoughtful online news editor. 'Since your bosses cannot raise your salary or give you a bonus, they reward you through trips funded by companies that want you to write about them. I came back from one of these trips just now. When I used to write for lifestyle sections, I tried not to take gifts sent to us by PR people. But today, it's difficult to refuse. You see your friends in high-tech companies earning twice as much as you, working half the hours. It also makes it hard for people who care about journalism. I mean, when the prime minister targets journalists every other day, your first instinct is to defend journalism, but it is difficult to do with journalism looking the way it does.'

The practices described by this editor are prevalent in lifestyle sections – less so in beats like politics. However, she points at a broader phenomenon, which other journalists expressed too: how to defend a news industry you yourself find flawed? The correlation between diminishing working conditions and deteriorating ethical standards makes it harder to defend journalism, even for its greatest fans. Regardless of how different journalists' media criticism was to that expressed by hostile populists, it still made them more hesitant to support fellow reporters. 'I will not defend a journalist who thinks he can publish whatever he wants at the expense of my own professional reputation, in which I invested much time and energy,' one investigative reporter told me angrily. 'I don't ask journalists or the public to defend me when I'm bullshitting. Making a symbol out of a sloppy journalist only harms journalism and equips Netanyahu with very powerful tools to go after us.' He has a point. Any little mistake committed by the media is now a cause for a full-on carnival celebrated by the populist movement and its loyalist anti-media media. The stakes are high.

Is Competition ... a Good Thing?

But there was something else. The most visceral response I received from journalists I interviewed over the years did not refer to the political or economic changes, but rather to competition as a value in and of itself. When asked about the possibility of responding to political attacks by collaborating with others, many interviewees were either uncomfortable, doubtful or fully against it. They associated their sentiment with the profession itself, claiming that it was inherently antithetical to any type of collective action. 'It is a profession that has always been extraordinarily individualistic,' explained a leading political correspondent.

In the past, however, competition was considered a practical obstacle with which journalists are forced to cope.[243] The fact that news outlets compete over scoops, exclusives and deadlines was considered an obstacle to 'good journalism', something that led reporters to compromise their professional practices in exchange for publishing first. In the last decade, this dynamic has been chiefly associated with the rising competition with digital and social media, which were portrayed as pushing journalists to prioritise speed, immediacy and clickbait over accuracy, fact-checking and deep investigations.[244] But based on years of research, I found that competition has become part and parcel of the journalistic ethos. It has been idealised, romanticised and embraced – glorified in movies and celebrated in newsrooms – making collective action against populists a non-starter. My interviewees see competition as part of their professional identity and ethos, not a necessary evil but a signal of journalistic excellence. It was therefore not a source of regret but of content.

In the spirit of the American tradition, competition became an integral part of journalists' understanding of what makes 'good journalism'. In this respect, there was little to no difference between those working for commercial and public media. This similarity indicates that the superiority of competition does not originate from a particular ownership model but from a shared journalistic culture. Since the 1970s, American ideas about media and politics have penetrated and shaped the Israeli news industry, forming a new journalistic ethos for the previously partisan state-owned media.[245] This liberal tradition favours private ownership over state or public ownership, presuming that competition between various actors will create the best news product. The basic assumption was that competition is essentially good. It was seen as the way to produce independent quality journalism that serves the public good and safeguards journalism from becoming subjugated to state propaganda. This is not a surprising outcome for the liberal democratic tradition of modern journalism, which was shaped by the trauma of journalism serving fascist and Nazi regimes earlier in the 20th century. The problem is, we are currently sliding into a different type of trauma. The new censorship requires different coping mechanisms from the old one.

Media Workers of the World – Unite?

Will unions save us? Not if you ask my interviewees. Israel has famously transformed from a fledgling socialist enterprise to a neoliberal state, which cut most public funding, encouraged privatisation of public services and broke labour unions, in large part due to the 'free market' policy reforms steered by Benjamin Netanyahu in his role as finance minister from 2003–2005.[246] The news industry shifted from collective agreements to individual contracts over the years, increasing inequality among journalists.[247] This shift, however, was not only technical, it also involved a cultural shift towards a libertarian approach that trusts in competition to deliver optimal journalistic outcomes.[248] One online political correspondent told me that she had 'a very serious beef' with the idea of journalists' associations intervening in the confrontation between populists and the media: 'I find the entire idea of unions and associations defunct,' she said. 'They create jobs for a few unemployed journalists, but they are irrelevant in a time of individual contracts. Because, you know, I would not sacrifice anything for the sake of the junior editor on the news desk. So, to me, these are really quite archaic organisations.'

This might sound like a harsh analysis, but another TV news editor, himself a member of the Israeli Press Council, agreed: 'What can we do about it?' he asked me, surprised at my implied expectation that journalists' associations play a role when the profession is under political attack. 'Nothing, really,' he answered. 'Should we publish a statement? If people stop trusting the news, what can the Press Council do about it? It's a problem, it really is. We're very limited.' So, paradoxically, adhering to unbounded competition was my interviewees' way of expressing belonging to their journalistic community. American journalism scholar Barbie Zelizer proposed that we think about journalists not only as professionals but as members of an interpretive community, suggesting that journalists' stories about themselves and their profession are their way of uniting as a community. Interestingly, what united the reporters I talked to was, to a large extent, the same vicious competitiveness that prevented them from working together. Their collective identity as journalists was based on their hostility towards collective action. The lack of solidarity was a substantial part of what united them as a community. Yet it prevented them from capitalising on their membership of this community through joint efforts to defend their well-being and social status together. Competition united them, yet pulled them apart.

Don't get me wrong, the problem is not that journalists never collaborate. As the opening to this chapter makes clear, journalists around the world are, at some points in time and in certain instances, capable of collaborating to confront the new censorship. This was more likely to happen when someone was targeted personally rather than the general attacks on 'the media', or when legal action was taken to harm news organisations rather than when the public campaign to undermine journalism was exploding. There were cases over the years when journalists were viciously attacked personally and certain colleagues felt bad enough to comfort them personally or text their support, but not as eager to express solidarity in public and certainly not to collaborate around this storm of hate. Some journalists tweeted their support to Ilana Dayan, whose story was laid out in the introduction to this book. Others came to protest when the public broadcasting corporation was threatened to be shut down by the government.

I also found that it was easier for journalists who were not direct competitors to express solidarity: journalists from the same news outlet, for instance, but also journalists from different mediums (e.g. print journalists and TV broadcasters), or different beats (e.g. legal correspondents and political pundits). The more direct the competition was, the more difficult it was for my interviewees to express their support. This may sound petty and discouraging but it also opens new paths for future collaborations. If networks of solidarity are easier to establish between non-direct competitors, this could be one first short-term goal.

Too often, though, journalists chose to turn a blind eye to the war on the media. This is a form of self-disarmament: why not use your means, skills and powers when fighting to protect the public's right to know, journalism's independence and, essentially, our beaten and challenged democracies?

Deride and conquer plays a big role in populist politics, not just when spreading hate and pitting groups in society against each other. It also neutralises solidarity among the targets of the smear – in this case, journalists – by portraying them as an elitist, conspiring, 'deep state' cartel. It was true in the Philippines after years of Rodrigo Duterte's populist leadership.[249] The urge to prove that, in my interviewees' words, 'we're no elders of Zion' compels journalists under attack to put down one of their most powerful weapons in the fight over truth: solidarity.

Welcome to the Upside Down: The World of Anti-Media Media

'You're not the BBC, you actually get your facts right!'
Former UK PM Liz Truss on GB News.

WILL WE KNOW who won the next elections?

Sounds like a ridiculous question. In many countries, readers might be lucky enough to shrug. Yes, there are bad faith actors, propaganda machines, ruthless bot farms and disinformation campaigns, but enough voters have regular access to good enough information, right? It should be fine. It always has been.

And yet, if one looks closely at the very recent histories of the United States, India, Brazil, Israel or Hungary, the question no longer seems so hyperbolic. In a July, 2023 survey, almost 40 per cent of the US public (and almost 70 per cent of Republicans) reported they reject the legitimacy of the 2020 elections. If you were to ask American voters only a couple of years earlier, 'Will we agree on who won the next election?', they, too, would probably shrug. However, today – after five people died, 174 police officers were injured, the entire congress was rushed into saferooms and 1,200 rioters were charged for their role in invading the US capitol on 6th January – they may no longer take this question so lightly.

This shift did not happen overnight. The enormous and complex sphere of denialism and conspiracies took years, money and sweat to establish. And elections are merely one – highly consequential – example. What will we know when the next pandemic hits? Will we get credible information on protecting ourselves or will we all be bathing in bleach? Will we know who perpetrates the next round of violence in the streets or will we be fed bigotry and lies? All these questions tend to one which encompasses all: what might our future look like if our right to know is lost?

The new censorship operates as a dual mechanism: undermining journalism on the one hand while establishing what looks like news (but operates as propaganda) on the other. Prominent political and legal scholar Kim Lane Scheppele, who saw up close democracy declining in Hungary, analyses in her work the three different ways in which 'legal authoritarians' – that is, politicians who gain power legally but then manipulate democratic tools to establish an autocratic regime – take over the media. The first, is the use of regulation to punish news outlets which refuse to align with the populist leader, and the second is the constant assault against critical and independent journalists and newsrooms. The third is starting what appears to be ordinary, profit-driven newspapers and TV channels, but in fact they operate to misinform and spread propaganda to support the populist leader or government. If we wish to agree on election results in the future – or anything else, for that matter – we must dive into the muddy water of anti-media media.

What is Anti-Media Media?

For decades, we have been told that news is necessary for democracy to work. Philosophers, policymakers, journalists and other advocates emphasised how the mass media allows citizens to vote based on somewhat relevant and hopefully credible information.[250] The idea was that journalism is good for democracy, primarily because it informs people of public affairs and holds the powerful accountable. Nevertheless, a growing body of research demonstrates that, while journalism is essential, the media can misinform as much as it informs, mislead as much as it scrutinises, and conceal more than it reveals. In fact, things have got so terribly out of hand that consuming news today might lead to people knowing *less* than those who weren't exposed to it at all.[251] Fox News viewers were found again and again to be less informed than any other group of Americans.[252] They knew less about current affairs, even when compared to people who reported not consuming any news at all. This was true for a wide range of topics: from the Iraq war to climate change, from economic issues to election results, from death penalty policies to Covid restrictions. And while Fox News is the most studied case to date, it has by now been outdone by far worse 'anti-media media'. How can we effectively stop such dark rabbit holes from grinding down our right to know?

As a former journalist, I can say with absolute certainty: journalists get things wrong, by mistake, negligence and various other flaws. However, anti-media media is different. In its intentions, loyalties, professional ethos and journalistic norms. Anti-media media is a political operation which uses the apparatus of news – the round table with suit-wearing panellists, the breaking news terminology and the familiar graphic design – to do something quite different. If journalism is ideally about informing the public, scrutinising the powerful and providing a space for public debate, anti-media media is about obfuscating and concealing information, providing disinformation and propaganda, and spreading hate speech and incitement. It's not always easy to make that distinction, but it is necessary to get better at it to defeat the new censorship.

The reason I do not call it 'non-media', or 'pseudo-media', but rather 'anti-media' is that this operation does not only follow a very different mission from journalism but also fights journalism heads-on. One of the core missions of anti-media media – from GB News in the UK to Fox News in the US, from Channel 14 in Israel to OpIndia in India – is to discredit journalism and demonise journalists as individuals. So, it is not only non-journalistic but rather anti-journalistic, spearheading the war against critical journalists and valuable news. How do they do it? By targeting individual reporters who criticise the populist right, suing for defamation, pushing for anti-democratic regulation and supporting the populist leadership unabashedly. Anti-media media provides a platform for hateful populists using the style of news as a shield, protecting and entrenching authoritarians in power and those in the making.

In the UK, certain tabloids have specialised in what came to be known as 'beeb-bashing'. Between 2008 and 2018, the

Daily Mail published no fewer than 4,000 news stories bashing the BBC, including 500 front-page stories and 2,500 opinion columns.[253] OpIndia, the most-visited right-wing news website in India, which supports Modi's ruling Hindu-nationalist party BJP, consistently undermined the Indian media for allegedly 'suppressing the voices and opinions of the Hindu majority, while favouring minorities and working against India's interests by tarnishing the country's global image'.[254] The website published more than 1,000 stories attacking and delegitimising the mainstream media over the years, where journalists were labelled 'Islamist propagandists' and accused of viciously spreading 'fake news', censoring right-wing views and 'hoping [their reporting] hurts PM Modi's image, even if it hurts India's image in the process.'[255] In Greece, Eugenia Siapera and Lambrini Papadopoulou describe the rise of 'hate journalism': journalism that emerged during the debt crisis years and is ideologically aligned with neo-fascist and ethnonationalist groups.[256] They give *Makeleio* – a Greek daily newspaper and news website – as the most successful example of Greek hate journalism. '*Makeleio's* hate journalism is mirroring, reproducing and reinforcing the nationalist, xenophobic, misogynist, homophobic and anti-Semitic values of conservative Greece,' they write. It is a popular news outlet – quite a rarity nowadays – thanks to what Siapera and Papadopoulou call 'the affective economy of hate'. But we should not fail to recognise that much of the anti-media media today is not truly a commercial enterprise. News outlets like GB News are losing millions of pounds per year, and yet their owners gain something out of it: access, influence, power.

Back in Israel, Channel 14 not only serves as Netanyahu's mouthpiece but also smears journalists daily. The channel's lead presenter Yinon Magal even announced on his radio programme that, 'If I were Netanyahu, I would have pulled out a submachine gun and shot a long time ago ... like Rocky, like Rambo, with the ammo belt going down. If I were Netanyahu, I would shoot all the journalists who criticise me with a semi-automatic gun.' After his outrageous statement drew some criticism, Magal claimed – conveniently – this was a joke. He never explained what was supposed to make it funny – the 'it's a joke' line has become an easy, effortless excuse popular among populist right-wing propagandists.

Yinon Magal is the perfect embodiment of anti-media media. Formerly a professional journalist at the public broadcaster over the years, Magal turned into a parliament member for The Jewish Home, a hard-right party associated with the Jewish settler's movement, until he was forced out due to allegations of sexual harassment. Magal turned into a die-hard Netanyahu loyalist, who spends half his time praising the Israeli prime minister on TV and the other half bashing 'the media'. Instead of breaking stories, corroborating facts, building contacts, exposing injustices or scrutinising power, he spreads conspiracy theories about 'enemies from within' and encourages his followers to harass and intimidate 'lefty traitors'. In his reading, anyone who criticises Netanyahu falls under this category.

Unfortunately, the anti-media media is not just about talk – it also tends to walk the walk. The anti-media media plays a significant and often disregarded part in all different types of warfare against the media. Channel 14 sued Israeli reporters who dared uncover its apparent biases (only to be rejected by the courts), and campaigned for the Israeli government to stop publishing ads on liberal media outlets. In Hong Kong, *Ta Kung Pao* and *Wen Wei Po* newspapers accused *Stand News* – a news website critical of the police during the 2019 protests – of inciting violence and terrorism, demanding police intervention and a criminal investigation into their reporting. By the end of 2021, *Stand News* offices were searched by the police, its top executives were arrested on suspicion of breaching the sedition law, and finally, the newsroom announced its closure.[257] In the United States, OANN (One America News Network), the 'Foxier' version of Fox News, filed a 10-million-dollar SLAPP lawsuit against the liberal TV cable network MSNBC, arguing that the network's talent, Rachel Maddow, defamed them. It ended with OANN paying MSNBC 250,000 dollars in legal fees, but it doesn't mean no damage was done: the time, energy, resources, legal teams – all went to waste. Instead of working on her journalism, Maddow had to defend her reputation and public standing against a bad faith, conspiratorial propaganda operation. While pretending to produce news, anti-media media is essentially an instrumental part of the populist war against news.

It's Not (Just) About Partisanship

To be clear, the problem is not partisan media. While GB News, Fox News and Channel 14 are harmful, 'partisan' media is not in itself a problem for public knowledge and our social lives. Discussing current affairs with like-minded people could be, in fact, wonderful for democracy and political engagement. The problem is not partisanship. The problem with anti-media media is that it does not deliver us reliable information and useful knowledge, and certainly does not scrutinise those in power or even enforce some social cohesion, but rather quite the opposite: to promote misinformation, propaganda and hate. This is significant. According to research by economist Leonardo Bursztyn and his colleagues, watching Tucker Carlson's TV show on Fox News had 'significantly affected behaviour and downstream health outcomes'.[258] What this scientific wording means in practice is that people who consumed Carlson's wild anti-vaccines campaign on their telly were more likely to hold false beliefs, avoid any prevention measures and eventually die from Covid-19. Yes, the stakes are *that* high: for Tucker's viewers, but also their neighbours, clients and friends. Misinformation, literally, kills. Yet the measures taken to counter it seem, to put it mildly, insufficient.

'Partisan media' has become a global buzzword in recent years, although its definition remains vague. Partisan media has been accused of becoming a central driver of disinformation, polarisation, hate and racism.[259] Unfortunately, it is not defined in a way that helps us make sense of it.[260] 'Partisan media' is an incredibly vague, all-embracing and therefore misleading term, used to amass together quite disparate entities with distinct missions, ethos, norms and societal implications.

The New York Times, *Wall Street Journal*, *Washington Post*, Fox News, Breitbart and Rush Limbaugh's TV show have all been studied by respected researchers in the US as 'partisan media'.[261] In fact, *The New York Times* and Fox

News outlets 'are regularly held up as exemplars of a partisan media establishment',[262] according to some. Quite odd, isn't it? Any news consumer who ran into *The New York Times* and Fox News – regardless of their ideological inclination or professional training – would probably be able to tell how distinct the two were. But there is a lot to be lost by binding them together.

While these news outlets might all somehow divert from the traditional model of objective and balanced journalism, they do so in an extremely different manner, which is crucial to acknowledge to reach useful conclusions about knowledge, disinformation and democracy. *The New York Times*, for instance, might be biased in favour of certain liberal values; Rush Limbaugh's talk radio show or GB News are still a substantially different type of media, indifferent to professional norms, willingly spreading debunked falsehoods.[263] Treating these media organisations as mirroring each other is disingenuous and risks undermining the efforts to defend our right to know. I would even argue it is the outcome of academics under populist attack turning to strategic bias themselves, trying to force balance on asymmetrical realities, just like journalists tend to do.

Let's look at the most common example of this blind spot: the frequent comparison between Fox News as a right-wing TV channel and MSNBC as a left-wing one. Comparing Fox and MSNBC is like comparing rotten apples to oranges – the outcomes are bound to be distorted, blurring the substantial disparities between the two, as if those were equivalent sources of information whose distinctive feature is their political slant.[264]

For instance, studies found that the effects of Fox News and MSNBC on American voters are different. 'Watching Fox News for additional 2.5 minutes per week increases the vote share of the Republican presidential candidate,' while 'the corresponding effect of watching MSNBC is an imprecise zero,' write Martin and Yurukoglu.[265] Surveys indicated 'significant pro-Republican effects on change in attitudes toward candidates from exposure to Fox News, but no effects from exposure to MSNBC'.[266] Meirick found that 'regular radio and news use was associated with greater likelihood of misperception among Republicans, but not non-Republicans'.[267] Morris and Morris discovered that 'exposure to Republican partisan media did have a significant negative effect on feelings toward Hillary Clinton,' whereas 'consumption of Democratic partisan television, however, had no influence on feelings toward Donald Trump'.[268]

You can see researchers reaching what seems to be a series of mysterious findings, which may well be the result of comparing very different animals. While Fox News promotes a Republican agenda and MSNBC hosts support Democrats, the nature of the content with which they feed their partisan audience – and particularly their approach to facts, lies and conspiracy theories – is substantially different. Do news outlets with declared conservative, liberal, communist or any other ideological affiliation operate similarly to those that hide their unabashed support for Trump, Netanyahu or Modi? Are party-owned media comparable to those that openly promote certain ideas? Should they be regulated similarly? And how could we distinguish better conspiratorial propaganda tools from partisan yet fact-based journalism?

Political alignment is not necessarily contradictory to trustworthy, professional and excellent news – just look at the *Guardian, Haaretz, Le Monde*.[269] They do, however, affect the media sphere: in the last election in the US, partly as a result of rising cable news channels like Fox and MSNBC, Democrats and Republicans were not consuming the same news. If the liberal-leaning media in the US still embraces journalistic norms like objectivity and balance but the right-wing media is operating as party propaganda, the broader information landscape is distorted. The general trend continues to push us further away from the truth, further away from accountability and further away from our right to know.

Press Freedom Against Press Freedom

Professor Cherian George, a kind, bearded, middle-aged Singaporean journalist-turned-academic, knows a thing or two about censorship. George's book was banned in 2021 by the government in his home country, Singapore.[270] Ironically, the book was titled *Red Lines: Political Cartoons and the Struggle against Censorship*. The former journalist, who was willing to challenge an authoritarian regime at the cost of his own professional standing, has seen press and academic freedoms eroded first-hand. Today, he teaches media and politics at Hong Kong Baptist University. When he moved there, Hong Kong seemed to be a haven of free speech compared to Singapore. Following the 2019–2020 protests, however, and China's fight to take over, things escalated quickly.

As someone who was publicly bashed by Israel's far-right minister of education as early as 2016 and slandered again by Netanyahu loyalists in 2024, I cannot but sympathise with Cherian's years-long mission. I know how hard it is to be cast as a danger to your country, having your work tarnished and your loyalty to your society questioned. But Cherian keeps speaking up, and we should all be grateful for that – press freedom and academic freedom are bound together. Both are prey to the populist effort to strangle our right to knowledge and truth.

'Some media,' George writes, 'do not subscribe to the Golden Rule of press freedom, that journalists should treat other journalists as they would want to be treated themselves.' He is not writing about Fox News or GB News but rather about the illiberal Hong Kong newspapers *Ta Kung Pao* and *Wen Wei Po*. 'They do not merely provide *post hoc* support for government repression of media,' he points out, 'they also call out potential targets and encourage the authorities to attack.' I would take George's argument one step further. Anti-media media – what he calls 'press vs press freedom' – cannot and should not be considered as press at all.

In the 2024 Hollywood film *Civil War*, which tells the story of a dystopian future in the US, there is a touching moment where Lee Smith, a heroic war photojournalist played by Kirsten Dunst, gives her PRESS vest to a young, shy and inexperienced photographer. It is an emotional moment because – spoiler alert! – Dunst's character is eventually killed by a bullet the PRESS vest could have stopped. She has given her armour down to protect a clueless, rooky journalist who looks up to her. But if we think about it, why are PRESS vests supposed to protect anyone against anything?

Are journalists' lives more valuable than any other civilian's? What's so special about journalism?

The idea of press freedom only makes sense if we understand journalism as a public good[271] – something so valuable that, as a society, we are willing to grant it a unique status and special protections. Only if we accept that journalism is essential for our shared present and future does it makes sense to grant the media special treatment and sacred rights, which are unavailable to us as ordinary citizens. And if journalism is indeed public good, we cannot keep neglecting our media to populist manipulation. Press freedom is there to protect our right to know. Those who fight against our right to know – be they Fox News, Channel 14 or *Wen Wei Po* – should not enjoy the benefits and protections granted by press freedom.

Press freedom was not invented to guarantee that billionaire-owned TV networks can freely spread half-truths, bigotry and unhinged conspiracy theories. It was not established to allow tabloids to threaten critical voices or make the public more ignorant and hateful than before. Media which does not bother to do the hard work of journalism – seeking sources, verifying facts, corroborating details, challenging the powerful – should not be rewarded with the protections granted to the press.

This is the message we should all be yelling from the rooftops. Serious journalists should not approach anti-media propagandists as their peers or colleagues. Suing Fox News for defamation, or any other anti-media operation for that matter, is therefore not a breach or threat to press freedom – quite the opposite. It will be a long, messy and complicated struggle, but we must distinguish those who improve our information universe from those who crush it. This is not about censorship or thought police, it is about putting the public interest in the centre rather than that of wealthy media moguls and self-centred politicians.

Building a shiny TV studio is not enough to become a journalist. Wearing a suit does not make you Bob Woodward. Establishing the pretence of news, mimicking the apparatus of news and using the terminology of news journalism is not enough to deliver valuable reporting. Earning the protections that we, as a society, choose to grant journalists so that they serve as checks and balances on our political establishment requires work. Press freedom is not a blank cheque. Imagine a future where, by 2030, most Israelis rely on Channel 14 for news, most Britons turn to GB News and most Americans get their current affairs from Newsmax. This is the dystopian scenario we must keep in mind when debating the future of the public's right to know.

Anti-Media Media Evolves

You might be thinking, *well, that is a bit of a stretch*. After all, GB News is still lagging far behind the BBC, News 12 is much stronger in Israel than Channel 14, and OpIndia is far from being the leading news source in India. *Ta Kung Pao* has an estimated 40,000 copies circulating, and *Wen Wei Po* attracts less than 1 per cent of the readership in Hong Kong.[272] But the first lesson from the very recent history of anti-media media is that even if it seems like a marginal sight gag in your community at the moment, there is no guarantee that it will remain that way.

WELCOME TO THE UPSIDE DOWN: THE WORLD OF ANTI-MEDIA MEDIA

Let me tell you the twisted yet telling tale of Channel 14.

From an insignificant and even laughable 'Jewish Heritage Channel', with around 0 per cent ratings on average, Channel 14 has become – within a few years – Benjamin Netanyahu's top propaganda arm and one of Israel's most popular news providers nationally. Owned by Yitzchak Mirilashvili, the son of a Georgian billionaire and Likud supporter Michael Mirilashvili, the channel was founded one decade ago as Channel 20. But it did not take off until the right opportunity came up. It was 2023. Hundreds of thousands of protesters were marching in the streets all across Israel to stop the government's planned takeover of the courts. Political polarisation was souring, and clashes between protesters, counter-protesters and the police made headlines day in and day out. During these times of public turmoil, PM Netanyahu was boycotting all Israeli journalists, but chose to give several pampering interviews to Channel 20 (which later became Channel 14).

Before the dust of the 2023 protests settled, Channel 14's ratings exceeded that of the Israeli Public Broadcaster and other popular national media for the first time in its short history. From close to zero exposure, its evening newscast reached an average of 3.6 per cent of the viewing public in January, 4.6 per cent in February and, shockingly, an estimated 7 per cent in March, becoming the second most-viewed news show in the country. This process was accompanied – in line with the populist playbook – by consistent attacks on the ratings measurement in Israel. It was Channel 14's version of Trump's consistent rants about those measuring his rallies' crowd size. A media watchdog group found that Channel 14 broadcast 70 false and misleading claims between August 2022 and April 2023. The channel's commentators develop numerous exciting and utterly unfounded conspiracy theories, including claims that the CIA funded the protests against Netanyahu's government and that the demonstrators were somehow the far descendants of Jews who refused to fight against the Nazis during World War II.

The 2023–2024 war in Gaza was the next milestone for anti-media media in Israel. Like the wave of nationalism following George Bush's war on terror boosted Fox News ratings and became known as 'the Fox News war'[273] the Israel–Gaza war became a boon for Channel 14. When I was interviewing journalists under attack back in 2018, they often took a swipe at Channel 14 (then Channel 20). 'They whine about "the lefty media", but when they get a right-wing media channel, nobody watches!' targeted reporters cheered gleefully. They are no longer laughing.

As I have been trying to warn,[274] it takes time to build an effective anti-media media. But once the right formula, regulation loopholes and deep pockets are found, it becomes very difficult to neutralise. It took years to turn Fox News into the kingmaker of US politics. The prosperous US media empire – in its Rupert Murdoch and belated Roger Ailes version – was preceded by no less than four failed attempts to ultimately establish a conservative news channel that would serve the American right. The pre-Fox attempts to found a conservative TV channel – from National Empowerment Television (NET) to GOP-TV – were proven to be a total failure.[275] But in the end, it worked: Fox News found its way to the hearts of millions of Americans. Today, it is hard to turn back time on the MAGA machine.

The current success of Channel 14 is not, by any means, accidental – nor was it inevitable. Netanyahu's far-right government provided the channel with outrageously generous regulations and regulators over the years. Channel 14 was part and parcel of Netanyahu's efforts to silence the Israeli media, and it was rewarded for it. The Israeli version of Fox News was released from regulatory obligations that bind other TV broadcasters, reaping the channel benefits worth tens of millions of shekels per year. The prime minister and his family ply the channel with exclusive 'interviews', too. For over a year after 7th October, a national trauma of unprecedented scale, PM Netanyahu refused to grant any interviews to Israeli journalists, despite the many questions the Israeli public deserved to ask about the war, the policies that led to it or its conduct. The only 'interviews' that took place were for Channel 14.

A cold analysis of the American and Israeli experiences teaches us that GB News and its global versions can indeed become a central force in British politics in the foreseeable future, especially if Ofcom, the relevant media regulator, refuses to act. The good news? We are not there yet. There is nothing inevitable about the rise of anti-media media. It depends on how we – journalists, activists and particularly policymakers – approach this fight.

The groundbreaking Dominion vs Fox News case from 2021 demonstrated that a public price can and should be exacted for spreading lies and promoting conspiracy theories. When Tucker Carlson and Sean Hannity told Americans that the mechanisms of Dominion Voting Systems had been created by communists in Venezuela to falsify the results of the 2020 election, the company decided to break its silence. Through a lawsuit claiming damages worth $1.6 billion, Dominion forced the reckless channel to supply evidence for the groundless allegations it had broadcast. Fox was compelled to apologise and remove the defamatory content from its website. More importantly, the reporting around the lawsuit exposed Fox viewers to the fact they were deliberately, intentionally and consistently lied to.

The only problem was that Dominion had a commercial incentive to get to an agreement with Fox News outside the court – settle for a big chunk of dollars, enjoy the publicity and keep going. Smartmatic, another company smeared as part of the same deranged conspiracy theory, also settled its defamation lawsuit against Newsmax, a far-right cable news channel, around their denial of the 2020 elections. It was great that they managed to squeeze enough money out of these propaganda machines to make it hurt, and even now, years later, one can hear how cautious Fox presenters become when the name Dominion comes up. However, if they genuinely cared about the public, Fox viewers or the American democracy, none of these companies would settle. These anti-media media organisations, which benefit from spreading hate and false accusations, should stand trial. The ones who were wronged are not just Dominion workers or Smartmatic employees, it was us, all of us, whose information environment was polluted by the Big Lie. We need to build, in each country according to the local political and legal settings, the appropriate entity that could sue and sanction on our behalf, based on the violation of our right to know. Big corporations are not the only ones to have their rights protected in courts. The right to know should be litigated against intentional, consistent and outrageous deception and manipulation of the kind we witness all around us today.

As a society, we will have to start exacting a price for harm caused to our right to know. In some cases this requires new legislation and policies; in others it simply means enforcing existing laws and norms. How to fight the anti-media media will be explained in more detail in the last chapter of this book. For now, I will only note that it is crucial that targets of anti-media media, who have the resources, stamina and time for it, sue when smeared with baseless lies and conspiracy theories. This might help them protect their reputation and good name, but more importantly, present liars and propagandists with a price for their actions which victims with less money and contacts might not get the chance to extract.

The Secret Benefits of Anti-Media Media

If like me, you are based in the UK, you might be thinking, *Well, even if anti-media media booms in the future, we could fight it once it becomes popular.* As of May 2024, GB News reaches an average of 2.7 million monthly viewers – only 0.45 per cent of TV views in the UK. The thing is, even if anti-media media has not come to dominate the information environment in your country it can still cause significant damage. And you don't even need to watch to be affected.

The first thing many of us missed back when the Israeli version of Fox News was still in its infancy is that anti-media media serves its masters even when the ratings are zero. For instance, it provides the politicians it promotes with a convenient platform to disseminate messages in the guise of 'interviews'. When the Israeli prime minister or his wife choose to give exclusive interviews to one of their propaganda channels, mainstream outlets yield to the temptation to broadcast excerpts from those same 'interviews' in prime time. But these are not interviews: calling them that is irresponsible. Using clips from them on proper news outlets is chopping off the branch over which journalism lies. Effectively, not only are these not interviews, they are, in fact, anti-interviews. They are meant to prevent rather than deliver journalistic interviews that will hold those in power accountable.

The second point journalists in Israel failed to recognise in real-time was that the anti-media universe allows the populist right to hold an army of loyalists and cronies on the payroll – for years. Like American journalist and politician Upton Sinclair said back in 1935: 'It is difficult to get a man to understand something when his salary depends on his not understanding it.' In most countries, it would be impossible for media moguls to directly pay politicians, but here in the UK, as we know well, serving the public is not considered a full-time job, and politicians can work anywhere alongside this role – including in the media industry. The boldest recent example made headlines in August 2024, as Nigel Farage was revealed to be the UK's highest-earning MP – with almost £1.2m a year from GB News (in addition to the £4,000 per month he receives from the

Daily Telegraph and other substantial sums coming from other sources).[276] Days later it was also reported that former UK PM and an eccentric populist in his own right, Boris Johnson, has not yet hosted a single TV programme for GB News – ten months after being signed up as a presenter. Michael Gove is another fresh hire of the channel, and it goes on media channels of all political persuasions. In other words, if Ofcom – the UK regulator in charge of protecting the British public sphere – will not act fast, the populist war on our right to know might be determined.

Third, as I have recounted in previous pages, studies have already demonstrated how Fox News, on its own, shifted the entire national media agenda in the United States.[277] Anti-media media, despite its blatant lies and consistent conspiracy theories, has the power to not only shape public opinion but also the journalistic agenda. It happened when the Fox News Decision Desk, literally led by George W. Bush's cousin, pushed other news outlets to declare victory for Bush in 2000 long before it was clear by the vote counts. It happened when Fox's overexposure to the Tea Party movement, with Fox talents setting their studios in the movement's rallies, was followed by journalists dedicating immense attention to the orchestrated protests too. Something similar occurred in Hong Kong. While the popularity of *Ta Kung Pao* and *Wen Wei Po* newspapers remains limited, 'what makes them important is who reads them and why ... Media gatekeepers and other opinion leaders, and even Hong Kong and central government officials follow them for on-the-ground readings of developments in Hong Kong through Beijing-loyalist eyes.'[278] The anti-media media, perceived as the unaccountable mouthpiece of authoritarian leaders and parties, gained a unique status among a particularly powerful milieu.

On top of shaping the entire information environment, anti-media media conveniently provides the populist right with 'plausible deniability'. In their last debate before the heated 2024 US elections, for instance, Donald Trump and Kamala Harris were doing their best to convince the American voters that they were the ones most qualified to lead the free world. In what became an immediate hit and generated endless memes and hilarious mash-ups since, Trump went on one of his strange, racist, rants in which he touted the debunked conspiracy theory that Haitian immigrants in Springfield, Ohio were 'eating the dogs, the people that came in, they're eating the cats. They're eating the pets of the people that live there, and this is what's happening in our country, and it's a shame.' As this was a blatant, debunked and hateful fabrication, in a televised debate where the moderators were unusually fearless in fact-checking Trump's lies, ABC's David Muir quickly explained to viewers that Trump's bizarre allegations were science fiction. 'ABC News did reach out to the city manager there,' Muir said. 'He told us there had been no credible reports of specific claims of pets being harmed, injured or abused by individuals within the immigrant community.'

What was Trump's reaction? 'Well, I've seen people *on television!*' Trump insisted. 'The people on television say, "my dog was taken and used for food".' Muir wasn't impressed. 'I'm not taking this from television,' he responded sharply, 'I'm taking this from the city manager.' 'People are on television saying, "the dog was eaten by the people that went there",'

Trump replied. This is what anti-media media is for: giving excuses for people to believe baseless conspiracy theories, citing what they saw 'on TV'. It's a more sophisticated version of another of Trump's favourite sentences: 'many people are saying'. It grants fake legitimacy to fake accusations. And it's working.

This specific type of partisan media, which thrives on misinformation, propaganda and hate, has a much broader impact than its direct audiences – especially when world leaders and tech giants are touting it. By driving and pushing the editorial agenda of the entire media, anti-media media reaches audiences everywhere. It serves the populist right by normalising, amplifying, setting the agenda, providing plausible deniability, establishing false equivalences and maintaining a crowd of loyal sycophants on the payroll. Anti-media media doesn't need to become popular to be influential.

The Fight to Know

Are we the people we've been waiting for?

BACK IN 2017, I had the questionable honour of being labelled by Israel's then-Minister of Education, Naftali Bennett, as 'auto-anti-Semite' due to a report he didn't like, published by the Center for the Renewal of Israeli Democracy (Molad), a progressive think tank for which I was working at the time. As the granddaughter of four Holocaust survivors, all of whom were the soul remainers of their families, I must say I was taken aback for a second. These were still early days of populism in power, when we were still shaken and offended by labels like 'traitors' and 'Nazis'. It is hard to make me angry, but Bennett succeeded. The cynical use of my very personal ancestors to push forwards messianic Jewish supremacy made me furious. I chose to respond to the minister's wild allegations in an op-ed in *Haaretz*.[279]

'This week, Education Minister Naftali Bennett declared me an anti-Semite, officially inducting me into the ever-growing club of Israelis who, according to right-wing leadership, are self-hating Jews,' I wrote. 'The membership list includes everyone from moderate Likudniks to radical leftists. We have all been branded as traitors with superpowers – somehow both running the country and conspiring to destroy it at the same time' (a famous anti-Semitic trope, by the way). 'Within just a few short years, it seems, anyone who dissents from Bennett's worldview has magically disappeared,' the op-ed continued. 'Those who dare to criticise Netanyahu have simply vanished into thin air. Only the loyalists who echo the party line remain – the rest are all traitors. After all, what other possible reason could there be for citizens to protest a prime minister mired in corruption investigations? Or to oppose a government with skewed priorities? Or to call out ministers who routinely lie to us? Surely, only foreign funding and sinister motives. And foreign agents, naturally, should not be debated or compromised. Traitors must be silenced.' This was the populist textbook 101.

At the time, I was mainly annoyed by the silence of those who thought they could escape the populist hit themselves if they only kept their heads low. 'Through their silence,' I wrote, 'these centre-left leaders are legitimising the idea that in Israel of 2017, it's perfectly acceptable to call political opponents anti-Semites, and that political activists are indeed enemies of the state. This silence is not just a moral failure; it is also a strategic blunder. Many before them believed that if they just distanced themselves from the "radical" left and kept their heads down low enough, the smear campaign would pass them by. To put it mildly, that didn't work. Voters are now left with an "extreme" left, that is silenced, and a "moderate" left, that chooses to stay silent. But those who think their "moderate" branding will protect them fail to grasp what has been happening here in recent years. Dear silent ones, you will always be on the side of the traitors – unless you open your eyes and remember that neither you nor your supporters are betraying anyone, and that it's time you start representing and defending them. If you don't start stating the obvious (that when the right has no answers, it calls everyone traitors), there will soon be no political positions left to squabble over'.

Fast-forward to 2024, when I scrambled again into the hateful machine of the populist right. This time, the trigger was an interview I gave to a sweet and wise podcaster called Ariel Klachkin, where I mentioned the lack of media representation of Palestinian citizens of Israel in the Israeli media. Reminder: Palestinian citizens of Israel, also known as Israeli Arabs, consist of around 20 per cent of the population. Yet, a recent report found their media representation as of 2024 has been lower than ever, borderline non-existent, ranging from 1 to 2.5 per cent.[280] I dared to mention these numbers on the podcast. Then all hell broke loose. Let's say the 'Nazi' comments were the softer ones this time around. The scale of the backlash was unbelievable – I didn't think the podcast had such a broad audience. The riddle was quickly solved, as my activist friends who monitor far-right groups online texted me: 'Congrats! you feature on the Likud WhatsApp groups.' One of the many groups used by Likud members and loyalists had posted a short bit of the interview, labelling me an 'extremist lefty'. It was a moment where I got to feel the online war myself. I made sure to keep the dozens of intimidating messages from my mom (let's hope she doesn't read this chapter, and if she does, sorry Mom!). I was lucky enough to experience all that from my quiet home in London, far away, feeling invincible. Still, the magnitude of the online abuse struck me. It was not that violent or intrusive last time around, only seven years earlier.

You can say many things about me, but brave is not one of them. My very short period working to advance refugee rights in the Israeli Parliament, back in 2014, ended with clinical depression that neutralised me for months and started a decade (and counting) of therapy and anti-depressants. And what I did not know by then, but perhaps my body was trying to warn me, was that it was only about to get worse. This wild bit of TMI is here because I wish to clarify beyond doubt that I do not judge anyone who chooses to have better lives for themselves by leaving the profession that puts them or their families at risk. We all have some resources (family, money, contacts, friends, skills, networks) and lack others. However, for those of us who do remain in the newsroom, for those of us who sit in the fancy studios as the war on the media plays out, those who enjoy holding the mic and making a living from storytelling, to them, I say, this comes at a price. The price is telling the truth. If you only wish to show people what they are willing to see, you would be better off in showbiz. With great power comes great responsibility, and this is true both in front of the mic and behind it.

Revolutionising our Media

Like many generations before us, ours will need to fight to know. Overcoming the populist war on the media is not easy or simple – nor can it be fought alone. For too many years, most of us took news for granted. At this point, securing our right to know in the future requires us to take on the mission of revolutionising our information environment.

In this short guide, I explain what each one of us – regardless of our location, resources or profession – could do to fight the new censorship within our communities and societies. Let's start with journalists caught between hostile populists, wild broligarchs and resentful audiences.

(1) Don't Let the Populist Become Your Editor-in-chief.

Lies and hate – the bread and butter of the populist war against the media – are easy to produce and spread in the current information environment. Debunking them, however, requires many more resources. Fact-checking is important, but also costly and time-consuming. Even if you have miraculously managed to perfect your fact-checking skills and successfully chase the moving target of populist manipulation you still end up discussing whatever it is the populist 'ordered' you to discuss that day. Decades of communication research tell us that often, determining what we discuss – for instance, immigration rather than health care – can be as influential as what we say about either of these. Instead of making considerate and active editorial decisions about what matters and requires public attention today, journalists lag behind an ever-changing and bogus agenda.

This is what the populist machine counts on: by the time reporters figure out how best to refute the daily lie by the populist in chief, the lie has already become 'common knowledge' and ten others were spread online to support it. As long as our gatekeepers keep chasing the last ridiculous made-up dazzling extreme statement, the populist right will keep running, *de facto*, our public sphere. Don't let the populists turn journalistic norms against you. Impartiality, balance and fairness are all means to a goal – the goal itself is truth. We don't need you to balance out verifiable facts, hide inconvenient truths or pretend the world is symmetrical and all truth claims are equal. When someone lies to you repeatedly they are not to be trusted. Even if they become president.

(2) Don't Surrender to Loyalty Tests

In legendary historian Tim Snyder's words: never obey in advance. We have seen news organisations like MSNBC and tech giants like Meta trying to signal to Trump, following his re-election, that they are 'open for business'. The lesson they should have learned from journalists in Israel, India and Brazil is that taking the knee won't save them from the populist rage. Strategic bias doesn't work.

Since the loyalty test is not really about 'the people', but rather about 'the populist', there are two options for journalists ahead: total surrender, deeming your newsroom to endless flattery, pretending to respect intentional lies and increasingly unhinged conspiracy theories; or standing up for your principles, your audiences and truth. Kissing the ring is never enough – the loyalty tests keep coming. Remember how Nigel Farage turned on the *Daily Mail* the second they scrutinised his position on Russia? This is the nature of the populist playbook. Populist politics demands total loyalty; unless you're willing to surrender entirely, it is not worth it.

You have a cruel choice to make: live the rest of your professional lives bound to ever-shifting populist talking points with loose ties to reality, or take the excruciating, long, complicated route of fighting back. Imagining you could somehow wink to the populist crowd yet keep practising serious, reliable, critical journalism is an illusion. By now, many reporters can attest to that.

Decades ago, after four different publishers rejected *Animal Farm*, Orwell wrote that 'the chief danger to freedom of thought and speech at this moment is not the direct interference of the Minister of Information or any official body. If publishers and editors exert themselves to keep certain topics out of print, it is not because they are frightened of prosecution but because they are frightened of public opinion. In this country, intellectual cowardice is the worst enemy a writer or journalist has to face, and that fact does not seem to me to have had the discussion it deserves.' A lot has changed since, particularly in the ways public opinion manifests itself, directly and immediately, to journalists' and publishers' social media accounts. The easy access each of us has to anyone's smartphone, the physical proximity of death threats made online, the distorted way algorithms amplify the most toxic voices of all – all of these made Orwell's point here ever more valid. In Silvio Waisbord's terms: 'mob censorship'.[281] But mob censorship does not work. Caving won't shield journalists against future bashing. It won't prevent further attacks on public knowledge. It won't regain the public's trust. The current war on our right to know is one we must fight with as much zeal and persistence as authoritarian populists use to take it away.

(3) Take Fun Seriously

Don't let fun become the villains' kingdom! Smart and valuable content can be funny, real and moving. Back in 2016, American reporter Salena Zito wrote an op-ed for the *Atlantic*, titled 'Taking Trump Seriously, Not Literally.' 'The press takes him literally, but not seriously; his supporters take him seriously, but not literally,' explained Zito, who used to work for the campaigns of President Bush Senior, President Bush Junior and fringe neocon Rick Santorum. The catchphrase quickly caught fire in the post-2016 elections US news industry, where everyone was baffled and embarrassed by a presidential victory they did not see coming. The number of articles and magazine stories where New York-based journalists were sent to rural Trump-voting communities to bring in the MAGA wisdom was ridiculous. But it was not necessarily the right lesson that was learned.

To this day, I am not sure what people mean by taking Trump 'seriously', apart from trying to make him sound more exceptional, serious or consistent than he actually is. What I do know is that data shows we should all take fun more seriously. Particularly the journalists among us. News avoidance is growing worldwide,[282] with people investing considerable efforts in actively avoiding news. And for good reasons: to be fair, the news is often frustrating, depressing, heartbreaking, even maddening. Entertainment has been an enormous advantage and weapon for populists worldwide – from Trump to Farage, from Modi to Milei. If the only fun characters in politics are right-wing authoritarians, the world as we know it is doomed.

The algorithmic mechanisms behind the current attention economy turned fun into a powerful magic trick.[283] Fun means attention, and attention is everything. In a world of abundant content and endless rabbit holes, getting people to listen and watch is precious. Attention is money, eyeballs, engagement, support. To establish an alternate factual universe, one needs tonnes of attention. Unfortunately, fun doesn't necessarily correlate with the skills required to become a leading politician or reporter. Well, they'll have to learn. Our journalists and leaders (even the boring ones! I'm looking at you, Sir Keir) must find ways to make politics a bit more fun. It doesn't mean ignoring the harsh reality, being criminally simplistic or faking some positive takes. And yet, fun plays a significant role when likes and shares determine who will see your messages and how many times. Make news fun again. We don't need bigots with ridiculous hair for that. Shiny objects don't have to be racist. Like AI, fun is another secret weapon journalists will need to learn how to excel in the upcoming years. It's a serious matter, and integral part of democracy's survival kit.

(4) Campaign for Journalism

It sounds terrible, I know. Nobody likes campaigning. But as the populist right takes over the conversation about news and its role within society, it's become inescapable: journalists and newsrooms must start campaigning for journalism. If the word gives you an allergic reaction, let's call it educating or informing the people about journalism and why it actually matters. Research from recent years indicates that the populist demonising of journalists shape what people think about the media. Who is there to tell a counterstory?[284]

Initial evidence also suggests that making counterarguments to the speculative accusations against critical journalism is crucial to maintain, or regain, the public's trust in the news.[285] But much too often journalists refrain from making such explicit arguments, worrying that they might be seen as biased and self-interested. Keeping quiet – hoping that the public sees the populist strategy for what it is or waiting for these dark days to pass – has not been proven useful, in Israel or anywhere else. By campaigning for journalism, I don't refer to the type of self-indulgent self-promotion that journalists tend to do on social media. It's the commitment to promote and explain journalism as a (flawed yet) necessary social institution. As media-savvy journalists should know, vague arguments about 'saving democracy' or 'checks and balances' won't do – they're too abstract and carry little sentimental resonance.

What would a wiser campaign look like? If journalists genuinely believe that journalism is essential for society, they shouldn't shy away from stating exactly how and why. Dear reporter, editor and news host: How have you actually contributed to people's everyday lives this past year? What have you done to expose discrimination, corruption or exploitation? Have you asked the powerful tough questions? How does your work protect us against disinformation and propaganda operations or voter suppression? How about publishing accessible annual reports, where journalists tell their audiences simply and directly how their reporting has been helpful for us this year? How have real people truly benefited from your reporting?

What did you do for the community? If the 'watchdog of democracy' remains a vague term with little to do with people's lives, no one will care to join the fight when it crumbles.

Educating the public about the role of journalism in society requires deliberate efforts and sincerity, and that's easier said than done. But there's no way around it – the risk is just too great, and other strategies have been proven futile. Even if the media industry takes urgent and much-needed steps like diversifying newsrooms and empowering local media, the populist media-bashing won't go away. Ignoring it is not a sustainable way forwards.

For all their flaws, most journalists I speak to genuinely and overwhelmingly believe in journalism. However, they don't usually stop to ask themselves why, and they certainly don't turn to discuss it with their audiences. Advocating for what journalism is and should be (how it benefits us, what it can save us from or shield us against) should be the job of vital democratic education, not journalists. At the moment, however, this type of education simply doesn't work in many societies worldwide. Journalists can no longer wait for others to change it. Neither can we. Journalists should lead the way, but those among us who still believe in the future of news must follow suit.

Remember the rainbow drawings British kids hung on the windows during Covid times, to express gratitude to the NHS? As a foreigner to the UK, I cannot stress strongly enough how striking it was to see a nation so in love with, well, an institution. In my dreams, many years from now, children will be hanging drawings of press vests on their windows, because they know that journalism is how we protect ourselves. Against neglect, tyranny, pandemics, disinformation. Journalists are essential workers for a reason. They should be respected for it.

By advocating for proper journalism, we would gain another substantial side benefit: re-orienting the news industry towards journalism's real-world, concrete, societal value. In times of generative AI, this is more urgent than ever. For too many years, ratings and traffic replaced journalists' concerns with the added value they provide to their audiences. By trying to promote better journalism, journalists might find that they themselves dramatically alter their priorities, if they are to make a public case for journalism and why it matters, perhaps more than ever before. This is what we should encourage our knowledge producers to pursue. This is the kind of work we should encourage and support. This is the type of news we should be amplifying, sharing, subscribing to, donating to and pushing forwards – if we are to save our information environment.

(5) Collaborate

If you are lucky enough to work in a country that maintains certain liberties, you still have significant power. Use it! Unionise. Work together. Join forces. Collaborate. Take inspiration from journalists worldwide who have fought this war before you. Use your wisdom, creativity and savviness to protect your profession and improve it. Journalists have immense power when they resist the populist 'deride and conquer' strategy.

There are lessons to learn from courageous journalists who refused to surrender. In Brazil, journalists openly defended their right to report. Despite the risk, the TV network Rede Globo, for instance, refused to screen Bolsonaro's speeches directly and had journalists read them instead.[286] During the January, 2023 uprising in Brazil – the rerun of the storming into the US capitol on 6th January, 2021 – Bolsonaro supporters sought to overturn the election results, harassing and injuring dozens of reporters they deemed hostile.[287] Read Maria Ressa's book about standing up to populist authoritarian Rodrigo Duterte in the Philippines. Look at the independent media's coalition in India around the last elections. Check your own histories to see how your professional ancestors collaborated in times of crisis. Prepare for the next crackdown against you and your colleagues – invest in building those collegiate alliances before it's too late, or at least much harder.

(6) Find New Ways of Belonging

One of the most difficult challenges for journalists in hyperpolarised societies is the challenge of finding rituals of loyalty that are not nationalistic, racist or otherwise excluding. In Israel, journalists sometimes try to refute the allegations of 'leftist traitors' by drawing on their military service. 'If I can show my people I was risking my life for this country, surely the treason allegations will go away?' is the rationale. If you have made it to this section of the book, you probably know how it went down (spoiler: not well).[288]

Research shows that affective polarisation – the hate towards political adversaries – is about which identities are salient.[289] Try to build inclusive identities. We have many identities: we may be single, we may be parents, we may be Londoners or Brummies, NHS patients, sci-fi fans, taxpayers, good people or maybe volunteers. Which identities we think of more often matter. What have you got in common with your audience? Who are 'the people' when we don't allow opportunist populists to define it based on our voting?

Leading polarisation scholar Matt Levendusky showed that in the US emphasising American identity, for instance, reduces partisan hatred.[290] People who had their American identity primed were 25 per cent less likely to declare animosity towards the other party and 35 per cent more likely to rate the other party as less hated.[291] We need journalism that does not appeal to our most harmful, exclusionary identities; journalism that does not appeal to people's partisan identity (like partisan media does) or nationalist identity (like much news media does, especially in times of war and conflict). We need to find better, safer, happier common ground. Journalists who wish to approach varied audiences have a role to play here. Don't shy away.

(7) Reject Anti-Media Media

Be clear about the difference between your journalistic work and the work of anti-media media: Breitbart, Channel 14, OpIndia and their copycats. One of the things we need to do if we wish to counter polarisation is to realise that there are bad faith actors who are manipulating noble ideas like press freedom to undermine democracy, freedom and equality.[292] The polarising forces in our society should be recognised, not allowed to hide behind the protections granted by the liberal democracy they seek to spoil.[293]

*

But saving our right to know is not only for journalists. What can we all do about it?

(1) Become a Media Warrior

This journey begins with reading this book, so you're already halfway there! Next is the uncomfortable realisation that institutional media may be boring, grey, biased and unforgivingly uncool, yet indispensable. We cannot count on influencers to save us from the most powerful tycoons, corporations, tyrants or predators. We need strong institutions to hold them accountable. We must hear our politicians answering tough questions, being fact-checked and challenged. For political campaigns and other forms of propaganda they can always turn to billboard campaigns, Facebook Live or politicians' Telegram channels.

As you can probably imagine, getting your news from a trustworthy, caring, professional news source is an important first step. So is media literacy. But at this moment in time, securing our future requires more than that: it requires media activism. Basically, media activism includes two paths of action. First, support and empower 'the good guys' – those producing reliable, relevant and valuable information, providing us with useful reporting, monitoring governments and corporations, and helping us to know and act. Second, less pleasant but no less important: fight and shame 'the bad guys' – those injecting fake news and propaganda into our communities, lying on purpose, helping the powerful to evade accountability and entrenching the darkest forces in society. But how?

(2) Support Relevant, Courageous, Truthful Journalism

One principle is acting to save those islands of good, committed, independent news out there. Don't be complacent: that news app you like? That podcast you enjoy? No one can guarantee it will still be around in a year, or two, or five. Wherever you live, illiberal forces may rise to power, and once they do they are sure to put any dissenting voices on their target board. Even without their massive efforts, the current attention economy – which forces investigative reporters to compete with reality shows, video games and porn – might drive them out of business. We must therefore educate ourselves and others, get involved and bring change.

We cannot hold those in power to account on our own. We don't have the time, energy, resources, money, legal advice and professional qualifications to do this type of reporting, commentary and analysis, which is expensive, time-consuming and essential.

Invest in journalism. Spend on journalism. Provide support for newsrooms and journalists prosecuted by SLAPPs (Strategic Lawsuit Against Public Participation, or: silencing lawsuit), smears or cyberbullying. Establish public organisations protecting whistleblowers, investigative reporters, truthtellers. We need them. It's our public good – the infrastructure for truth and accountability.

Supporting our right to know means consuming news you trust and respect. Subscribe to good sources of news whenever possible. Not only in order to overcome paywalls, but also as a form of political activism and informational futureproofing. We do not always have time to read all the stories in our local newspaper, but it does not mean that we are willing to live in a world where it disappears, leaving our elected officials unscrutinised. So yes, when possible, pay for news – even those you do not consume at the moment. If your favourite news sources are not based on subscriptions, consider donating.

However, this is not just about the money. News outlets have become more and more dependent on social media corporations and regulatory rules determined by populist governments to reach their audiences and survive financially. So please, start spreading the news. Literally. Share the content you find valuable. Comment on it. Your clicks mean a lot. Ratings and traffic are monitored obsessively in the newsroom. This is your way to reward your sources of knowledge and send them a message. Encountered a brave journalistic investigation? An insightful piece of commentary? A news clip saying it like it is? Send it to everyone you know. Like it, share it, comment on it. Help improve the balance between excellent and awful information around us.

Apart from the news organisations and news stories, support good journalists: you cannot imagine how much they have to endure for it. For any story that scrutinises those in power, they *will* be bashed. Be the counterpressure. Help them work for us. Contact them, provide feedback. They are dying for it. You have no idea what it means for a journalist who gets online harassment, death threats or graffiti sprayed on their doorstep to know that someone is touched, influenced and appreciative of their work. It does not cost anything. Help them stand up to colleagues and bosses who might be more willing to compromise on the public interests or surrender to populist threats. The news industry will not be doing the right thing unless we push it to.

In fact, expressing your support does more than encourage journalists to be better. It also guarantees the people who serve us are not trapped in misperceptions about who 'the public' is and where it stands. According to research conducted in Belgium, journalists tend to believe that the support for the populist right is more pervasive than it actually is.[294] Why could it be? In an original large-scale survey, conducted with three stellar scholars, we found that right-wing voters and Netanyahu's supporters were way more likely to reach out to journalists to complain about the news and scrutinise their work.[295] It is therefore not surprising that the CEO of the most popular newsroom in Israel was quoted saying that when the left-wing pundit speaks 'our switchboard collapses,' whereas when the right-wing pundit speaks nothing happens. This bias has significant implications: journalists get the sense that the most vocal, racist, extremist voices in our societies – some operated by bots and fake profiles abroad – are way more ubiquitous and numerous than they are. To counter them, we will have to show up for the fight.

Support public media. If like health care journalism is a public good, it needs to be funded. When threats are made to the BBC in the UK, Kan in Israel or Voice of America in the US, we should all go out and protest. The link between public media broadcasting and democratic resilience have been made clear by research over and over again.[296]

This does not mean we should not demand more from our news sources – quite the opposite. No need to be mean, rude or uncivil. But remember, algorithms amplify the most hateful voices. Make your voices heard too: let journalists know when you're happy and unhappy about their work, promote valuable content when they produce it and demand more. Journalism is there for us. Despite what the populists want us to believe, we too are 'the people'.

While you might personally resort from time to time to getting your news from TikTok or detoxing from news altogether, make sure you keep subscribing or even donating to news organisations you trust to tell you the truth when the next pandemic or tsunami hits. Make sure to share and spread news content you value. Support NGOs that protect journalism under attack. We need to make sure we have news organisations that are secure, powerful and resourceful enough to speak truth to power for us.

(3) Fight Info Pollution: Sue, Report, Complain, Deplatform

Unfortunately, protecting democracy in times of 'flooding the zone with shit' might also be, well, dirty. Some of us might feel more comfortable empowering great journalists who take their public service seriously than fighting those who hide behind 'press freedom' to disseminate hate, violence and harmful lies. But it is necessary to fight the polluters of the public conversation. There has to be implications – legal, political, reputational – for destroying our right to know. How to do it, though?

On a very basic level we must adopt a more proactive approach to the information around us. Report disinformation online – research shows that deplatforming works. Complain to ombudsmen and TV networks when they are being reckless. When appropriate, sue for libel. Think about the Dominion lawsuit against Fox News after the network spread the unfounded conspiracy about the company's relations to Hugo Chávez and their alleged defrauding of the presidential elections in 2020. As detailed earlier, Dominion sued because Fox News's conspiracies hurt them financially, and they settled when they were offered a good enough deal.

The Dominion lawsuit, while initially promising, did not end well. It did for Dominion: they got massive publicity, global brand recognition and a significant payout from Rupert Murdoch. But it did not end well for us, the people. While it exposed the tip of the iceberg that is Fox News's manipulation of its viewers, satisfying the commercial and reputational interests of Dominion, this TV channel's worst sin – knowingly and consistently lying to the American people – was not addressed at all.

Some of you might be thinking: 'We shouldn't censor anyone, not even these liars.' Well, the freedom of the press is not there to protect the Tucker Carlsons of the world who knowingly lie to the public about the most sacred organising principle of democracy: free and fair elections. 'Press freedom' was intended to protect us against governments taking over the media. Those spreading incitement, bad faith and conspiracies do not deserve this protection. Quite the opposite: they should pay, in money, power and prestige, lose advertisers and be publicly shamed.

On the structural level we have become too comfortable with the idea that certain figures and corporations – from Rupert Murdoch's empire to Elon Musk's global experiment in humans – control our information environment unmonitored. This has to change. But this is not a mission individuals can accomplish on their own. Those of us willing to resist the new censorship will have to organise against it. Protest against propaganda operations and corruption Petri dishes masked as news. Mobilise when governments try to take over public media and minds. Get involved. The 'bad guys' have a plan; it is about time we have one too.

(4) Media Policy – Now

Above all, media must become a central political issue – just like the economy, immigration and climate change – as it determines the framing and attention granted to each and every aspect of our shared lives. Any other political policy, from net zero to affirmative action, is shaped, and often determined, by its mediation. How do we find out about it? How much exposure does it get on national media? What is hidden and who is silenced? Media activism must be on the agenda of any concerned individual or community who wants to improve this world. Just like we all know where we stand on our government's policies, budget, alliances, wars and even gender-neutral bathrooms – we all need to take a stand on media. Otherwise, others will determine it for us.

This battle will not be won solely by liking, sharing or even subscribing and paying for excellent news. We will have to organise, mobilise and take action if we are to change the future of knowledge. What would you do if a huge corporation were to spill its sewage into your garden? Surely not nothing? This is how we should start thinking about parties and corporations who intentionally pollute our information environment. Sue super-spreaders of conspiracy theories. Support those who run long legal wars on liars and propagandists. Party platforms must reflect how politicians intend to protect our information environment. Candidates should be questioned about it in election debates and constituency surgeries and town halls.

Policymakers and public servants have significant power to protect us against the new censorship. They can build an infrastructure for flourishing knowledge producers, they can regulate the harms caused by algorithm-based media, they can break down the broligarchy, embolden journalism and sanction those polluting the public conversation. But they won't do it alone. Activists, pressure groups and civil society must enter the shit-flooded scene and take action to make them do just that. If we are to save anything at all – the planet, human rights, gender equality, religious freedom or the wealth gap – media activism will have to become part of our lives. Instead of worrying about being accused of bias we need to embrace a new bias towards the principles (rather than bureaucracies and procedures) of democracy. Professor Jay Rosen and

Professor Stephen Ward have already called for the media to adopt a pro-democracy approach. However, for this to work, we will all have to take part. We have to pressure our representatives to build incentives, regulations and mechanisms of accountability to make sure our right to know is no longer infringed so blatantly, so consistently and so brazenly. We have to take responsibility over our information, not just in terms of data privacy but also in terms of value, transparency and quality. That is the only cure for the rise of the new censorship.

(5) Go Local, Go Global

This struggle will take a different form in different countries. While the new censorship is evident everywhere, the forces at play, the historical grievances, cultural sensitivities and political economies vary significantly. Learn your local context, and what would be the best way to advance your right to know.

In the UK, for instance, one first tangible step forwards for media activists would be organising and mobilising to ban British politicians from being paid by news organisations. There is no good explanation for why the political elite in this country – the most powerful people in the nation, who have increased access to influence the news as is – should also be funded generously by self-interested billionaires to be psuedo-journalists. 'Without fear or favour' becomes a joke when someone like Nigel Farage is hosting current affairs programmes. Anyone who pretends that GB News is simply the right-wing equivalent of Channel 4 News is pulling the rug from underneath the future of journalism. If we rebuild the media as a democratic institution in a way that serves the public, politicians should be monitored by it, not running it. Another useful pressure could be applied to sanction GB News or empower Ofcom to work more fiercely for the people. Make sure hate speech and dangerous lies are being sanctioned, because shame is no longer a powerful enough deterrent.

Eventually, just like climate change, the fight against the new censorship must go global. Without international collaboration – between journalists, policymakers and activists – there is no chance to fix the technological infrastructure that grants enormous power to wealthy donors, dark political operations and populist coalitions of hate. To break our dependency on Elon Musk and his views on disinformation or white supremacy, an international coalition will be needed. This, too, will not happen without public pressure to protect our collective right to know.

The UK is in a wonderful position – surprising, I know – to lead this global shift. The Labour government does not owe anything to the Murdoch empire, to GB News, to Elon Musk, the lie spreaders, hate inciters and conspirators. Unlike Tony Blair back in the day, Keir Starmer did not spend his precious campaign time flying over to kiss Murdoch's ring. For the first time in decades, the man who runs the country can fix – or at least improve – our information environment. Starmer has the opportunity, and none of the barriers of his predecessors, to revolutionise the media. Apart from being the right thing to do, it might even be wise. Not because he should aim for loyalist media that pats his back, but rather because currently the asymmetric media sphere in the UK and beyond means that racists, bigots and right-wing extremists are getting a fore.

An Antidote to Anti-Media Media

What can we do against the infectious influence of anti-media media? 'In a political environment of heightened risk and uncertainty, targeted media organisations cannot afford to ignore anti-liberal media outlets' expressions of outrage and indignation,' Professor Cherian George writes about journalism under attack in Hong Kong. 'While they possess no direct coercive power, these media contribute to a culture of fear and self-censorship.' I couldn't agree more. Time to stop waiting for the tide to pass – history tells us it won't.

First, expose anti-media media for what it is: a fraud. An attempt to fool the public into thinking that its manipulative messaging, hateful campaigns and fake news are what press freedom is all about. The fact that Rupert Murdoch and his son were both invited to give the James MacTaggart Memorial Lecture – perhaps the most renowned event in British broadcasting – is shameful, and honestly, plain dumb. By granting legitimacy and credibility to people who actively work to undermine the profession, threaten and smear journalists and file SLAPP lawsuits, British journalists are cutting off the branch we're all sitting on. The Murdochs should be facing the consequences of their responsibility for the spread of fake news, conspiracy theories and lies in the anti-media they own. They should be answering tough questions in journalistic interviews, Ofcom investigations or congressional hearings, not applauded for corrupting the public sphere for political power and financial gain. No wonder Murdoch Junior spent the time he got on stage bashing, you guessed it, the BBC.

Second, campaign, protest and take legal action when possible. How to do that? While the right-wing campaign against the BBC, for instance, focuses on its so-called lack of 'due impartiality', it often neglects and blurs the rest of the Communications Act 2003, which states that the regulator must ensure that 'news, in whatever form, is reported with *due accuracy* and presented with due impartiality.' How about this accuracy, then? Ofcom, the British media regulator, will have to make much more effort in this direction to protect our right to know. 'The free marketplace of ideas' was supposed to prevent such journalistic flops: according to the classic political theory of liberal democracy, audiences were supposed to punish news outlets that lie to them, thus ensuring that those who provide the best news product win. But the time has long come for us to give up on the free-market illusion when it comes to news. Without proper, robust regulation the 'invisible hand' of the news market (and certainly its 'invisible algorithms') might be serving various interests, but certainly not the public.

Third, demand better policies, better regulation and better enforcement. It is not a coincidence that for many years Sky News was a much more credible, reliable and journalistic TV channel than Fox News across the pond – although the same Rupert Murdoch owned both.[297] The reason is, in one word, regulation. For decades, the TV landscape in the UK was regulated much better than the US broadcasting jungle.

We need a good media policy that advances our right to know in these hectic times, and we need a proper, courageous regulator to pursue them for us. However, as GB News is challenging Ofcom's authority and Ofcom seems to avoid sanctioning those polluting our information environment, the situation might deteriorate rapidly.[298] If there are no sanctions for spreading lies and hate, for using airtime for biased propaganda and outrageous conspiracies, why would anyone bother doing the difficult, time-consuming and expensive work called journalism?

Afterword

This book is intended to set us free from the populist takeover. It traces the use of the new censorship to transform our collective mind, step by step: the manipulation of impartiality and balance against press freedom, the establishment of anti-media media and propaganda-disguised-as-news operations, the mainstreaming of the far right, the threats to public media funding, the legal intimidation and the incitement of media-hate. It also offers a way out: a concrete guide for saving our information environment, with everything we know – based on rigorous, cross-national research and history – that could help us save our right to know. Knowledge is, still, power; otherwise, the most powerful people in the world would not be in a frantic frenzy to control it.

The case of Netanyahu's takeover of the Israeli media uncovers how the populist war on news – riding on unprecedented technological opportunities, unleashed monopolies and outdated journalistic standards – turned journalists less independent, and us all less informed. Strikingly, in the attempt to prevent further media-bashing and save what remained of the public's trust in the media, those in charge of holding the powerful accountable ended up bending over, self-censoring, virtue-signalling and shifting the entire public conversation, slowly but surely, further to the far right. The language of democracy and freedom was abused to obfuscate authoritarian efforts to crush our fundamental rights.

The sheer scale of content bombarding us has not only provided a rich information environment but also more propaganda, surveillance, gaslighting, incitement, fearmongering and lies. It has changed us as audiences, but not the way we hoped it would. Rather than better informed, we ended up exhausted, disappointed, resentful, suspicious and angry.

The populist war against the media has real-world casualties, whether it is led by Netanyahu, Trump, Farage, Modi or Milei. Just like we came to realise that we will have to fight for the planet if we want to keep living on it, it is time we all become actively responsible for our information environment. Our right to know can no longer be left unguarded in the hands of populist leaders, fundamentalist pressure groups, wealthy tech giants, their cronies or scared gatekeepers.

For too many years, most of us neglected to protect the public sphere and took our democratic institutions for granted. At this point, securing our right to know requires revolutionising our media. No battle will be won without a victory in our fight to know.

Endnotes

Prologue

1. Bhat & Chadha, 2020; Egelhofer & Lecheler, 2019; Engesser et al., 2017; Farhall et al., 2019; Figenschou & Ihlebæk, 2019; Fuchs, 2018; Haller & Holt, 2018; Waisbord & Amado, 2017.
2. Carlson et al., 2022; Committee to Protect Journalists, 2019; Egelhofer et al., 2021; Fawzi, 2019; Lawrence & Moon, 2021; Meeks, 2020; van der Linden et al., 2020; Relly, 2021; Duyn & Collier, 2019; Waisbord, 2020; Wasserman & Madrid-Morales, 2019; Schulz et al., 2020.
3. Tumber, 2004; Waisbord, 2002.
4. Cardiff School of Journalism, Media and Cultural Studies, 2003; for similar findings in the US see Silcock et al., 2008.
5. Nygren et al., 2018; Roman et al., 2017.
6. Hallin, 1989.
7. Elbaz & Bar-Tal, 2019; Zandberg & Neiger, 2005.
8. Philo & Berry, 2004, 2007.

Between the Li(n)es

9. https://www.thetimes.com/article/bbc-is-now-the-enemy-declares-furious-farage-after-tv-grilling-zrmf0bdv5
10. https://rsf.org/en/czech-republic-czech-president-threatens-journalists-mock-kalashnikov-0

11. Savage, 2025; 'Serbia Transforming from Pariah to EU Partner', 2014.
12. Berl Katzanelson Hate Speech Report, 2018; 2019.
13. Nilsson & Örnebring, 2016.
14. Kim & Shin, 2022.
15. Benzaquen, 2019.
16. Bein-Lebovitch & Maanit, 2021; Benzaquen, 2019b, 2019a.
17. Panievsky et al., 2025.
18. Donaway et al., 2024.
19. Krämer, 2018b; McChesney, 2004; Postman, 1985.
20. Klumpp et al., 2016.
21. Nielsen, 2017, p. 1252.
22. Stiglitz, 2003.
23. Jasser et al., 2022.
24. Chama, 2015; Florini, 2007; Meyers, 1993; Wright, 1967.
25. Bass & MacLean, 1993; Cate et al., 1994; Lewis, 2009; Mokrosinska, 2018; Papandrea, 2005; Schudson, 2015.
26. Watson, 2021.
27. Tambini, 2021.
28. Tufekci, 2018.
29. Reuters Digital News Report
30. Toff et al., 2023.
31. Mannell & Meese, 2022.
32. Usher, 2021.
33. Neff et al., 2022; Noble, 2018.
34. Gerbaudo, 2018; Kim et al., 2021; Rhodes, 2021.
35. Rogenhofer & Panievsky, 2020.
36. Ball, 1996.
37. Carlson et al., 2022; Egelhofer & Lecheler, 2019; Jones & Sun, 2017.
38. Levi & Agmon, 2020; Panievsky et al., 2025; Talshir, 2018.

39. Peri, 2004; Rogenhofer & Panievsky, 2020; Talshir, 2018.
40. Dugard & Reynolds, 2013.
41. Levi & Agmon, 2020; Talshir, 2018.
42. Ginosar & Reich, 2022; Kampf & Daskal, 2011; Markowitz-Elfassi et al., 2018; Peri, 2007; Tsfati & Meyers, 2012.
43. Caspi, 2010; Lachover and Lemish, 2018; Markowitz-Elfassi et al., 2018; Peri 2011b; Reich, Barnoy, & Hertzog, 2016; Schejter & Yemini, 2016; Tsfati & Meyers, 2012.
44. https://rsf.org/en/turkish-journalists-arrested-reporting-covid-19-cases
45. https://rsf.org/en/journalists-new-wave-arrests-turkey
46. https://rsf.org/en/turkey-media-purge-intensifies-coup-attempts-wake
47. https://cpj.org/special-reports/2024-is-deadliest-year-for-journalists-in-cpj-history-almost-70-percent-killed-by-israel/

The Populist War on Our Right to Know

48. https://x.com/elonmusk/status/1879426713035436199?lang=en-GB
49. Koliska and Assmann, 2021.
50. Mudde, 2007.
51. Müller, 2016.
52. Krämer, 2018.
53. https://www.theguardian.com/politics/article/2024/jun/24/nigel-farage-attacks-mail-newspapers-over-putin-ally-reports
54. Gans, 1979.
55. Davis, 2019.
56. Davis, 2009.
57. Cage, 2016.
58. Egelhofer et al., 2021.

59. Engesser et al., 2017; Gerbaudo, 2018; Moffitt, 2018.
60. Antunovic, 2019; Waisbord, 2022.
61. Rathje et al. 2021; 2024.
62. Heltzel & Laurin, 2024.
63. Keen, 2008.
64. S. C. Lewis & Molyneux, 2018; Waisbord, 2020.
65. Ferrier and Garud Patkar, 2018; Neilson and Ortiga, 2022; Waisbord, 2022.
66. Panievsky, 2023; Relly, 2021.
67. Quandt, 2018; Quandt & Klapproth, 2023; Westlund, 2021.
68. Curran et al. 2016.
69. de Albuquerque & Alves, 2023.
70. Hendricks & Denton, 2010; Katz et al., 2013; Kreiss, 2012.
71. Shoham et al., 2018.
72. https://pressgazette.co.uk/news/news-deserts-research-newspapers-closed/?utm_source=chatgpt.com
73. https://pressgazette.co.uk/publishers/regional-newspapers/local-newspaper-closures-uk-2022-to-2024/?utm_source=chatgpt.com
74. https://www.cjr.org/business_of_news/the-journalism-crisis-across-the-world.php?utm_source=chatgpt.com
75. https://pressgazette.co.uk/media_business/journalism-job-cuts-2023/?utm_source=chatgpt.com
76. https://www.bbc.co.uk/news/articles/c0m07g49004o?utm_source=chatgpt.com
77. https://www.theguardian.com/world/2024/apr/10/new-zealand-warner-bros-discovers-closes-newshub-tvnz-programs-bulletins-cuts?utm_source=chatgpt.com
78. https://www.theguardian.com/global-development/2025/feb/11/trump-usaid-cuts-freeze-press-freedom-ukraine-afghanistan-media-rsf?utm_source=chatgpt.com

79. Curran, 2011; Schudson, 2018; Starr, 2008.
80. Haskell, 2000; Lewis, 2012.
81. Starr, 2008, pp. 35–36.
82. Galston, 2018; Müller, 2016.
83. Baker, 2001, pp. 129–153; Ferree et al., 2002; Hallin & Mancini, 2004; Strömbäck, 2005.
84. Flores, 2016.
85. https://www.youtube.com/watch?v=DxgmI1vgq5Y
86. Hadjicostis & Wilson, 2024.
87. Spike, 2024.
88. Shirky, 2008, pp. 143–160.
89. Castells, 2010, pp. 11–15.
90. Palfrey & Gasser, 2008; Tapscott, 2009.
91. Rushkoff, 2003, p. 118.
92. Castells, 2012, pp. 315–316.
93. Dutton, 2008; Shirky, 2008.
94. Curran, 2016; Morozov, 2012; Turner, 2018.
95. Cammaerts, 2009.
96. Keen, 2008.
97. Gillmor, 2006.

The Playbook: Choose Your Weapon

98. https://www.cnbc.com/2018/05/22/trump-told-lesley-stahl-he-bashes-press-to-discredit-negative-stories.html
99. Wodak, 2015.
100. Scheppele, 2018; Sharon, 2023.
101. https://fom.coe.int/en/alerte/detail/107637394
102. https://www.politico.eu/article/romania-journalist-media-freedom-emilia-sercan-cristian-pantazi-g4media-rule-law-nicolae-ciuca/

103. https://www.indexoncensorship.org/2023/11/argentinas-milei-ushers-in-atrocity-denialism-trolling-and-attacks-on-the-media/
104. Reporters Without Borders, 2017.
105. According to the NGO the Journalism Society, cited in Oxford Reuters Institute Report on press freedom in Poland from 2022: https://reutersinstitute.politics.ox.ac.uk/digital-news-report/2022/poland
106. Committee to Protect Journalists Impunity Index, 2024.
107. Reporters Without Borders, 2023.
108. Pintak, 2023.
109. Carson & Wright, 2022; Lim & Bradshaw, 2023.
110. Moyakine & Tabachnik, 2021.
111. Suebsaeng, 2022.
112. https://ipi.media/germany-rising-attacks-against-journalists-covering-protests/
113. Schneider, 2021.
114. Bein-Lebovitch & Maanit, 2021.
115. https://www.the7eye.org.il/521986
116. https://www.theguardian.com/us-news/2017/feb/24/media-blocked-white-house-briefing-sean-spicer
117. Bajomi-Lázár, 2013; Bleyer-Simon & Benedek, 2024; Griffen, 2020.
118. Persico, 2024.
119. Ross Arguedas et al., 2024.
120. Chen et al., 2020; Genç, 2014; Høiby, 2020; Ivask, 2020; Jamil, 2020; Koirala, 2020; Le Vu Phung, 2020; Panievsky & Blumell, 2025; Stahel, 2023; Stahel & Schoen, 2020.
121. UNESCO, 2019.
122. Fahmy et al., 2024.
123. Callison et al., 2020; Forde, 2021.
124. e.g. https://reutersinstitute.politics.ox.ac.uk/news-powerful-and-privileged-how-misrepresentation-and-underrepresentation-disadvantaged

The Nigel Farage Effect: Mainstreaming the Far Right

125. https://www.theguardian.com/politics/2023/dec/10/nigel-farage-finishes-third-in-im-a-celebrity-get-me-out-of-here
126. Aisch, 2015; Confessore & Yourish, 2016.
127. Reporters Without Borders, 2017.
128. Bos et al., 2010.
129. Bolet & Foos, 2023; Halperin, 2024; Smith, 2010.
130. Maltz, 2016.
131. Amir, 2022; Peretz, 2021; Rubin & Parker, 2022.
132. https://www.facebook.com/watch/?v=790712165683845
133. Mazzoleni et al., 2003; Pickard, 2019.
134. Broockman & Skovron, 2018.
135. Pilet et al., 2024.
136. Beckers et al., 2021, p. 255.
137. Hopmann & Schuck, 2023.
138. Banaji & Bhat, 2022; Kenyon et al., 2022; Lajevardi et al., 2022; Riebe et al., 2018.
139. Coddington et al., 2021; Nelson, 2021.
140. https://reutersinstitute.politics.ox.ac.uk/trust-gap-how-and-why-news-digital-platforms-viewed-more-sceptically-versus-news-general
141. Chong & Druckman, 2007; Druckman, 2001; Miller & Krosnick, 2000.
142. Ellinas, 2018.
143. Committee to Protect Journalists Impunity Index, 2024.
144. Hall et al., 1978; Harcup and O'Neill, 2017; Tuchman, 1978.
145. Herpen, 2021.
146. de Jonge & Gaufman, 2022.
147. Downs, 2002.
148. Turnbull-Dugarte, 2024.
149. Wright et al., 2024

150. Valentim, 2021.
151. Hagemeister, 2022.
152. https://www.dw.com/en/far-right-afd-how-should-german-media-deal-with-the-party/a-68982940
153. Bolet & Foos, 2023, p. 4.

Strategic Bias: How Our News Universe Shifts to the Right

154. Quoted in Ayton & Tumber, 2001, p. 14.
155. Hayes, 2003.
156. Koltay, 2013.
157. Limor and Helman 2003.
158. Surčulija-Milojević, 2015, p. 226.
159. Georgantopoulos, 2016.
160. Ladd, 2011; Smith, 2010.
161. Farhall et al., 2019.
162. Crawford, 2007, p. 27.
163. Koliska et al., 2020.
164. Egelhofer et al., 2022; Ladd, 2011; Smith, 2010; Watts et al., 1999.
165. Egelhofer et al., 2022; Pingree et al., 2018.
166. e.g. https://www.bbc.co.uk/news/world-middle-east-48652986, https://www.timesofisrael.com/criminal-probe-launched-into-sara-netanyahu-over-allegations-of-witness-tampering/, https://edition.cnn.com/2024/12/26/middleeast/israel-sara-netanyahu-investigation-allegation-intl-latam/index.html, https://www.france24.com/en/20190616-sara-netanyahu-israeli-premiers-scandal-plagued-wife
167. Peri, 2011.
168. Maras, 2012.
169. Tuchman, 1972.
170. Maras, 2012, p. 188.

171. Rosen, 1999; Rosen & Merritt, 1994.
172. https://x.com/jayrosen_nyu/status/1303495521244512256
173. Deacon, 2016; more on the media coverage of Brexit see Cooper, 2021; Gaber & Fisher, 2021; Gavin, 2018; Rone, 2023.
174. Watson, 2018, p. 3028.
175. Grossmann & Hopkins, 2016; Lovett, 2023; van der Linden et al., 2020.
176. Bennett, 2012, pp. 189–193.
177. Voltmer, 2013, p. 183.
178. Cohen-Almagor, 2007; Fitzgerald, 2019; Levitsky and Ziblatt, 2018.
179. Panievsky, 2022.
180. Entman, 2007; Herman and Chomsky, 1988; Lichter, 2017.
181. Hallin, 1989.
182. Maras, 2012.
183. Fletcher, 2020.
184. Alamo-Pastrana and Hoynes, 2020; Anderson, 2022; Burrows, 2018; Callison et al., 2020; Schmidt, 2023; Usher, 2021; Wallace, 2019.
185. Donegan, 2021.
186. Chandler and Munday, 2020.
187. Schudson, 1981.
188. Hallin, 2000, pp. 47–48; Ward, 2008, pp. 75–80.
189. Harding, 1992; Wahl-Jorgensen et al., 2017; Wallace, 2019.
190. Lynch & McGoldrick, 2005.
191. Newman et al., 2020.
192. Ryan, 2001, pp. 16–17.
193. Davis, 2007, p. 40; McChesney & Nichols, 2002, p. 60; Tuchman, 1972.
194. Bagdikian, 2004, p. 25; Hall et al., 1978, pp. 57–60.
195. Cohen-Almagor, 2007; Deuze, 2005; Tuchman, 1978; Ward, 2006.
196. Bagdikian, 2004; Herman and Chomsky, 1988; Lichter, 2017.

197. Entman, 2007, p. 166.
198. Entman, 2007, p. 163.
199. Koliska et al., 2020; Koliska & Assmann, 2021.
200. Koliska et al., 2020.
201. Krämer & Langmann, 2020.
202. Krämer, 2018a.
203. Krämer & Langmann, 2020, p. 142.
204. Barwise & York, 2020, p. 156.
205. Shamir and Rahat, 2017; Talshir, 2018.

When the War on the Media Meets War

206. Duyn & Duyn, 2021.
207. Hemmer, 2016.
208. Hallin, 1989.
209. Caspi, 1981, p. 191.
210. Liebes, 1997; Sheafer and Weimann, 2005; Wolfsfeld, 2012; Zandberg and Neiger, 2005.
211. Markowitz-Elfassi et al., 2018, p. 643.
212. Rogenhofer and Panievsky, 2020.
213. Noelle-Neumann, 1974.
214. Based on Daniel Hallin's celebrated theory of 'spheres of legitimacy', 1989, pp. 116–118.
215. Hayes & Guardino, 2010.
216. Persico, 2024.
217. Cohen, 2025.

Deride and Conquer: The Populist Crackdown on Solidarity

218 https://x.com/laderechadiario/status/1859197498981597458?ref_src=twsrc%5Etfw%7Ctwcamp%5Etweetembed%7Ctwterm%5E1859197498981597458%7Ctwgr%5E4

f095e644494c343534a0212cabe0777556a3247%7Ctwcon%5Es1_&ref_url=https%3A%2F%2Fwww.eldiarioar.com%2Fpolitica%2Fmilei-lanzo-amenaza-periodismo-les-llego-momento-bancarse-vuelto-haber-mentido_1_11836665.html
219. Taberez, 2024.
220. Aberbach & Rockman, 2002; Harvey, 2011.
221. Najjar, 1996, p. 118.
222. Kantola & Harju, 2021; Miller & Lewis, 2020.
223. Juntunen, 2010; Phillips, 2013; Usher, 2014.
224. Arteaga Rojas, 2022; Farhall et al., 2019; Varma, 2023.
225. Pain & Korin, 2021, p. 82.
226. Bustamante & Relly, 2016.
227. Ashraf & Brooten, 2017.
228. Svensson, 2012, p. 22.
229. Kantola & Harju, 2021.
230. Selva, 2020.
231. Harrison & Pukallus, 2021, p. 309.
232. Huddy, 2013.
233. Karpf, 2018.
234. Bassan-Nygate & Weiss, 2020; Gidron et al., 2022.
235. Anderson, 2013; McChesney, 2013; Tsfati & Meyers, 2012.
236. Caspi, 2010, p. 5; Markowitz-Elfassi et al., 2018b; Tsfati & Meyers, 2012, p. 445.
237. Benzaquen, 2015; Grossman et al., 2022; Yahav, 2015.
238. Megiddo, 2018.
239. Bhat, 2023; Bhat & Chadha, 2020; Figenschou & Ihlebæk, 2019; Peck, 2019; Selva, 2020.
240. Tsfati and Meyers, 2012, pp. 445–46.
241. Aberneithie & Tobitt, 2024.
242. https://www.politico.com/news/2024/02/01/journalism-lay-offs-00138517

243. Juntunen, 2010; Phillips, 2013.
244. Usher, 2014.
245. Peri, 2004.
246. Filc, 2009; Mandelkern, 2015, pp. 285–287; Rogenhofer & Panievsky, 2020.
247. Tsfati and Meyers, 2012.
248. Curran, 2011; Marzolf, 1990; Wyatt, 2007.
249. Tapsell, 2022.

Welcome to the Upside Down: The World of Anti-Media Media

250. Aalberg & Curran, 2011; Alexander, 2016; Curran, 2011.
251. Ash et al., 2024; Bartlett, 2015; Kizito, 2021; Meirick, 2013; Seol et al., 2024; Vultee, 2009.
252. Cassino, 2016; Kull et al., 2003.
253. Barwise & York, 2020, p. 96.
254. Bhat & Chadha, 2020.
255. Chadha & Bhat, 2022.
256. Siapera & Papadopoulou, 2021.
257. George, 2023.
258. Bursztyn et al., 2020.
259. Ash, Galletta, Pinna, et al., 2024; Benkler et al., 2018; Bennett & Livingston, 2018; Iyengar et al., 2019; Levendusky, 2013; Wu & Shen, 2022.
260. Bauer et al., 2022.
261. Budak et al., 2016; Frisby, 2018; Nicola, 2010; Suk et al., 2022.
262. Budak et al., 2016.
263. Bacon, 2016; Jamieson & Cappella, 2008; Reifowitz, 2021.
264. Freiling et al., 2021; Suk et al., 2022.
265. Martin & Yurukoglu, 2017, p. 2567.

266. Morris & Francia, 2010.
267. Meirick, 2013.
268. Morris & Morris, 2022.
269. Voltmer, 2013.
270. George, 2024.
271. Pickard, 2019.
272. George, 2023; Lo & Wong, 2021.
273. Oates, 2008.
274. Panievsky, 2020.
275. Peck, 2019.
276. https://www.theguardian.com/politics/article/2024/aug/16/nigel-farage-revealed-to-be-uks-highest-earning-mp
277. Jamieson & Cappella, 2008; Peck, 2019; Levendusky, 2013; McKnight, 2010; Williamson et al., 2011.
278. George, 2024.

The Fight to Know

279. https://www.haaretz.co.il/opinions/2017-08-29/ty-article-opinion/.premium/0000017f-defd-db5a-a57f-deff06960000
280. https://www.haaretz.co.il/gallery/media/2025-03-09/ty-article/.premium/00000195-79e6-d46d-a3f7-f9ef5f770000
281. Waisbord, 2020.
282. Toff et al., 2023.
283. Hayes, 2025.
284. Duyn & Collier, 2019; Ladd & Podkul, 2020; Panievsky et al., 2025; Watts et al., 1999.
285. Pingree et al., 2018.
286. Sbaraini Fontes & Marques, 2022.
287. Committee to Protect Journalists Impunity Index, 2024.
288. Panievsky, 2023.

289. Iyengar et al., 2019.
290. Levendusky, 2017.
291. Carlin & Love, 2018 reached similar findings.
292. Nadler & Bauer, 2019.
293. George, 2023.
294. Wagrave et al., 2018.
295. Panievsky et al., 2024.
296. Moore, 2024.
297. Cushion & Lewis, 2009.
298. Barnett & Petley, 2021.

Bibliography

Aalberg, T., & Curran, J. (Eds.). (2011). *How Media Inform Democracy: A Comparative Approach*. Routledge.

Aberbach, J. D., & Rockman, B. A. (2002). Conducting and Coding Elite Interviews. *PS: Political Science & Politics*, 35(4), 673–676. https://doi.org/10.1017/S1049096502001142

Aberneithie, C., & Tobitt, C. (2024, January 4). At least 8,000 journalism job cuts in UK and North America in 2023. *Press Gazette*. https://pressgazette.co.uk/media_business/journalism-job-cuts-2023/

Aisch. (2015, August 7). Trump Wins the Airtime Contest in the Republican Debate. *The New York Times*. https://www.nytimes.com/interactive/2015/08/05/us/republican-debate-charts.html, https://www.nytimes.com/interactive/2015/08/05/us/republican-debate-charts.html

Alamo-Pastrana, C., & Hoynes, W. (2020). Racialization of News: Constructing and Challenging Professional Journalism as "White Media". *Humanity & Society*, 44(1), 67–91. https://doi.org/10.1177/0160597618820071

Alexander, J. C. (2016). Introduction: Journalism, Democratic Culture, and Creative Reconstruction. In J. C. Alexander, E. B. Breese, & M. Luengo (Eds.), *The Crisis of Journalism Reconsidered: Democratic Culture, Professional Codes, Digital Future* (pp. 1–30). Cambridge University Press. https://doi.org/10.1017/CBO9781316050774

Amir, I. (2022, August 29). The Media Play Major Role in Ben-Gvir's Meteoric Rise. *Haaretz*. https://www.haaretz.com/opinion/2022-08-29/ty-article-opinion/.premium/the-media-play-major-role-in-ben-gvirs-meteoric-rise/00000182-eb55-da50-af83-fbf552f30000

Anderson, C. W. (2013). *Rebuilding the News: Metropolitan Journalism in the Digital Age*. Temple University Press.

Anderson, C. W. (2022). News and the Public Sphere. In S. Allan (Ed.), *The Routledge Companion to News and Journalism*. Routledge London.

Antunovic, D. (2019). "We wouldn't say it to their faces": Online harassment, women sports journalists, and feminism. *Feminist Media Studies*, 19(3), 428–442. https://doi.org/10.1080/14680777.2018.1446454

Artega Rojas, R. D. (2022). *The Journalist as Neoliberal Lone Wolf: On Mexico's Imaginary Reporters and Collaborative Resistance in a Divided Guild* [University of Cambridge]. https://www.repository.cam.ac.uk/handle/1810/339031

Ash, E., Galletta, S., Hangartner, D., Margalit, Y., & Pinna, M. (2024). The Effect of Fox News on Health Behavior during COVID-19. *Political Analysis*, 32(2), 275–284. https://doi.org/10.1017/pan.2023.21

Ash, E., Galletta, S., Pinna, M., & Warshaw, C. S. (2024). From viewers to voters: Tracing Fox News' impact on American democracy. *Journal of Public Economics*. https://doi.org/10.1016/j.jpubeco.2024.105256

Ashraf, S. I., & Brooten, L. (2017). Tribal Journalists under Fire: Threats, impunity and decision making in reporting on conflict in Pakistan. In U. Carlsson & R. Pöyhtäri (Eds.), *The Assault on Journalism: Building Knowledge to Protect Freedom of Expression* (pp. 147–158). Nordicom.

Ayton, P., & Tumber, H. (2001). The Rise and Fall of Perceived Bias at the BBC. *Intermedia*, 29(4), 12–15.

Bacon, J. (2016). The Rush Limbaugh Show and the expanding culture war: Whiteness, masculinity, and conservative media denials of climate change and sexism. In *Systemic Crises of Global Climate Change*. Routledge.

Bagdikian, B. H. (2004). *The New Media Monopoly*. Beacon Press.

Bajomi-Lázár, P. (2013). The Party Colonisation of the Media: The Case of Hungary. *East European Politics and Societies*, 27(1), 69–89. https://doi.org/10.1177/0888325412465085

Baker, C. E. (2001). *Media, Markets, and Democracy*. Cambridge University Press.

Ball, C. H. (1996, June 5). Professor recalls Netanyahu's intense studies in three fields. *MIT News | Massachusetts Institute of Technology*. https://news.mit.edu/1996/netanyahu-0605

Banaji, S., & Bhat, R. (2022). *Social Media and Hate*. Taylor & Francis.

Barnett, S., & Petley, J. (2021). Why Ofcom must find its backbone. *British Journalism Review*, 32(1), 29–36. https://doi.org/10.1177/0956474821998991

Bartlett, B. (2015). How Fox News Changed American Media and Political Dynamics. *SSRN Electronic Journal*. https://doi.org/10.2139/ssrn.2604679

Barwise, P., & York, P. (2020). *The War Against the BBC: How an Unprecedented Combination of Hostile Forces Is Destroying Britain's Greatest Cultural Institution ... And Why You Should Care*. Penguin.

Bass, G. D., & MacLean, A. (1993). Enhancing the Public's Right-to-Know about Environmental Issues. *Villanova Environmental Law Journal*, 4, 287.

Bassan-Nygate, L., & Weiss, C. M. (2020). It's Us or Them: Partisan Polarization in Israel and Beyond. *APSA MENA Politics Newsletter*.

Bauer, A. J., Nadler, A., & Nelson, J. L. (2022). What is Fox News? Partisan Journalism, Misinformation, and the Problem of Classification. *Electronic News*, *16*(1), 18–29. https://doi.org/10.1177/19312431211060426

Beckers, K., Walgrave, S., Wolf, H. V., Lamot, K., & Van Aelst, P. (2021). Right-wing Bias in Journalists' Perceptions of Public Opinion. *Journalism Practice*, *15*(2), 243–258. https://doi.org/10.1080/17512786.2019.1703788

Bein-Lebovitch, A., & Maanit, C. (2021, May 18). Increase in threats against journalists. *Globes*. https://www.globes.co.il/news/article.aspx?did=1001371318

Benkler, Y., Faris, R., & Roberts, H. (2018). *Network Propaganda: Manipulation, Disinformation, and Radicalization in American Politics*. Oxford University Press.

Bennett, W. L. (2012). *News: The Politics of Illusion*. Longman.

Bennett, W. L., & Livingston, S. (2018). The disinformation order: Disruptive communication and the decline of democratic institutions. *European Journal of Communication*, *33*(2), 122–139. https://doi.org/10.1177/0267323118760317

Benzaquen, I. (2015, March 17). How Israel Today Served Netanyahu in the Runup to the 2015 Elections. *Ha'ayin Hashviit*. http://www.the7eye.org.il/151820

Benzaquen, I. (2019, September 17). Netanyahu's Attack on the Media, September 2019 Election: Summary and Analysis. *Ha'ayin Hashviit*. https://www.the7eye.org.il/344716

Bhat, P. (2023). Hindu-Nationalism and Media: Anti-Press Sentiments by Right-Wing Media in India. *Journalism & Communication Monographs*, *25*(4), 296–364. https://doi.org/10.1177/15226379231201455

Bhat, P., & Chadha, K. (2020). Anti-media populism: Expressions of media distrust by right-wing media in India. *Journal of International and Intercultural Communication*. https://doi.org/10.1080/17513057.2020.1739320

Bleyer-Simon, K., & Benedek, K. (2024). State capture of Romani ethnic media in Hungary. *European Journal of Communication*. https://doi.org/10.1177/02673231241282509

Bolet, D., & Foos, F. (2023). *Media platforming and the normalisation of extreme right views*. OSF. https://doi.org/10.31235/osf.io/urhxy

Bos, L., Brug, W. van der, & Vreese, C. de. (2010). Media coverage of right-wing populist leaders. *Communications*, 35(2), Article 2. https://doi.org/10.1515/comm.2010.008

Broockman, D. E., & Skovron, C. (2018). Bias in Perceptions of Public Opinion among Political Elites. *American Political Science Review*, 112(3), 542–563. https://doi.org/10.1017/S0003055418000011

Budak, C., Goel, S., & Rao, J. M. (2016). Fair and Balanced? Quantifying Media Bias through Crowdsourced Content Analysis. *Public Opinion Quarterly*, 80(S1), 250–271. https://doi.org/10.1093/poq/nfw007

Burrows, E. (2018). Indigenous media producers' perspectives on objectivity, balancing community responsibilities and journalistic obligations. *Media, Culture & Society*, 40(8), Article 8. https://doi.org/10.1177/0163443718764807

Bursztyn, L., Rao, A., Roth, C. P., & Yanagizawa-Drott, D. H. (2020). *Misinformation During a Pandemic*. National Bureau of Economic Research. https://doi.org/10.3386/w27417

Bustamante, C. G. de, & Relly, J. E. (2016). Professionalism Under Threat of Violence: Journalism, reflexivity, and the potential for collective professional autonomy in northern Mexico. *Journalism Studies*, 17(6), 684–702. https://doi.org/10.1080/1461670X.2015.1006903

Callison, C., Young, M. L., Callison, C., & Young, M. L. (2020). *Reckoning: Journalism's Limits and Possibilities*. Oxford University Press.

Cammaerts, B. (2009). Radical pluralism and free speech in online public spaces: The case of North Belgian extreme right discourses. *International Journal of Cultural Studies*, 12(6), 555–575. https://doi.org/10.1177/1367877909342479

Carlin, R. E., & Love, G. J. (2018). Political Competition, Partisanship and Interpersonal Trust in Electoral Democracies. *British Journal of Political Science*, 48(1), 115–139. https://doi.org/10.1017/S0007123415000526

Carlson, M., Robinson, S., & Lewis, S. C. (2022). *News After Trump: Journalism's Crisis of Relevance in a Changed Media Culture*. Oxford University Press.

Carson, A., & Wright, S. (2022). Fake news and democracy: definitions, impact and response. *Australian Journal of Political Science*, 57(3), 221–230. https://doi.org/10.1080/10361146.2022.2122778

Caspi, D. (1981). On politicians' criticism of the mass media. *Journal of Broadcasting*, 25(2), 181–193. https://doi.org/10.1080/08838158109386441

Caspi, D. (2010). Israel: Media System. In *The International Encyclopedia of Communication* (pp. 2536–2541). Blackwell.

Cassino, D. (2016). Fox News and Political Knowledge. In *Fox News and American Politics*. Routledge.

Castells, M. (2010). *The Rise of the Network Society: The Information Age: Economy, Society, and Culture*. Wiley.

Castells, M. (2012). *Networks of Outrage and Hope: Social Movements in the Internet Age*. Polity Press.

Cate, F. H., Fields, D. A., & McBain, J. K. (1994). The Right to Privacy and the Public's Right to Know: The Central Purpose of the Freedom of Information Act. *Administrative Law Review*, 46, 41.

Chadha, K., & Bhat, P. (2022). Alternative News Media and Critique of Mainstream Journalism in India: The Case of OpIndia. *Digital*

Journalism, *10*(8), 1283–1301. https://doi.org/10.1080/21670811. 2022.2118143

Chama, B. (2015, March 1). Tabloid journalism and philosophical discourses surrounding the right to privacy and press freedom. *International Journal of Media & Cultural Politics*. https://doi.org/10.1386/macp.11.1.105_1

Chandler, D., & Munday, R. (2020). Bias. In *A Dictionary of Media and Communication*. Oxford University Press. https://www.oxfordreference.com/view/10.1093/acref/9780198841838.001.0001/acref-9780198841838-e-209

Chen, G. M., Pain, P., Chen, V. Y., Mekelburg, M., Springer, N., & Troger, F. (2020). 'You really have to have a thick skin': A cross-cultural perspective on how online harassment influences female journalists. *Journalism*, *21*(7), 877–895. https://doi.org/10.1177/1464884918768500

Chong, D., & Druckman, J. N. (2007). Framing Theory. *Annual Review of Political Science*, *10*(Volume 10, 2007), 103–126. https://doi.org/10.1146/annurev.polisci.10.072805.103054

Coddington, M., Lewis, S. C., & Belair-Gagnon, V. (2021). The Imagined Audience for News: Where Does a Journalist's Perception of the Audience Come From? *Journalism Studies*. https://doi.org/10.1080/1461670X.2021.1914709

Cohen, I. D. (2025, January 13). Israeli Channel Drops Foreign News Editor From Appearances After Calling for End to War. *Haaretz*. https://www.haaretz.com/israel-news/2025-01-13/ty-article/.premium/israeli-channel-drops-foreign-news-editor-from-appearances-after-calling-for-end-to-war/00000194-6089-d4d0-a1f4-fbed26f00000

Cohen-Almagor, R. (2007). *The Limits of Objective Reporting*. Social Science Research Network.

Sugars, S. (2019, January 30). From fake news to enemy of the people: An anatomy of Trump's tweets. *Committee to Protect Journalists*. https://cpj.org/blog/2019/01/trump-twitter-press-fake-news-enemy-people.php

Committee to Protect Journalists Impunity Index. (2024). https://cpj.org/thematic-reports/haiti-israel-most-likely-to-let-journalists-murders-go-unpunished-cpj-2024-impunity-index-shows/

Confessore, N., & Yourish, K. (2016, March 15). $2 Billion Worth of Free Media for Donald Trump. *The New York Times*. https://www.nytimes.com/2016/03/16/upshot/measuring-donald-trumps-mammoth-advantage-in-free-media.html

Cooper, G. (2021). Populist rhetoric and media misinformation in the 2016 UK Brexit referendum. *The Routledge Companion to Media Disinformation and Populism*. Routledge.

Crawford, C. (2007). *Attack the Messenger: How Politicians Turn You Against the Media*. Rowman & Littlefield Publishers.

Curran, J. (2011). *Media and Democracy*. Taylor & Francis.

Curran, J. (2016). The Internet of Dreams: Reinterpreting the Internet. In J. Curran, N. Fenton, & D. Freedman (Eds.), *Misunderstanding the Internet* (pp. 1–47). Routledge.

Cushion, S., & Lewis, J. (2009). Towards a 'Foxification' of 24-hour news channels in Britain?: An analysis of market-driven and publicly funded news coverage. *Journalism*, *10*(2), 131–153. https://doi.org/10.1177/1464884908100598

Davis, A. (2007). *The Mediation of Power: A Critical Introduction*. Routledge.

Davis, A. (2019). *Political Communication: A New Introduction for Crisis Times*. Polity.

de Albuquerque, A., & Alves, M. (2023). *Bolsonaro's Hate Network: From the fringes to the presidency*. Freie Universität Berlin. https://doi.org/10.48541/DCR.V12.2

de Jonge, L., & Gaufman, E. (2022). The normalisation of the far right in the Dutch media in the run-up to the 2021 general elections. *Discourse & Society*, *33*(6), 773–787. https://doi.org/10.1177/09579265221095418

De Launey, G. (2014, January 21). Serbia transforming from pariah to EU partner. *BBC News*. https://www.bbc.com/news/world-europe-25808463

Deacon, D. (2016, June 27). Media coverage of the EU Referendum. *Centre for Research in Communication and Culture*. https://blog.lboro.ac.uk/crcc/eu-referendum/uk-news-coverage-2016-eu-referendum-report-5-6-may-22-june-2016/

Deuze, M. (2005). What is journalism?: Professional identity and ideology of journalists reconsidered. *Journalism: Theory, Practice & Criticism*, *6*(4), Article 4. https://doi.org/10.1177/1464884905056815

Donaway, R. R., Silva, D. E., & Hutchens, M. J. (2024). Different Year, (Mostly) Same Coverage: Comparing the 2016 and 2020 Election News Posted on Facebook. *Journalism & Mass Communication Quarterly*. https://doi.org/10.1177/10776990241260832

Donegan, M. (2021, March 30). Why did the Washington Post ban a sexual assault survivor from reporting on rape? *The Guardian*. https://www.theguardian.com/commentisfree/2021/mar/30/washington-post-felicia-sonmez-sexual-assault-sexism

Downs, W. M. (2002). How Effective is the Cordon Sanitaire? Lessons from Efforts to Contain the Far Right in Belgium, France, Denmark and Norway. *Journal Für Konflikt Und Gewaltforschung (JKG)*, *4*(1), Article 1. https://doi.org/10.11576/jkg-5614

Druckman, J. N. (2001). On the Limits of Framing Effects: Who Can Frame? *The Journal of Politics*, *63*(4), 1041–1066. https://doi.org/10.1111/0022-3816.00100

Duyn, E. V., & Collier, J. (2019). Priming and Fake News: The Effects of Elite Discourse on Evaluations of News Media. *Mass Communication and Society*, 22(1), 29–48. https://doi.org/10.1080/15205436.2018.1511807

Duyn, E. V., & Duyn, E. V. (2021). *Democracy Lives in Darkness: How and Why People Keep Their Politics a Secret*. Oxford University Press.

Egelhofer, J. L., Aaldering, L., & Lecheler, S. (2021). Delegitimizing the media? Analyzing politicians' media criticism on social media. *Journal of Language and Politics*, 20(5), 653–675. https://doi.org/10.1075/jlp.20081.ege

Egelhofer, J. L., Boyer, M., Lecheler, S., & Aaldering, L. (2022). Populist attitudes and politicians' disinformation accusations: effects on perceptions of media and politicians. *Journal of Communication*. https://doi.org/10.1093/joc/jqac031

Egelhofer, J. L., & Lecheler, S. (2019). Fake news as a two-dimensional phenomenon: a framework and research agenda. *Annals of the International Communication Association*, 43(2), Article 2.

Elbaz, S., & Bar-Tal, D. (2019). Voluntary silence: Israeli media self-censorship during the Second Lebanon War. *Conflict & Communication Online*, 18(2), Article 2.

Ellinas, A. A. (2018). *Media and the Radical Right*. The Oxford Handbook of the Radical Right.

Engesser, S., Ernst, N., Esser, F., & Büchel, F. (2017). Populism and social media: how politicians spread a fragmented ideology. *Information, Communication & Society*, 20(8), 1109–1126. https://doi.org/10.1080/1369118X.2016.1207697

Entman, R. M. (2007). Framing Bias: Media in the Distribution of Power. *Journal of Communication*, 57(1), 163–173. https://doi.org/10.1111/j.1460-2466.2006.00336.x

Fahmy, S. S., Salama, M., & Alsaba, M. R. (2024). Shattered lives, unbroken stories: journalists' perspectives from the frontlines of the Israel–Gaza war. *Online Media and Global Communication*, *3*(2), 151–180. https://doi.org/10.1515/omgc-2024-0012

Farhall, K., Carson, A., Wright, S., Gibbons, A., & Lukamto, W. (2019). Political Elites' Use of Fake News Discourse Across Communications Platforms. *International Journal of Communication*, *13*, 4353–4375.

Fawzi, N. (2019). Untrustworthy News and the Media as "Enemy of the People?" How a Populist Worldview Shapes Recipients' Attitudes toward the Media. *The International Journal of Press/Politics*, *24*(2), Article 2. https://doi.org/10.1177/1940161218811981

Ferree, M. M., Gamson, W. A., Gerhards, J., & Rucht, D. (2002). Four models of the public sphere in modern democracies. *Theory and Society*, *31*(3), 289–324. https://doi.org/10.1023/A:1016284431021

Figenschou, T. U., & Ihlebæk, K. A. (2019). Challenging Journalistic Authority. *Journalism Studies*, *20*(9), Article 9. https://doi.org/10.1080/1461670X.2018.1500868

Filc, D. (2009). Netanyahu's post-populism. *The Political Right in Israel*. Routledge.

Fitzgerald, A. A. (2019). Letting the Fascists Speak for Themselves: The Enabling of Authoritarians and the Need for a Partisan Press. *Journal of Communication Inquiry*, *43*(1), Article 1. https://doi.org/10.1177/0196859918786938

Fletcher, R. (2020, January 9). Trust will get worse before it gets better. *Reuters Institute Digital News Report*. https://www.digitalnewsreport.org/publications/2020/trust-will-get-worse-gets-better/

Flores, R. (2016, November 12). In '60 Minutes' interview, Donald Trump weighs Twitter use as president. *CBS News*. https://www.cbsnews.com/news/donald-trump-60-minutes-interview-weighs-twitter-use-as-president/

Florini, A. (2007). *Right to Know: Transparency for an Open World*. Columbia University Press.

Forde, K. R. (Ed.). (2021). *Journalism and Jim Crow*. UI Press.

Freiling, I., Krause, N. M., Scheufele, D. A., & Brossard, D. (2021). Believing and sharing misinformation, fact-checks, and accurate information on social media: The role of anxiety during COVID-19. *New Media & Society*. https://doi.org/10.1177/14614448211011451

Frisby, C. (2018). 'Oh, See What We Say:' A Content Analysis of Partisan Media's Framing of the 'take a knee' silent protest by the NFL. *International Journal of Humanities and Social Science*, 4, 6.

Fuchs, C. (2018). *Digital Demagogue: Authoritarian Capitalism in the Age of Trump and Twitter*. Pluto Press.

Gaber, I., & Fisher, C. (2021). "Strategic Lying": The Case of Brexit and the 2019 U.K. Election. *The International Journal of Press/Politics*. https://doi.org/10.1177/1940161221994100

Galston, W. A. (2018). *Anti-Pluralism: The Populist Threat to Liberal Democracy*. Yale University Press.

Gans, H. J. (1979). *Deciding What's News: A Study of CBS Evening News, NBC Nightly News, Newsweek, and Time*. Pantheon Books.

Gavin, N. T. (2018). Media definitely *do* matter: Brexit, immigration, climate change and beyond. *The British Journal of Politics and International Relations*, 20(4), 827–845. https://doi.org/10.1177/1369148118799260

Genç, K. (2014). Turkey's "treacherous" women journalists: Dangerous times for female reporters. *Index on Censorship*, 43(4), 88–92. https://doi.org/10.1177/0306422014560506

Georgantopoulos, M. A. (2016, October 14). *CNN's President Says It Was A Mistake To Air So Many Trump Rallies And 'Let Them Run'*. BuzzFeed News. https://www.buzzfeednews.com/article/maryanngeorgantopoulos/cnn-president-mistake-to-air-so-many-trump-rallies

George, C. (2023). Left or Right, Reactionary Anti-Liberal Media Are Worth Closer Study. *Journalism & Communication Monographs*, *25*(4), 365–369. https://doi.org/10.1177/15226379231201457

George, C. (2024, June 11). From scandal to business as usual: normalising controls over academia. *Knowledge Praxis*. https://knowledgepraxis.academia.sg/blog/2024/06/11/cherian-george/

Gerbaudo, P. (2018). Social media and populism: An elective affinity? *Media, Culture & Society*, *40*(5), Article 5. https://doi.org/10.1177/0163443718772192

Gillmor, D. (2006). *We the Media: Grassroots Journalism by the People, for the People*. O'Reilly Media.

Ginosar, A., & Reich, Z. (2022). Obsessive–Activist Journalists: A New Model of Journalism? *Journalism Practice*, *16*(4), 660–680. https://doi.org/10.1080/17512786.2020.1816488

Griffen, S. (2020). Hungary: a lesson in media control. *British Journalism Review*, *31*(1), 57–62. https://doi.org/10.1177/0956474820910071

Grossman, G., Margalit, Y., & Mitts, T. (2022). How the Ultra-Rich Use Media Ownership as a Political Investment. *The Journal of Politics*. https://doi.org/10.1086/719415

Grossmann, M., & Hopkins, D. A. (2016). *Asymmetric Politics: Ideological Republicans and Group Interest Democrats*. Oxford University Press.

Hadjicostis, M., & Wilson, J. (2024, June 17). 2 political outliers claim seats in European Parliament by leveraging social media's viral power. *AP News*. https://apnews.com/article/election-panayiotou-social-media-spain-alvise-perez-b19afbc4e56d71143bb513de111fef1a

Hagemeister, F. (2022). Populism and propagation of far-right extremism. *European Journal of Political Economy*, *72*, 102116. https://doi.org/10.1016/j.ejpoleco.2021.102116

Hall, S., Roberts, B., Clarke, J., Jefferson, T., & Critcher, C. (1978). *Policing the Crisis: Mugging, the State, and Law and Order*. Macmillan.

Haller, A., & Holt, K. (2018). Paradoxical populism: how PEGIDA relates to mainstream and alternative media. *Information, Communication & Society*. https://doi.org/10.1080/1369118X.2018.1449882

Hallin, D. (2000). A Fall from Grace? In R. Giles & R. W. Snyder (Eds.), *What's Fair?* (pp. 47–52). https://doi.org/10.4324/9781351299404-10

Hallin, D. C. (1989). *The Uncensored War: The Media and Vietnam*. University of California Press.

Hallin, D. C., & Mancini, P. (2004). *Comparing Media Systems: Three Models of Media and Politics*. Cambridge University Press.

Halperin, E. (2024). *Footnote: How We Let Hate and Extremism Tear Us Apart*. Kinneret Zmora Beitan. [Hebrew]

Harcup, T., & O'Neill, D. (2017). What is News? *Journalism Studies*, 18(12), 1470–1488. https://doi.org/10.1080/1461670X.2016.1150193

Harding, S. (1992). After the Neutrality Ideal: Science, Politics, and 'Strong Objectivity'. *Social Research*, 59(3), 567–587.

Harrison, J., & Pukallus, S. (2021). The politics of impunity: A study of journalists' experiential accounts of impunity in Bulgaria, Democratic Republic of Congo, India, Mexico and Pakistan. *Journalism*, 22(2), 303–319. https://doi.org/10.1177/1464884918778248

Harvey, W. S. (2011). Strategies for conducting elite interviews. *Qualitative Research*, 11(4), 431–441. https://doi.org/10.1177/1468794111404329

Haskell, J. (2000). *Direct Democracy Or Representative Government? Dispelling The Populist Myth*. Perseus.

Hayes, D., & Guardino, M. (2010). Whose Views Made the News? Media Coverage and the March to War in Iraq. *Political Communication*, 27(1), 59–87. https://doi.org/10.1080/10584600903502615

Hayes, J. (2003). The Right to Reply: A Conflict of Fundamental Rights. *Columbia Journal of Law and Social Problems*, 37, 551.

Heltzel, G., & Laurin, K. (2024). Why Twitter Sometimes Rewards What Most People Disapprove of: The Case of Cross-Party Political Relations. *Psychological Science*, 35(9), 976–994. https://doi.org/10.1177/09567976241258149

Hemmer, N. (2016). *Messengers of the Right: Conservative Media and the Transformation of American Politics*. University of Pennsylvania Press.

Hendricks, J. A., & Denton, R. E. (2010). *Communicator-in-Chief: How Barack Obama Used New Media Technology to Win the White House*. Lexington Books.

Herman, E. S., & Chomsky, N. (1988). *Manufacturing Consent: The Political Economy of the Mass Media*. Pantheon Books.

Herpen, M. H. V. (2021). A plea for a *cordon sanitaire*. The end of populism. https://www.manchesterhive.com/display/9781526154156/9781526154156.00018.xml

Hirsch-Hoefler, S., & Mudde, C. (2020). *The Israeli Settler Movement: Assessing and Explaining Social Movement Success*. Cambridge University Press.

Høiby, M. (2020). The "triple effect" silencing female journalists online: A theoretical exploration. *Journalist Safety and Self-Censorship*. Routledge.

Hopmann, D. N., & Schuck, A. R. T. (2023). Journalists' Misjudgement of Audience Opinion. *The International Journal of Press/Politics*, 28(3), 648–670. https://doi.org/10.1177/19401612211052297

Huddy, L. (2013). From Group Identity to Political Cohesion and Commitment. In L. Huddy, D. O. Sears, & J. S. Levy (Eds.), *The Oxford Handbook of Political Psychology*. Oxford University Press. https://doi.org/10.1093/oxfordhb/9780199760107.013.0023

Ivask, S. (2020). A way to silence journalists? Estonian female journalists' experiences with harassment and self-censorship. In *Journalist Safety and Self-Censorship*. Routledge.

Iyengar, S., Lelkes, Y., Levendusky, M., Malhotra, N., & Westwood, S. J. (2019). The Origins and Consequences of Affective Polarization in the United States. *Annual Review of Political Science*, 22(1), 129–146. https://doi.org/10.1146/annurev-polisci-051117-073034

Jamieson, K. H., & Cappella, J. N. (2008). *Echo Chamber: Rush Limbaugh and the Conservative Media Establishment*. Oxford University Press.

Jamil, S. (2020). Suffering in Silence: The Resilience of Pakistan's Female Journalists to Combat Sexual Harassment, Threats and Discrimination. *Journalism Practice*, 14(2), 150–170. https://doi.org/10.1080/17512786.2020.1725599

Jasser, J., Garibay, I., Scheinert, S., & Mantzaris, A. V. (2022). Controversial information spreads faster and further than non-controversial information in Reddit. *Journal of Computational Social Science*, 5(1), 111–122. https://doi.org/10.1007/s42001-021-00121-z

Jones, R. A., & Sun, L. G. (2017). Enemy Construction and the Press. *SSRN Electronic Journal*. https://doi.org/10.2139/ssrn.2929708

Juntunen, L. (2010). Explaining the Need for Speed: Speed and Competition as Challenges to Journalism Ethics. In S. Cushion & J. Lewis, *The Rise of 24-Hour News Television: Global Perspectives* (pp. 167–182). Peter Lang.

Kampf, Z., & Daskal, E. (2011). When the Watchdog Bites: Insulting Politicians On Air. In M. Ekström & M. Patrona (Eds.), *Talking Politics in Broadcast Media: Cross-cultural perspectives on political interviewing, journalism and accountability* (pp. 177–200). John Benjamins Publishing.

Kantola, A., & Harju, A. A. (2021). Tackling the emotional toll together: How journalists address harassment with connective practices. *Journalism.* https://doi.org/10.1177/14648849211055293

Katz, J., Barris, M., & Jain, A. (2013). *The Social Media President: Barack Obama and the Politics of Digital Engagement.* Springer.

Keen, A. (2008). *The Cult of the Amateur: How blogs, MySpace, YouTube and the rest of today's user-generated media are killing our culture and economy.* Nicholas Brealey Publishing.

Kenyon, J., Binder, J., & Baker-Beall, C. (2022). Understanding the Role of the Internet in the Process of Radicalisation: An Analysis of Convicted Extremists in England and Wales. *Studies in Conflict & Terrorism.* https://doi.org/10.1080/1057610X.2022.2065902

Kim, C., & Shin, W. (2022). Harassment of Journalists and Its Aftermath: Anti-Press Violence, Psychological Suffering, and an Internal Chilling Effect. *Digital Journalism.* https://doi.org/10.1080/21670811.2022.2034027

Kim, J. W., Guess, A., Nyhan, B., & Reifler, J. (2021). The Distorting Prism of Social Media: How Self-Selection and Exposure to Incivility Fuel Online Comment Toxicity. *Journal of Communication.* https://doi.org/10.1093/joc/jqab034

Kizito, K. (2021). Media: Fox News, Racism, and White America in the Age of Trump. In D. W. Austin & B. P. Bowser (Eds.), *Impacts of Racism on White Americans In the Age of Trump* (pp. 137–149). Springer International Publishing.

Klumpp, T., Mialon, H. M., & Williams, M. A. (2016). The Business of American Democracy: Citizens United, Independent Spending, and Elections. *The Journal of Law and Economics*, 59(1), 1–43. https://doi.org/10.1086/685691

Koirala, S. (2020). Female Journalists' Experience of Online Harassment: A Case Study of Nepal. *Media and Communication*, 8(1), Article 1. https://doi.org/10.17645/mac.v8i1.2541

Koliska, M., & Assmann, K. (2021). Lügenpresse: The lying press and German journalists' responses to a stigma. *Journalism*, 22(11), 2729–2746. https://doi.org/10.1177/1464884919894088

Koliska, M., Chadha, K., & Burns, A. (2020). Talking Back: Journalists Defending Attacks Against their Profession in the Trump Era. *Journalism Studies*, 21(11), 1496–1513. https://doi.org/10.1080/1461670X.2020.1763190

Koltay, A. (2013). The right of reply in a European comparative perspective. *Acta Juridica Hungarica*, 54(1), 73–89. https://doi.org/10.1556/ajur.54.2013.1.6

Krämer, B. (2018a). How Journalism Responds to Right-Wing Populist Criticism. In K. Otto & A. Köhler (Eds.), *Trust in Media and Journalism* (pp. 137–154). Springer Fachmedien Wiesbaden. https://doi.org/10.1007/978-3-658-20765-6_8

Krämer, B. (2018b). Populism, Media, and the Form of Society. *Communication Theory*, 28(4), Article 4. https://doi.org/10.1093/ct/qty017

Krämer, B., & Langmann, K. (2020). Professionalism as a Response to Right-Wing Populism? An Analysis of a Metajournalistic Discourse. *International Journal of Communication*, 14(2020), 5643–5662.

Kreiss, D. (2012). *Taking Our Country Back: The Crafting of Networked Politics from Howard Dean to Barack Obama*. Oxford University Press.

Kull, S., Ramsay, C., & Lewis, E. (2003). Misperceptions, the Media, and the Iraq War. *Political Science Quarterly*, 118, 569.

Ladd, J. M. (2011). *Why Americans Hate the Media and How It Matters*. Princeton University Press.

Ladd, J. M., & Podkul, A. R. (2020). *Sowing Distrust of the News Media as an Electoral Strategy*. The Oxford Handbook of Electoral Persuasion. https://doi.org/10.1093/oxfordhb/9780190860806.013.17

Lajevardi, N., Oskooii, K. A. R., & Walker, H. (2022). Hate, amplified? Social media news consumption and support for anti-Muslim policies. *Journal of Public Policy*, 42(4), 656–683. https://doi.org/10.1017/S0143814X22000083

Lawrence, R. G., & Moon, Y. E. (2021). "We Aren't Fake News": The Information Politics of the 2018 #FreePress Editorial Campaign. *Journalism Studies*, 22(2), 155–173. https://doi.org/10.1080/1461670X.2020.1831399

Le Vu Phung, N. (2020). The Influences of Misogynist Online Harassment on German Female Journalists and their Personal and Professional Lives [Master's thesis, Ohio University]. http://rave.ohiolink.edu/etdc/view?acc_num=ohiou1594828390923411

Levendusky, M. (2013). *How Partisan Media Polarize America*. University of Chicago Press.

Levendusky, M. S. (2017). Americans, Not Partisans: Can Priming American National Identity Reduce Affective Polarization? *The Journal of Politics*, 80(1), 59–70. https://doi.org/10.1086/693987

Levi, Y., & Agmon, S. (2020). Beyond culture and economy: Israel's security-driven populism. *Contemporary Politics*, 27(3), 292–315. https://doi.org/10.1080/13569775.2020.1864163

Levitsky, S., & Ziblatt, D. (2018). *How Democracies Die: The International Bestseller: What History Reveals About Our Future*. Viking.

Lewis, A. (2009). A Public Right to Know About Public Institutions: The First Amendment as Sword. In *Media Freedom and Contempt of Court* (pp. 35–60). Routledge. https://doi.org/10.4324/9781315091297-4

Lewis, D. (2012). *Direct Democracy and Minority Rights: A Critical Assessment of the Tyranny of the Majority in the American States.* Routledge.

Lewis, S. C., & Molyneux, L. (2018). A Decade of Research on Social Media and Journalism: Assumptions, Blind Spots, and a Way Forward. *Media and Communication*, 6(4), Article 4. https://doi.org/10.17645/mac.v6i4.1562

Lichter, S. R. (2017). Theories of Media Bias. *The Oxford Handbook of Political Communication.* https://doi.org/10.1093/oxfordhb/9780199793471.013.44

Liebes, T. (1997). Internalizing censorship: How journalists reconcile freedom of expression with national loyalty and responsibility. In *Reporting the Arab-Israeli Conflict: How Hegemony Works* (pp. 28–48). Routledge.

Lim, G., & Bradshaw, S. (2023). *Chilling Legislation: Tracking the Impact of "Fake News" Laws on Press Freedom Internationally.* Center for International Media Assistance. https://www.cima.ned.org/publication/chilling-legislation/

Limor, Y., & Helman, E. (2003). 'No Reply?' The Right of Reply in Journalistic Ethics and the Ruling by the Press Council in Israel. *Kesher*, 33(May), 16–31.

Lo, W. H., & Wong, T. C. (2021). Hong Kong: Free Press Under Existential Threat. In *The Media for Democracy Monitor 2021* (pp. 231–274). https://doi.org/10.48335/9789188855428-6

Lovett, A. (2023). The ethics of asymmetric politics. *Politics, Philosophy & Economics*, 22(1), 3–30. https://doi.org/10.1177/1470594X221133445

Lynch, J., & McGoldrick, A. (2005). *Peace journalism.* Hawthorn Press.

Maltz, J. (2016, January 4). The lawyer for Jewish terrorists who started out by stealing Rabin's car emblem. *Haaretz*. https://www.haaretz.com/israel-news/2016-01-04/ty-article/.premium/jewish-terrorisms-star-lawyer/0000017f-eda1-da6f-a77f-fdaff1f00000

Mandelkern, R. (2015). A Brief History of Neoliberalism in Israel. In D. Harvey, *A Brief History of Neoliberalism [Hebrew]*. Molad – Centre for the renewal of Israeli democracy.

Mannell, K., & Meese, J. (2022). From Doom-Scrolling to News Avoidance: Limiting News as a Wellbeing Strategy During COVID Lockdown. *Journalism Studies*, 23(3), 302–319. https://doi.org/10.1080/1461670X.2021.2021105

Maras, S. (2012). *Objectivity in Journalism*. Polity Press.

Markowitz-Elfassi, D., Sheafer, T., Tsfati, Y., Weimann, G., & Wolfsfeld, G. (2018). Political Communication and Israeli Politics. *The Oxford Handbook of Israeli Politics and Society*. https://doi.org/10.1093/oxfordhb/9780190675585.013.38

Martin, G. J., & Yurukoglu, A. (2017). Bias in Cable News: Persuasion and Polarization. *American Economic Review*, 107(9), 2565–2599. https://doi.org/10.1257/aer.20160812

Marzolf, M. T. (1990). *Civilizing Voices: American Press Criticism, 1880–1950*. Addison-Wesley Longman.

Mazzoleni, G., Stewart, J., & Horsfield, B. (2003). *The Media and Neo-Populism: A Contemporary Comparative Analysis*. Bloomsbury.

McChesney, R. W. (2004). Understanding U.S. Journalism: Right-Wing Criticism and Political Coverage. In *The Problem of the Media*. Monthly Review Press.

McChesney, R. W. (2013). *Digital Disconnect: How Capitalism is Turning the Internet Against Democracy*. The New Press.

McChesney, R. W., & Nichols, J. (2002). *Our Media, Not Theirs: The Democratic Struggle Against Corporate Media*. Seven Stories Press.

McKnight, D. (2010). Rupert Murdoch's News Corporation: A Media Institution with A Mission. *Historical Journal of Film, Radio and Television*, *30*(3), 303–316. https://doi.org/10.1080/01439685.2010.505021

Meeks, L. (2020). Defining the Enemy: How Donald Trump Frames the News Media. *Journalism & Mass Communication Quarterly*, *97*(1), 211–234. https://doi.org/10.1177/1077699019857676

Megiddo, G. (2018, May 4). Making water from air: Why is Netanyahu doing PR for this Israeli startup. *Haaretz*. https://www.haaretz.com/israel-news/.premium-making-water-from-air-why-is-netanyahu-doing-pr-for-this-startup-1.6054458

Meirick, P. (2013). Motivated Misperception? Party, Education, Partisan News, and Belief in "Death Panels". *Journalism & Mass Communication Quarterly*, *90*, 39–57. https://doi.org/10.1177/1077699012468696

Meyers, C. (1993). Justifying Journalistic Harms: Right to Know Vs. Interest in Knowing. *Journal of Mass Media Ethics*, *8*(3), 133–146. https://doi.org/10.1207/s15327728jmme0803_1

Miller, J. M., & Krosnick, J. A. (2000). News Media Impact on the Ingredients of Presidential Evaluations: Politically Knowledgeable Citizens Are Guided by a Trusted Source. *American Journal of Political Science*, *44*(2), 301–315. https://doi.org/10.2307/2669312

Miller, K. C., & Lewis, S. C. (2020). Journalists, harassment, and emotional labor: The case of women in on-air roles at US local television stations. *Journalism*, 1464884919899016. https://doi.org/10.1177/1464884919899016

Moffitt, B. (2018). Populism 2.0: Social media and the false allure of 'unmediated' representation. In *Populism and the Crisis of Democracy*. Routledge.

Mokrosinska, D. (2018). The People's Right to Know and State Secrecy. *Canadian Journal of Law & Jurisprudence*, *31*(1), 87–106. https://doi.org/10.1017/cjlj.2018.4

Moore, M. (2024). Keeping Democracies Alive: The Role of Public Service Media. *The Political Quarterly*, *95*(1), 108–112. https://doi.org/10.1111/1467-923X.13359

Morozov, E. (2012). *The Net Delusion: The Dark Side of Internet Freedom*. PublicAffairs.

Morris, D. S., & Morris, J. S. (n.d.). Partisan media exposure, polarization, and candidate evaluations in the 2016 general election. *Social Science Quarterly*. https://doi.org/10.1111/ssqu.13182

Moyakine, E., & Tabachnik, A. (2021). Struggling to strike the right balance between interests at stake: The 'Yarovaya', 'Fake news' and 'Disrespect' laws as examples of ill-conceived legislation in the age of modern technology. *Computer Law & Security Review*, *40*, 105512. https://doi.org/10.1016/j.clsr.2020.105512

Müller, J.W. (2016). *What Is Populism?* University of Pennsylvania Press.

Nadler, A., & Bauer, A. J. (2019). *News on the Right: Studying Conservative News Cultures*. Oxford University Press.

Najjar, O. A. (1996). From enemies to 'colleagues': Relations between Palestinian journalists and Israeli West Bank beat reporters, 1967–1994. *Gazette*, *55*(2), Article 2. https://doi.org/10.1177/001654929605500203

Neff, T., Popiel, P., & Pickard, V. (2022). Philadelphia's news media system: Which audiences are underserved? *Journal of Communication*, *72*(4), 476–487. https://doi.org/10.1093/joc/jqac018

Nelson, J. L. (2021). *Imagined Audiences: How Journalists Perceive and Pursue the Public*. Oxford University Press.

Newman, N., Fletcher, R., Schulz, A., And, S., & Nielsen, R. K. (2020). *Reuters Institute Digital News Report 2020*.

Nicola, N. (2010). Black face, white voice: Rush Limbaugh and the "message" of race. *Journal of Language and Politics*, 9(2), 281–309. https://doi.org/10.1075/jlp.9.2.06nic

Nielsen, R. K. (2017). The One Thing Journalism Just Might do for Democracy. *Journalism Studies*, 18(10), 1251–1262. https://doi.org/10.1080/1461670X.2017.1338152

Nilsson, M. L., & Örnebring, H. (2016). Journalism Under Threat. *Journalism Practice*, 10(7), Article 7. https://doi.org/10.1080/17512786.2016.1164614

Noble, S. U. (2018). *Algorithms of Oppression: How Search Engines Reinforce Racism*. New York University Press.

Noelle-Neumann, E. (1974). The Spiral of Silence. *Journal of Communication*, 24(2), Article 2. https://doi.org/10.1111/j.1460-2466.1974.tb00367.x

Nygren, G., Glowacki, Michal, Hök, Jöran, Kiria, Ilya, Orlova, Dariya, & and Taradai, D. (2018). Journalism in the Crossfire: Media coverage of the war in Ukraine in 2014. *Journalism Studies*, 19(7), 1059–1078. https://doi.org/10.1080/1461670X.2016.1251332

Oates, S. (2008). Media and War. In *Introduction to Media and Politics* (pp. 112–133). SAGE Publications. https://doi.org/10.4135/9781446211809

Pain, P., & Korin, E. (2021). 'Everything is dimming out, little by little:' examining self-censorship among Venezuelan journalists. *Communication Research and Practice*, 7(1), 71–88. https://doi.org/10.1080/22041451.2020.1824435

Palfrey, J., & Gasser, U. (2008). *Born digital: Understanding the first generation of digital natives*. Basic Books.

Panievsky, A. (2021). The Strategic Bias: How Journalists Respond to Antimedia Populism. *The International Journal of Press/Politics*, 27(4), 808–826. https://doi.org/10.1177/19401612211022656

Panievsky, A., & Blumell, L. E. (2025). The safety threats experienced by UK journalists and their physical, emotional, and mental well-being. In *UK Journalists in the 2020s*. Reuters Institute for the Study of Journalism. https://reutersinstitute.politics.ox.ac.uk/uk-journalists-2020s/6-safety-threats-experienced-uk-journalists-and-their-physical-emotional

Panievsky, A., David, Y., Gidron, N., & Sheffer, L. (2024). Imagined Journalists: New Framework for Studying Media–Audiences Relationship in Populist Times. *The International Journal of Press/Politics*, 30(1), 38–62. https://doi.org/10.1177/19401612241231541

Papandrea, M.R. (2005). Under Attack: The Public's Right to Know and the War on Terror. *Boston College Third World Law Journal*.

Peck, R. (2019). *Fox Populism: Branding Conservatism as Working Class*. Cambridge University Press.

Peretz, S. (2021). Israeli Media Also Helped Itamar Ben-Gvir. *Haaretz*. https://www.haaretz.com/opinion/2021-02-17/ty-article-opinion/.premium/israeli-media-also-helped-itamar-ben-gvir/0000017f-f506-d044-adff-f7ff6b070000

Peri, Y. (2004). *Telepopulism: Media and Politics in Israel*. Stanford University Press.

Peri, Y. (2007). Intractable Conflict and the Media. *Israel Studies*, 12(1), 79–102.

Peri, Y. (2011). The Impact of National Security on the Development of Media Systems: The Case of Israel. In D. C. Hallin & P. Mancini (Eds.), *Comparing Media Systems Beyond the Western World* (pp. 11–25). Cambridge University Press.

Persico, O. (2024). *Women's Representation Index 2023: More than two-thirds of the journalists appearing on current affairs programmes are men*. Ha'ayin Hashviit. https://www.the7eye.org.il/507811

Phillips, W. (2013). The House That Fox Built: Anonymous, Spectacle, and Cycles of Amplification. *Television & New Media*, 14(6), Article 6. https://doi.org/10.1177/1527476412452799

Philo, G., & Berry, M. (2004). *Bad News From Israel*. Pluto Press.

Philo, G., & Berry, M. (2007). *More Bad News From Israel*. Pluto Press.

Pickard, V. (2019). *Democracy Without Journalism?: Confronting the Misinformation Society*. Oxford University Press.

Pilet, J.B., Sheffer, L., Helfer, L., Varone, F., Vliegenthart, R., & Walgrave, S. (2024). Do Politicians Outside the United States Also Think Voters Are More Conservative than They Really Are? *American Political Science Review*, 118(2), 1037–1045. https://doi.org/10.1017/S0003055423000527

Pingree, R. J., Watson, B., Sui, M., Searles, K., Kalmoe, N. P., Darr, J. P., Santia, M., & Bryanov, K. (2018). Checking facts and fighting back: Why journalists should defend their profession. *PLOS ONE*, 13(12), Article 12. https://doi.org/10.1371/journal.pone.0208600

Pintak, L. (2023). Journalism in MENA. In *The Handbook of Media and Culture in the Middle East* (pp. 107–121). John Wiley & Sons. https://doi.org/10.1002/9781119637134.ch11

Postman, N. (1985). *Amusing Ourselves to Death*. Penguin.

Quandt, T. (2018). Dark Participation. *Media and Communication*, 6(4), Article 4. https://doi.org/10.17645/mac.v6i4.1519

Quandt, T., & Klapproth, J. (2023). Dark Participation: A Critical Overview. In *Oxford Research Encyclopedia of Communication*. https://doi.org/10.1093/acrefore/9780190228613.013.1155

Reich, Z., Barnoy, A., & Hertzog, L. (2016). Journalists in Israel. In *Worlds of Journalism Study*. www.worldsofjournalism.org

Reifowitz, I. (2021). The Legacy of Rush Limbaugh Will Always Be Tied to Donald Trump. *The Forum*, 19(3), 439–458. https://doi.org/10.1515/for-2021-0022

Relly, J. E. (2021). Online harassment of journalists as a consequence of populism, mis/disinformation, and impunity. In *The Routledge Companion to Media Disinformation and Populism*. Routledge.

Reporters Without Borders. (2017a). *Journalism weakened by democracy's erosion*. https://rsf.org/en/journalism-weakened-democracys-erosion

Reporters Without Borders. (2017b). *Who owns the Media in Serbia?* https://rsf.org/en/who-owns-media-serbia

Reporters Without Borders. (2023). *Hungary's sovereignty law is Viktor Orban's new dangerous provocation targeting independent media*. https://rsf.org/en/hungary-s-sovereignty-law-viktor-orban-s-new-dangerous-provocation-targeting-independent-media

Rhodes, S. C. (2021). Filter Bubbles, Echo Chambers, and Fake News: How Social Media Conditions Individuals to Be Less Critical of Political Misinformation. *Political Communication*. https://doi.org/10.1080/10584609.2021.1910887

Riebe, T., Pätsch, K., Kaufhold, M.-A., & Reuter, C. (2018). *From Conspiracies to Insults: A Case Study of Radicalisation in Social Media Discourse*. https://dl.gi.de/handle/20.500.12116/16795

Rogenhofer, J. M., & Panievsky, A. (2020). Antidemocratic populism in power: Comparing Erdoğan's Turkey with Modi's India and Netanyahu's Israel. *Democratization*, 27(8), 1394–1412. https://doi.org/10.1080/13510347.2020.1795135

Roman, N., Wanta, W., & Buniak, I. (2017). Information wars: Eastern Ukraine military conflict coverage in the Russian, Ukrainian and U.S. newscasts. *International Communication Gazette*, 79(4), 357–378. https://doi.org/10.1177/1748048516682138

Rone, J. (2023). "Enemies of the people"? Diverging discourses on sovereignty in media coverage of Brexit. *British Politics*, 18(4), 519–537. https://doi.org/10.1057/s41293-021-00157-9

Rosen, J. (1999). *What Are Journalists For?* Yale University Press.

Rosen, J., & Merritt, D. (1994). *Public Journalism: Theory and Practice.* Kettering Foundation.

Rubin, S., & Parker, C. (2022). How Israeli media propelled Netanyahu and Itamar Ben Gvir to power. *The Washington Post.* https://www.washingtonpost.com/world/2022/11/03/israel-election-netanyahu-ben-gvir/

Rushkoff, D. (2003). *Open Source Democracy: How Online Communication is Changing Offline Politics.* Demos.

Ryan, M. (2001). Journalistic Ethics, Objectivity, Existential Journalism, Standpoint Epistemology, and Public Journalism. *Journal of Mass Media Ethics*, 16(1), 3–22. https://doi.org/10.1207/S15327728JMME1601_2

Savage, M. (2025, March 23). Press freedom in Serbia is facing a dangerous turning point, editors warn. *The Guardian.* https://www.theguardian.com/world/2025/mar/23/press-freedom-in-serbia-is-facing-a-dangerous-turning-point-warn-editors

Sbaraini Fontes, G., & Marques, F. P. J. (2022). Defending democracy or amplifying populism? Journalistic coverage, Twitter, and users' engagement in Bolsonaro's Brazil. *Journalism.* https://doi.org/10.1177/14648849221075429

Schejter, A. M., & Yemini, M. (2016). Media Ownership and Concentration in Israel. In *Who Owns the World's Media?* Oxford University Press. https://doi.org/10.1093/acprof:oso/9780199987238.003.0030

Scheppele, K. (2018). Autocratic Legalism. *University of Chicago Law Review*, 85(2). https://chicagounbound.uchicago.edu/uclrev/vol85/iss2/2

Schmidt, T. R. (2023). Challenging journalistic objectivity: How journalists of color call for a reckoning. *Journalism.* https://doi.org/10.1177/14648849231160997

Schneider, T. (2021, May 19). Covering unrest from up close, Israel's journalists increasingly in line of fire. *The Times of Israel.* https://

www.timesofisrael.com/covering-unrest-from-up-close-journalists-increasingly-in-the-line-of-fire/

Schudson, M. (1981). *Discovering The News: A Social History Of American Newspapers*. Basic Books.

Schudson, M. (2015). *The Rise of the Right to Know – Politics and the Culture of Transparency, 1945–1975*. Harvard University Press.

Schudson, M. (2018). *Why Journalism Still Matters*. Polity.

Schulz, A., Wirth, W., & Müller, P. (2018). We Are the People and You Are Fake News: A Social Identity Approach to Populist Citizens' False Consensus and Hostile Media Perceptions. *Communication Research*. https://doi.org/10.1177/0093650218794854

Selva, M. (2020). *Fighting Words: Journalism Under Assault in Central and Eastern Europe*. https://reutersinstitute.politics.ox.ac.uk/fighting-words-journalism-under-assault-central-and-eastern-europe

Seol, S., Mejia, J., & Dennis, A. (2024). Lying for Viewers: Commingled Partisan Falsehoods Increase Viewing and Sharing of News Media. *MIS Quarterly*, 48(2):551–582.

Shamir, M., Dvir-Gvirsman, S., & Ventura, R. (2017). Taken captive by the collective identity cleavage: Left and right in the 2015 elections. In *The Elections in Israel 2015* (pp. 139–164). Taylor and Francis. https://doi.org/10.4324/9781315112121

Sharon, A. (2023, July 11). Israel Is Hurtling Toward a New Kind of Illiberal Regime. *Haaretz*. https://www.haaretz.com/israel-news/2023-05-20/ty-article-magazine/.highlight/israel-is-hurtling-toward-a-new-kind-of-illiberal-regime/00000188-35a8-d7fd-adec-ffebca370000

Sheafer, T., & Weimann, G. (2005). An Empirical Analysis of the Issue of Media Bias in Israeli Elections, 1996-2003. In A. Arian & M. Shamir (Eds.), *The Elections In Israel: 2003* (pp. 123–142).

Shirky, C. (2008). *Here Comes Everybody: The Power of Organizing Without Organizations*. Allen Lane.

Shoham, S., Bolzman, L., & Birger, L. (2018). *Moving under Threats: The Treacherous Journeys of Refugees who 'Voluntary' Departed from Israel to Rwanda and Uganda and Reached Europe*. https://blogs.law.ox.ac.uk/research-subject-groups/centre-criminology/centreborder-criminologies/blog/2018/10/moving-under

Siapera, E., & Papadopoulou, L. (2021). Hate as a 'hook': The political and affective economy of 'hate journalism'. *Journalism*, 22(5), 1256–1272. https://doi.org/10.1177/1464884920985728

Silcock, B. W., Schwalbe, Carol B., & and Keith, S. (2008). "Secret" Casualties: Images of Injury and Death in the Iraq War Across Media Platforms. *Journal of Mass Media Ethics*, 23(1), 36–50. https://doi.org/10.1080/08900520701753205

Smith, G. R. (2010). Politicians and the News Media: How Elite Attacks Influence Perceptions of Media Bias. *The International Journal of Press/Politics*, 15(3), 319–343. https://doi.org/10.1177/1940161210367430

Spike, J. (2024, July 31). How Hungary's Orbán uses control of the media to escape scrutiny and keep the public in the dark. *The Associated Press*. https://www.ap.org/news-highlights/spotlights/2024/how-hungarys-orban-uses-control-of-the-media-to-escape-scrutiny-and-keep-the-public-in-the-dark/

Stahel, L. (2023). Why Do Journalists Face Varying Degrees of Digital Hostility? Examining the Interplay Between Minority Identity and Celebrity Capital. *Communication Research*. https://doi.org/10.1177/00936502231158426

Stahel, L., & Schoen, C. (2020). Female journalists under attack? Explaining gender differences in reactions to audiences' attacks. *New Media & Society*, 22(10), 1849–1867. https://doi.org/10.1177/1461444819885333

Starr, P. (2008). Democratic theory and the history of communications. In B. Zelizer (Ed.), *Explorations in Communication and History*. https://doi.org/10.4324/9780203888605-8

Stiglitz, J. E. (2003). On Liberty, the Right to Know, and Public Discourse: The Role of Transparency in Public Life. In M. J. Gibney (Ed.), *Globalizing Rights: The Oxford Amnesty Lectures 1999*. Oxford University Press. https://doi.org/10.1093/oso/9780192803054.003.0008

Strömbäck, J. (2005). In Search of a Standard: four models of democracy and their normative implications for journalism. *Journalism Studies*, 6(3), 331–345. https://doi.org/10.1080/14616700500131950

Suebsaeng, R. B., Asawin. (2022, November 8). Trump Keeps Musing About Journalists Being Raped in Prison—He's Not Joking. *Rolling Stone*. https://www.rollingstone.com/politics/politics-news/trump-imagines-journalists-raped-prison-1234626493/

Suk, J., Shah, D. V., & McLeod, D. M. (2022). Breaking the "Virtuous Circle": How Partisan Communication Flows Can Erode Social Trust but Drive Participation. *Human Communication Research*, 48(1), 88–115. https://doi.org/10.1093/hcr/hqab015

Surčulija-Milojević, J. (2015). The right of reply: A tool for an individual to access the media. *Godišnjak Fakulteta Političkih Nauka*, 9(13), 225–238. https://doi.org/10.5937/GodFPN1513225M

Svensson, M. (2012). Media and civil society in China. *China Perspectives*, 2012(3), Article 3. https://doi.org/10.4000/chinaperspectives.5934

Taberez, N. (2024). Indian News Media. In Š. Ganguly, D. Mistree, & L. Diamond (Eds.), *The Troubling State of India's Democracy* (pp. 321–336). University of Michigan Press.

Talshir, G. (2018). Populist Rightwing Ideological Exposition: Netanyahu's Regime as a Case in Point. *Advances in Applied Sociology*, 08, 329. https://doi.org/10.4236/aasoci.2018.84019

Tambini, D. (2021). *Media Freedom*. Polity.

Tapscott, D. (2009). *Grown Up Digital: How the Net Generation is Changing Your World*. McGraw Hill.

Tapsell, R. (2022). Divide and rule: Populist crackdowns and media elites in the Philippines. *Journalism*, 23(10), 2192–2207. https://doi.org/10.1177/1464884921989466

Toff, B., Palmer, R., & Nielsen, R. K. (2023). *Avoiding the News: Reluctant Audiences for Journalism*. Columbia University Press.

Tsfati, Y., & Meyers, O. (2012). Journalists in Israel. In D. H. Weaver & L. Willant (Eds.), *The Global Journalist: News People Around the World* (pp. 443–457). Hampton Press.

Tuchman, G. (1972). Objectivity as Strategic Ritual. *American Journal of Sociology*, 77(4), 660–679.

Tuchman, G. (1978). *Making news: A study in the construction of reality*. Free Press.

Tufekci, Z. (2018). *Twitter and Tear Gas: The Power and Fragility of Networked Protest*. Yale University Press.

Tumber, H. (2004). Prisoners of News Values? Journalists, professionalism, and identification in times of war. S. Allan, B. Zelizer (Eds.) *Reporting War: Journalism in Wartime*. Routledge (pp. 190–205).

Turnbull-Dugarte, J. (2024). Public support for the cordon sanitaire: Descriptive evidence from Spain. *Party Politics*. https://journals.sagepub.com/doi/full/10.1177/13540688241246141

Turner, F. (2018). Trump on Twitter: How a Medium Designed for Democracy Became an Authoritarian's Mouthpiece. In P. J. Boczkowski & Z. Papacharissi (Eds.), *Trump and the Media* (pp. 143–150). The MIT Press. https://doi.org/10.7551/mitpress/11464.003.0023

UNESCO. (2019). *Intensified Attacks, New Defences: Developments in the Fight to Protect Journalists and End Impunity*.

Usher, N. (2014). *Making News at The New York Times*. University of Michigan Press.

Usher, N. (2021). *News for the Rich, White, and Blue: How Place and Power Distort American Journalism*. Columbia University Press.

Valentim, V. (2021). Parliamentary Representation and the Normalization of Radical Right Support. *Comparative Political Studies*, *54*(14), 2475–2511. https://doi.org/10.1177/0010414021997159

van der Linden, S., Panagopoulos, C., & Roozenbeek, J. (2020). You are fake news: political bias in perceptions of fake news. *Media, Culture & Society*, *42*(3), 460–470. https://doi.org/10.1177/0163443720906992

Varma, A. (2022). Moral solidarity as a news value: Rendering marginalized communities and enduring social injustice newsworthy. *Journalism*, 24(9), 1880–1898. https://doi.org/10.1177/14648849221094669

Voltmer, K. (2013). *The Media in Transitional Democracies*. John Wiley & Sons.

Vultee, F. (2009). Jump back jack, mohammed's here. *Journalism Studies*, *10*(5), 623–638. https://doi.org/10.1080/14616700902797333

Wahl-Jorgensen, K., Berry, M., Garcia-Blanco, I., Bennett, L., & Cable, J. (2017). Rethinking balance and impartiality in journalism? How the BBC attempted and failed to change the paradigm. *Journalism*, *18*(7), Article 7. https://doi.org/10.1177/1464884916648094

Waisbord, S. (2002). Journalism, Risk, and Patriotism. In B. Zelizer & S. Allan (Eds.), *Journalism After September 11* (pp. 201–219). Routledge.

Waisbord, S. (2020). Mob Censorship: Online Harassment of US Journalists in Times of Digital Hate and Populism. *Digital Journalism*, *8*(8), 1030–1046. https://doi.org/10.1080/21670811.2020.1818111

Waisbord, S. (2022). Online Trolling of Journalists, in S. Allan (Ed.) *The Routledge Companion to News and Journalism* (pp. 149–158).

Waisbord, S., & Amado, A. (2017). Populist communication by digital means: Presidential Twitter in Latin America. *Information, Communication & Society*, 20(9), Article 9. https://doi.org/10.1080/1369118X.2017.1328521

Wallace, L. R. (2019). *The View from Somewhere: Undoing the Myth of Journalistic Objectivity*. University of Chicago Press.

Ward, S. J. A. (2006). *The Invention of Journalism Ethics: The Path to Objectivity and Beyond*. McGill-Queen's University Press.

Ward, S. J. A. (2008). *Truth and Objectivity*. The Handbook of Mass Media Ethics; Routledge. https://doi.org/10.4324/9780203893043-13

Wasserman, H., & Madrid-Morales, D. (2019). An Exploratory Study of "Fake News" and Media Trust in Kenya, Nigeria and South Africa. *African Journalism Studies*, 40(1), 107–123. https://doi.org/10.1080/23743670.2019.1627230

Watson, L. (2018). Systematic Epistemic Rights Violations in the Media: A Brexit Case Study. *Social Epistemology*, 32(2), 88–102. https://doi.org/10.1080/02691728.2018.1440022

Watson, L. (2021). *The Right to Know: Epistemic Rights and Why We Need Them*. Routledge.

Watts, M. D., Domke, D., Shah, D. V., & Fan, D. P. (1999). Elite cues and media bias in presidential campaigns: Explaining public perceptions of a liberal press. *Communication Research*, 26(2), 144–175. https://doi.org/10.1177/009365099026002003

Westlund, O. (2021). Advancing Research into Dark Participation. *Media and Communication*, 9(1), 209–214. https://doi.org/10.17645/mac.v9i1.1770

Williamson, V., Skocpol, T., & Coggin, J. (2011). The Tea Party and the Remaking of Republican Conservatism. *Perspectives on Politics*, 9(1), 25–43. https://doi.org/10.1017/S153759271000407X

Wodak, R. (2015). *The Politics of Fear*. Sage Publications.

Wolfsfeld, G. (2012). *Political Communication: Five Things You Need to Know*. IDC (The Interdisciplinary Center).

Wright, J. S. (1967). Defamation, Privacy, and the Public's Right To Know: A National Problem and a New Approach. *Texas Law Review*, 46, 630.

Wu, Y., & Shen, F. (2022). Exploring the impacts of media use and media trust on health behaviors during the COVID-19 pandemic in China. *Journal of Health Psychology*, 27(6), 1445–1461. https://doi.org/10.1177/1359105321995964

Wyatt, W. N. (2007). *Critical conversations: A theory of press criticism*. Hampton Press.

Yahav, T. (2015). Petition: Instruct 'Israel Hayom' to stop publishing elections propaganda. *Ynet*. https://www.ynet.co.il/articles/0,7340,L-4624499,00.html

Zandberg, E., & Neiger, M. (2005). Between the nation and the profession: journalists as members of contradicting communities. *Media, Culture & Society*, 27(1), 131–141. https://doi.org/10.1177/0163443705049073

Acknowledgements

This book was written throughout long years of political and personal turmoil. One global pandemic, one judicial overhaul, five Israeli election cycles, and one ongoing, haunting, life-changing war later, I can safely say I was lucky enough to find the best people on earth with whom to survive these times and reflect on them.

I am immensely grateful to all the journalists who chose to share with me their experiences. Thanks for dedicating your time and opening your hearts. Some of you became close friends in the process, others argued with me endlessly over the years. Your work is essential; I hope you find this book useful in your mission to make journalism better, for the sake of us all. My special and heartfelt thanks to Emily Maitlis, a friend and an inspiration, who generously prefaced this book. You are the perfect partner for deep conversations – over countless Margaritas – about the future of news and the world.

Ella McPherson, co-director of the Centre of Governance and Human Rights at Cambridge University, was the optimistic and wise PhD supervisor I needed. Aeron Davis was the one who encouraged me to pursue this project to begin with, before becoming my academic mentor and dear friend. My exceptional viva examiners, Silvio Waisbord and Gina Neff, met with me shortly after October 7th, when I was still figuring out which parts of my life changed forever and what could be salvaged. Their advice made me believe that there might be a book hiding somewhere in there.

Along the way, I had the pleasure of meeting creative minds and kind hearts who supported me and my work in all these moments of uncertainty: Cristian Vaccari, Chris W. Anderson, Kate Wright, Mel Bunce, Seth C. Lewis, Jacob Nelson, Gadi Wolfsfeld, Yariv Tsfati, Andrea Carson, Zohar Kampf, Efrat Nechushtai, Keren Tenenboim-Weinblatt. I am particularly in debt to Assaf Sharon and Avner Inbar, who taught me politics, and to my close circle of thinkers and activists at Molad. It takes a village, and while annoyingly spread around the globe and across time zones – you are my village.

My genius friends and brain twins, Yonatan Levi and Shai Agmon, have probably read this book as many times as I did. Beyond true friendship, brainstorming sessions, and thousands of coffees, I often use their writing as a scaffolding for my own. By now, I cannot distinguish my ideas from theirs.

My besties back in Tel Aviv, who are always my home: Noa (Alfus) Alfia, Lior Birger, Lital Kaplan, Stav Shaffir, Alon-Lee Green, Nof Nathanzon, Ori Mark, Lior Sheffer, Tami Gilon, Or Ben-David, Ella Fainaro, Ziv Berkowitz, Sivan Shur, Maya Ilani, Callum Hood, Oren Eldar, Tuli Afek, Tomer Shenar, Assaf Harel, Ido Shlomo, Noam Gidron, Yossi David, Amitay Gilad, and my sweetest god-daughter Alex Gilad-Alfia. My Hackney gang, Noa Livnat-Agmon, Saide Mobayed, Alex Cullen, Mirna Pedalo, Jesse and Daniel, Maoz and Nelly, Ariel and Kinneret, Hanna and Oscar.

ACKNOWLEDGEMENTS

I couldn't have written this book – or anything else, really – without my lover, closest friend, and partner in crime, Daniel Mann, who spent years stuck in the same room with the worst version of me: the one who writes her PhD. Your imagination and sincerity shaped every bit of this book. More importantly, you make me a happy warrior, which isn't easy when researching authoritarianism.

To my brother, Guy Niv, who always asks the hardest questions: thanks for keeping me on alert and letting me have fun with Michael when I can no longer pretend to be working. Thanks to my crazy and loving family, who always has my back: Moshe Vainkrantz, Nurit Vainkrantz, Shiri Vainkrantz, Kfir Magen, Kobi Vainkrantz, Omri Zarbiv, Niv and Leo. You are my safe space. To my second family, who couldn't be more involved and caring: Kenneth Mann, Gabriela Mann, Itamar Mann, Shira Mann-Shmueli, Eytan Mann, Noa Mann-Shimshoni, Nit, Mormor, Yahli, Raf and Nuri.

Finally, and most importantly, everything I know and do is the direct outcome of having the absolute, unquestionably, objectively best mom in the world. This entire journey would have never taken place if I didn't have your endless love, unconditional support and daily advice. Your courage and compassion are my compass.